Realms of Gold

REALMS OF GOLD
*The colorful Writers
of
San Francisco
1850-1950*

George Rathmell

CREATIVE ARTS BOOK COMPANY
Berkeley • California • 1998

CREDITS

Grateful acknowledgment is made to the following publishers for permission to reprint copyrighted material:

To Stanford University Press for *Tamar,* by Robinson Jeffers, copyright 1924, by Robinson Jeffers. Reprinted by permission.

To Viking Penguin Press for *Cannery Row,* by John Steinbeck, copyright 1945, 1973, by John Steinbeck. Reprinted by permission.

PHOTOS

Cover, 5, 15, 23, 36, 144, 160.
Courtesy, San Francisco Public Library.

2, 6, 24, 86, 110, 115, 128, 134, 136, 140, 154,
163, 165, 200, 202, 222, 240, 246, 249, 264, 266.
Courtesy, Bancroft Library, University of California, Berkeley.

9 Courtesy, Oakland Public Library.

237 Courtesy, Corbis-Bettman Archives.

Realms of Gold is published by Donald S. Ellis
and distributed by Creative Arts Book Company

For Information contact:
Creative Arts Book Company
833 Bancroft Way
Berkeley, California 94710

For ordering information call:
1-800-848-7789
Fax: 1-510-848-4844

Graphics and Book Design by Pope Graphic Arts Center

ISBN 0-88739-162-1
Library of Congress Catalog Number 97-76373

Printed in the United States of America

ON FIRST LOOKING INTO CHAPMAN'S HOMER

Much have I traveled in the realms of gold,
    And many goodly states and kingdoms seen;
    Round many western islands I have been
Which bards in fealty to Apollo hold.
Oft of one wide expanse had I been told
    That deep-browed Homer ruled as his demesne;
    Yet did I never breathe its pure serene
Till I heard Chapman speak out loud and bold:
Then felt I like some watcher of the skies
    When a new planet swims into his ken;
Or like stout Cortez when with eagle eyes
    He stared at the Pacific—and all his men
Looked at each other with a wild surmise—
    Silent, upon a peak in Darien.

John Keats, 1816

LIST OF PHOTOGRAPHS

ACKNOWLEDGEMENTS

A book such as this one requires a great deal of research, and since I live two hours away from the nearest library, I am dependent on the Mendocino County Public Library Bookmobile that lumbers along the narrow, winding country roads from Ukiah every two weeks. For helping me with my research and locating books from librarians all over the country, I am deeply indebted to Bookmobile librarians Mary Luther and Allison Rea. I would also like to express my appreciation to the staffs at the San Francisco History Room of the San Francisco Public Library, the Oakland History Room of the Oakland Public Library, and the University of California; Bancroft Library.

I want to thank my friends JoAnn Ridley and Rob Diefenbach for their many helpful suggestions and continuing encouragement. I am especially grateful to Charles A. Fracchia of the San Francisco Historical Society for checking the content of the book for historical accuracy and for guiding me to valuable resources, and to Victoria Gill for her outstanding skill in editing the manuscript.

And for her patience and forbearance over the years it took to complete this project, I want to express to my wife Margaret—my most astute critic and my most ardent supporter—my gratitude and devotion.

For my father

CONTENTS

INTRODUCTION

The French have a word for it—*cachet*, the unique charm of a place. Paris has its cachet, thoroughly French but completely different from that of Nice or Honfleur. The cachet of San Francisco is unquestionably singular and considerably more complex than tourists can realize when they are infatuated with Victorian houses, cable cars, flower stands, and streets that swoop up and down like amusement park rides with stunning marine views. It is not just San Francisco's climate, topography, architecture, and blending of cultures that attracts more than eight and a half million visitors each year, it is also the subtle but palpable sense of ongoing history that you feel in this restless and improbable city. To discover, to attempt to define something of what it is that attracts so many people to the place (many of whom come to visit and then decide to stay), we can investigate it through one of the windows on its past, its literary history, the interwoven story of the artists who came—few were born here—in search of their own form of gold and whose efforts created a romance of the imagination. To understand the story of these artists, it is essential to have a sense of the three-century pageant of history that preceded their arrival, for that history was the source and inspiration for their work.

The Spanish Period, 1521 -1822

No place in America has a more obviously literary and legendary origin than California, at least in its name. When conquistador Hernan Cortés claimed Mexico for Charles V of Spain in 1521, California came along in the bargain. So far as the Spaniards knew, California was a huge island lying off the west coast of the unexplored continent recently discovered by Columbus. Before long they determined that what lay across the water from their Mexican garrisons was a peninsula (Baja

California), not an island, but European maps continued to show California as an island until 1700. Cortés officially named the land Santa Cruz, but the name that stuck among the sailors and eventually among the map-makers was *California.* The reason is no mystery. One of Cortés' lieutenants, after an excursion to the north, reported that Indians had told him of an island nearby that was rich in gold and pearls and inhabited exclusively by dark-skinned, warlike women. This account could bring only one thing to the minds of the Spaniards, for even those who were illiterate knew the stories in a best-seller of the time, Garcí Ordoñez de Montalvo's chivalric novel *Las Sergas de Esplandián,* written around 1510, which begins:

> Know ye that on the right hand of the Indies there
> is an island called California, very close to the side of
> the Terrestrial Paradise, which was inhabited by black
> women without a single man among them.

According to Montalvo's fanciful account, these Amazons, ruled by a Queen Califia, were robust warriors with weapons of gold, magnificent ships, and griffins (beasts that were half eagle, half lion) trained to kill and eat any man who ventured near the island. With such romance at hand, Cortés' efforts to give the new land a respectable Christian name were doomed. California was baptized with the holy water of fable.

As for the 105 tribes of Indians living in what is now California in the 16th century, they were unaware of the merging of European and Native American cultures that was taking place to the south of them. They lived their simple but highly spiritual lives for the next two hundred and fifty years in blissful ignorance that they were subjects of the King of Spain. They began to realize it in 1769 when the Franciscan friars under Junipero Serra began a mission at San Diego, the first of a series of twenty-one that would stretch six hundred miles up the coastal valleys along El Camino Reál as far as Sonoma.

The purpose of the missions was to convert the Indians of Alta California, teach them Spanish and agricultural and building skills, and then turn the missions over to them to run their own lives as civilized Christians. This process was expected to take ten years, but fifty years later the adobe compounds with their roofs of red tile molded over the thighs of Indian women were no closer to being administered by the Indians than they were when they had started. The "converts" had a bad habit of running off whenever the opportunity presented itself, and while they accepted the new religion as an appendage to their own metaphysical belief system, they were loath to forsake the customs that had sustained their ancestors for more than thirty centuries.

Certainly the missions should have been successful; they controlled hundreds of thousands of acres of the most fertile land in California and had over 30,000 "neophytes" who worked the land for food and lodging. But the experiment had not worked, and their source of support, the Pious Fund, eventually fell into the hands of a new independent Mexican government which secularized the missions and effectively set the Indians free, leaving them to their own devices.

The Mexican Period, 1822–1846

While the experiment to teach the natives to run the missions on their own never achieved its goal, it did provide a basis for the land grant program that began under Spanish and continued under Mexican rule. Anyone who felt worthy, mostly military veterans, could apply for a grant of 50,000 acres of land. These grants gave rise to the great ranchos, some of them comprising over half a million acres, that turned California into a vast system of cattle ranches.

Cattle were not raised for food but for the hides and tallow they produced, which could be shipped from one of the four California ports—San Diego, Santa Barbara, Monterey, and San Francisco—to the leather and soap factories in the U.S. and Britain. It was a very profitable business, and the Californio land owners, although they were mostly of common origins, experienced a style of living that would be the envy of landed aristocracy anywhere in the world. It was centered around the horse, the fundamental means of transportation as well as an essential element of ranch work. Horses were adorned with elaborately tooled saddles and bridles with engraved silver hardware, and Californios, men and women alike, seldom walked anywhere, preferring to mount their horses even for short distances. Although these rancheros were capitalists in the truest sense, they cared little for development. Their way of life was good with its frequent fiestas, fandangos, and celebrations that lasted for days, held at the slightest provocation. William Benjamin Davis, an early American pioneer in California who later became the first American mayor of Los Angeles (and grandfather of General George S. Patton), married into the Yorba family and participated in the life of the Californios. He later wrote:

> There was no place in the world where I could enjoy more true happiness and true friendship than among them. There were no courts, no juries, no lawyers, nor any need for them. The people were honest and hospitable, and their word was as good as their bond.

The Californios were completely dependent on their four ports for selling their hides and tallow and receiving manufactured goods, yet they made no effort to improve any of them. San Francisco in this period remained nothing more than an unsuccessful mission (aptly named Dolores, "sorrows") and a small fort at the opening to the Bay, the Presidio. These had been established in June of 1776 at the same moment in history when Thomas Jefferson, John Adams, and Benjamin Franklin were working on their final draft of an announcement to King George III that would become known as the Declaration of Independence. While the colonists on the East Coast struggled to establish a republic, Juan Bautista de Anza, a Spanish military officer, led a group of 240 soldiers, settlers, and monks from Sonora, Mexico to the windswept sand hills that would eventually be named San Francisco after St. Francis of Assisi.

Mission Dolores never really prospered, the converts being regularly decimated by successive epidemics of measles, smallpox, and venereal diseases; and the Presidio, as a defensive installation, was little more than a joke. British sea captain George

Vancouver described the place in 1792 as a "cattle pen with mud walls inhabited by thirty-five Spanish soldiers and their families." Under Mexican rule, it did not improve. For example, it was customary for ships preparing to enter the Bay to fire a salute with their cannon and for the fort to reply with a similar salute. On two occasions in the early nineteenth century, the ancient cannons exploded in the faces of the Presidio soldiers firing these salutes, and in 1806, when a Russian ship prepared to enter, the Presidio guards had to row out to the ship and borrow enough gunpowder to fire a greeting.

This lack of development and protection did not escape the notice of the English, Americans, French, and Russians who came to trade in California's ports. It was obvious to them that the land was a plum ripe for plucking, having been ignored for three centuries by the central governments of Spain and, later, by Mexico.

An English sailor by the name of William Richardson began to pluck the ripe fruit in 1822 when he jumped ship from the whaler *Orion*, converted to Catholicism, and married Maria Antonia Martinez, daughter of the Presidio commanding officer. He was given a lot at Yerba Buena Cove, and, in a shack on that lot, he established the area's first trading center, serving the increasing traffic of trading ships that were entering the Bay. The dusty street in front of his shack he named Calle de la Fundacion. Later it would become Dupont Street. Less than ten years after Richardson established his enterprise at Yerba Buena, there was a customs house at the pueblo, and the commercial district was under way.

While Richardson was developing a legitimate port at San Francisco, another European, John Sutter, was active in the northern region. He had come from Switzerland and, seeing vast opportunities in the undeveloped valleys of California, became a Mexican citizen and obtained a 50,000-acre land grant at the junction of two large rivers, the Sacramento and the American. There, in 1840, he constructed a fort and set up a huge agricultural domain called "Nueva Helvetia," using local Indians as serfs. The following year he purchased the Russian properties at Fort Ross and Bodega. The Russian fur traders, having hunted the sea otters out of existence, were abandoning their California outpost. Sutter's holdings became collection points for the numerous illegal immigrants from the Mississippi and Missouri Valleys who were coming into California to establish family farms. They were squatters with no legal claims to property, but they remained unmolested since there was no Mexican force in Northern California capable of chasing them out.

Sutter's Fort soon became the center of an American community of squatters who firmly believed that manifest destiny would soon make California a part of the United States. In June of 1846, John Charles Frémont, an officer in the Topographical Corps of the U.S. Army, arrived at Sutter's Fort with a band of sixty armed men. Stirring up the settlers by convincing them that the Mexican government planned to expel them as undesirable aliens, Frémont fomented the Bear Flag Revolt, in which Americans took over the town of Sonoma and proclaimed California to be an independent republic. A month later, the Bear Flaggers learned that President James Polk had declared war on Mexico over a border dispute in Texas. They shifted their allegiance to the local American commander, Commodore Sloat, who had occupied Monterey. The war ended two years later with the Treaty of Hidalgo, and California was on the road to statehood.

For the Californios, the defeat of Mexico brought little change at first. Instead of a red, white, and green flag, they now had a red, white, and blue one with twenty-eight stars. The soldiers at the forts were American rather than Mexican, and more settlers were coming in; but Spanish was still the language of the land, and the Californios continued to live as they had for the previous seventy-five years.

California literature officially begins in this pastoral Mexican period with the reports of a young student from Cambridge, Massachusetts, whose life was a prophetic initiation for a new literary realm. Richard Henry Dana was in his second year at Harvard when a bad case of measles left his eyesight so weak that he had to withdraw from the University. In 1834, at nineteen, restless and somewhat rebellious, Dana signed aboard the Yankee trading ship *Pilgrim* as a common sailor for a voyage around the Horn to California. His family could easily have afforded to provide him passage for an ocean voyage, but Dana was eager to prove himself capable of doing a man's job. When he returned to Cambridge two years later, the journals he had carefully kept throughout the voyage were lost; but despite that tragic loss and despite his Harvard course work, he sat down each evening and put his experiences on paper. The result was *Two Years Before the Mast.* There are more accurate pictures of the Californio period than that which Dana painted from memory, but none has ever captured the American reader's imagination so well. The *Pilgrim* carried liquor, coffee, tea, spices, molasses, hardware, shoes, fabrics, jewelry, furniture, and fireworks to sell in the California ports. In exchange, its hold was filled with "California banknotes," roughly-cured steer hides. Dana's fresh vision of a wondrous undeveloped land comes alive in his sharp descriptive prose as he arrives in San Francisco:

> Our anchorage was between a small island called Yerba Buena, and a gravel beach in a little bight or cove of the same name, formed by two small projecting points. Beyond, to the westward of the landing-place, were dreary sand hills, with little grass to be seen, and a few trees, and beyond them higher hills, steep and barren, their sides gullied by the rains. Some six miles beyond the landing-place to the right, was a ruinous Presidio, and some three or four miles to the left was the Mission of Dolores, as ruinous as the Presidio, almost deserted, with but a few Indians attached to it, and but little property in cattle. Over a region far beyond our sight there were no other human habitations, except that of an enterprising Yankee, [*probably William Richardson—G.R.*] years in advance of his time, put up on the rising ground above the landing, a shanty of rough boards, where he carried on a very small retail trade between the hide ships and the Indians.

Dana was obviously not much impressed with the settlement he found, but his description of San Francisco Bay as he departed indicates his appreciation of the area's potential:

> We sailed down this magnificent bay with a light wind, the tide, which was running out, carrying us at the rate of four or five knots. It was a fine day; the first of entire sunshine we had had for more than a month. We passed directly under the high cliff on which the Presidio is built, and stood into the middle of the bay from whence we could see small bays making up into the interior, large and beautifully wooded islands, and the mouths of several small rivers. If California ever becomes a prosperous country, this bay will be the centre of its prosperity. The abundance of wood and water; the extreme fertility of its shores; the excellence of its climate, which is as near to being perfect as any in the world; and its facilities for navigation, affording the best anchoring grounds in the whole western coast of America—all fit it for a place of great importance.

Two Years Before the Mast has never been out of print since its publication in 1840. It was a best-seller for ten years and would have made its young author a fortune if he had not sold the rights to it to his publisher for $250.

What happens to a young man who writes a best-seller at the age of twenty-five? In Dana's case, not much. He took his law degree from Harvard and practiced maritime law in Boston for forty years, seeking relief from a tedious career and an unhappy marriage in the same kind of New England respectability that had driven him away to seek adventure as a young man. He ran for Congress but was defeated, and was nominated as ambassador to England but not confirmed. Only once did he take up his pen again in an effort to reproduce the success of his youth. The result was *To Cuba and Back*, a travel book, but his gift had been dulled by years of drudgery and the work lacked the quality of his first book both in content and style.

The Gold Rush, 1848–1854

The cattle-based Californio life that Dana found in 1835 would continue in Southern California to some extent until the end of the century, but 1848 brought cataclysmic change to San Francisco and the waterways that fed into its bay. John Sutter, expanding his commercial operation at Sutter's Fort, wanted a sawmill constructed so he could sell lumber to the growing number of squatters in the Sacramento Valley. On January 24, 1848, the foreman of the mill construction crew, James Marshall, was deepening the millrace so the waterwheel could turn when he noticed something gleaming in the water. He bent over and picked up a shiny rock—it was a nugget of pure gold!

Sutter and Marshall resolved to keep the discovery quiet until they could determine the extent of it. The nearest population center was San Francisco, some eighty miles distant. They felt that if they were prudent, they could keep the world away. Nearby settlers would find out about it of course, but they would have an interest in keeping it to themselves as well. There were about 600 people living in San Francisco at the time—among them was Sam Brannan, a convert to the Mormon faith destined to thwart Sutter's and Marshall's plans. When Joseph Smith, founder of the Church of Latter Day Saints, was murdered by a mob in Carthage, Illinois in 1844, the majority of his followers decided to leave the United States and carve out a home for themselves in an unsettled part of Mexico. Most of them followed Brigham Young on an overland route, headed for California. A second group of 238 people, mostly Mormons led by Sam Brannan, left for San Francisco on the sailing ship *Brooklyn*.

When they arrived in July, 1846, after a six-month voyage, they encountered two disappointments. First, they learned that California had just become U.S. territory; and second, that Brigham Young, instead of being there to welcome them, had chosen a place in the Utah desert as the Promised Land. Brannan had little desire to work on making the desert bloom and decided to remain in San Francisco, where he constructed the little settlement's first flour mill and started its first newspaper. The 238 settlers more than doubled San Francisco's population and made Brannan one of the most important figures in the area. Quarrels with the Mormon hierarchy over the use of church funds to establish his own businesses led Brannan to be accused of embezzlement, but his trial—California's first jury trial—left him a free man due to a hung jury.

When Brannan learned of Marshall's discovery of gold, he established a general store at Sutter's Fort, stocked it to the ceiling with goods, and then returned to San Francisco with a quinine bottle filled with gold dust that he displayed all over town, proclaiming, "There's gold in the American River!" As the men of San Francisco raced off to the valleys to scoop their fortunes from the rivers, Sam Brannan began quietly buying up San Francisco real estate.

The word was out, and men from all over California, Mexico, and South American seaports on the Pacific began pouring into San Francisco and heading for Sutter's territory. Technically, all of the gold on Sutter's property belonged to him, but he had no means to enforce his legal rights. Mexican laws and grants were being ignored, and California was not yet a state. Since there were fifteen free states and fifteen slave states at the time, Congress blocked any effort that would upset the balance. Without statehood, there was no California militia. The only possible law enforcement around was the small number of U.S. troops at the forts. The territorial military governor, Colonel Richard Mason, reported:

> It was a matter of serious reflection to me how I could secure to the government certain rents or fees for the privilege of procuring the gold, but considering the large extent of the country, the character of the miners involved, and the small force at my command, I am resolved not to interfere but to permit all to work freely.

Colonel Mason had little choice. His soldiers received seven dollars a month in salary. In 1848, most miners could easily obtain fifty dollars a day, panning the icy waters running down from the melting snows of the Sierras. Before long, most of the soldiers had deserted.

Stories of gold lying on the ground began to circulate around the world, but most Americans in the East were skeptical. They assumed the stories were just exaggerated, just ballyhoo designed to attract settlers to the new territory. However, when President Polk, on December 5, 1848, displayed 230 ounces of California gold, doubts were dispelled, and tens of thousands of men started West with dreams of returning home wealthy.

There were four routes to San Francisco in 1849, none of them good. The first was a ship around the Horn. The trip took from four to eight months, and when ships were becalmed off the coast of South America, some men—tortured by the idea that they were sitting on a motionless ship while everyone else in California was collecting all the gold—literally lost their minds and had to be confined in an institution when they finally arrived. A faster way was to take a ship to the narrowest part of land between Central and South America, where the Panama Canal is now. From there, prospective miners would travel by Indian dugouts and then mules, exposed to bad water, hostile natives, and yellow fever, to get another ship going north at Panama City on the Pacific side. Tickets from the East were cheap, but the fare from Panama to San Francisco could run as high as a thousand dollars. A third route was to take a ship to Vera Cruz on the Gulf of Mexico and then cross the mountains—risking dehydration, cholera, and bandit attacks before reaching the port of Acapulco. But the majority of the forty-niners took the fourth way—across the plains in covered wagon trains. Some men who could not afford a vehicle were so desperate to go that they followed the wagon trains, pushing their belongings in a wheelbarrow. One out of five who took the overland route died along the way. Cholera was the primary cause of death, dehydration the second, floods the third, and Indian warriors the fourth. The overland crossing was the cheapest way to get to California. Many who came that way, it was said, later returned back East, but not one of them by the same route.

Those argonauts who did survive the journey found an instant city in San Francisco that had grown from a population of 600 to 40,000 in less than three years, nearly all the newcomers being men under the age of forty. Their ships could not reach

Yerba Buena Cove where Dana's *Pilgrim* had anchored because it was filled with more than seven hundred idle ships whose crews had run off to the gold fields. New arrivals had to tie up at the edge of the abandoned ships that lined the twelve piers stretching into the Bay, and the passengers and the crew would scramble toward land and the ticket office for steamboats headed up the Sacramento River. As they made for the shore, they noticed that not all of the abandoned ships were unoccupied. Some of the more enterprising of San Francisco's new residents realized that it was much easier to extract gold from the pockets of miners who came into town for a spree than from the rivers and creek beds up in the hills. Thus the empty ships became retail businesses: saloons, brothels, restaurants, and supply houses.

Once ashore, the new arrivals found a hodge-podge collection of tents and shanties made of packing cases. On the Plaza (now Portsmouth Square), they were astonished to see immense gambling houses: the El Dorado, the Bella Union, and the California. These establishments had started as huge tents with dirt floors and gaming tables consisting of planks laid across sawhorses, but by 1850 they were among the city's first permanent buildings, decorated with oriental carpets, rich velvet drapes, elaborate crystal chandeliers, gilt-framed paintings of lush nudes, and six-piece string ensembles competing with the clicking of the roulette wheel. It was a time of unbelievably rapid change. Bayard Taylor, a journalist for the New York Tribune, who arrived in 1849, wrote this description of the center of town:

> But see! the groups in the Plaza suddenly scatter; the city surveyor jerks his pole out of the ground and leaps on a pile of boards; the vendors of cakes and sweetmeats follow his example, and the place is cleared, just as a wild bull which has been racing down Kearny Street makes his appearance. Two vaqueros, shouting and swinging their lariats, follow at a hot gallop; the dust flies as they gallop across the Plaza.

Taylor left San Francisco for a visit to Monterey and was stunned when he returned six weeks later to discover three-story buildings where tents had been and new houses on the sides of Telegraph and Russian Hills. The population had leapt from 6,000 to 15,000 in his absence.

In the gambling halls around the Plaza, many of the dealers were cigar-smoking women deftly handling cards and gold dust. The clientele in these establishments was more international than anywhere else on earth. Among the boisterous Americans in their red flannel shirts were numerous Mexicans and South Americans; Irishmen fleeing the potato famine; French, Italians, and Germans fleeing political upheavals at home; Chinese fleeing the Taiping Rebellion and starvation; blacks fleeing slavery (slavery had been outlawed in Mexico since the early 19th century); and, here and there, a native American, fleeing nothing but overwhelmed by the changes going on in his homeland.

At night, standing out in the streets which alternated between dusty and knee-deep in mud according to the weather, the forty-niners were treated to a magic lantern show. In thousands of tents scattered over the hills of the city, residents were silhouetted by the lanterns in their tents as they prepared for bed or sat writing a letter to those who were counting on them to come home safe...and rich. Walking down toward North Beach, the newcomers would arrive at Little Chile, an area near the present intersection of Grant and Jackson, where men stood in long lines outside the tents of dark-skinned women plying the oldest profession— Mexican, Chilean, Peruvian, and Indian women whose fees were low but who made up for it by the volume of their business. Women were vastly outnumbered by men in the Gold Rush days, and virtuous women were rarer still. In a town filled with young men far from home, many with pockets heavy with gold dust, prostitution was a major industry, second only to gambling. Initially there was no law enforcement agency in the boom town, but when the activities of hoodlums such as the Hounds (anti-Catholic gang members from New York City) and the Sydney Ducks (ex-convicts from Australia) became too flagrant, a Vigilante Committee was formed by Sam Brannan. Brannan, excommunicated from the Mormon Church by Brigham Young, had become a successful businessman and publisher of San Francisco's first newspaper, *The California Star*. His Vigilante Committee put an end to the reign of terror brought on by the gangs, but made no effort to control vice.

Fancier brothels with elegant furnishings began to appear to serve those who could afford better than what Little Chile had to offer. This development was aided considerably by concurrent events in France. In 1848, Prince Louis Napoleon Bonaparte was elected President of the Republic and immediately set his mind to becoming emperor, as his uncle had been. His treasury was low, unemployment was high, and the streets of Paris were filled with political enemies plotting his overthrow. The solution to all these problems was the Lottery of the Golden Ingots, a huge national lottery with tickets at one franc and prizes that ranged from 1,000 francs to solid gold bars worth 400,000 francs. The ostensible goal of the lottery was to send five thousand unemployed skilled workers to San Francisco, where employment opportunities were great. What the ticket buyers did not realize was that the lottery was rigged so that prize money would go straight to the government, and that the people who would be sent to San Francisco were political undesirables and prostitutes. Alexandre Dumas fils was engaged to write the advertisement for the lottery, and the gold ingots, heavily guarded, were displayed in a store window at 10, boulevard Montmartre. Millions of tickets were sold, and the lottery increased the French population of San Francisco considerably. Little Chile soon became "Frenchtown," and as that section evolved into rows of brothels, saloons, and dance halls, it became known to sailors as the "Barbary Coast," a term that lingers today around lower Broadway. In the early days of the Gold Rush, American miners had given a pejorative nickname to Frenchmen: they called them "Kesskydees" because of their habit, when addressed in English, of looking at one another, hunching their shoulders, and asking *Qu'est-ce qu'il dit?* (What's he saying?). After the lottery, a new and even more pejorative term came along—"Ingot," synonymous with "deported undesirable"—whose use was often the cause of verbal and even physical battles.

Albert Benard de Russailh, one of the first chroniclers of the

French in California, arrived in San Francisco in March of 1851 to seek his fortune. He prospered but unfortunately died of cholera a year later. He was a meticulous, if some-what chauvinistic, journal writer and recorded his impressions on the arrival of the "Ingots."

> When I first arrived here there were only ten or twelve French women in San Francisco. Men would look hopefully at them in the streets....They much preferred the French women, who had the charm of novelty. Americans were irresistibly attracted by their graceful walk, their supple and easy bearing, and charming freedom of manner, qualities, after all, only to be found in France; and they trooped after a French woman whenever she put her nose out of doors....if the poor fellows had known what these women had been in Paris, how one could pick them up on the boulevards and have them for almost nothing, they might not have been so free with their offers of $500 or $600 a night....Many ships have reached San Francisco during the past three or four months, and the number of women in town is greatly increased....Nearly all these women at home were streetwalkers of the cheapest sort. But out here for a few minutes they ask a hundred times as much as they were getting in Paris....The beauties of San Francisco today are Marguet, Hélène, Marie, Artémise, Lucy, Emilie, Madame Mauget, Lucienne, Madame Weston, Eléonore, Madame St. Amand, Madame Meyer, Maria, Angèle, and others whose names I have forgotten.
>
> There are some honest women in San Francisco, but not very many.

However sordid their beginnings may have been, the "Ingots" did well in San Francisco and lent a Gallic air to the place that has never faded. As early as 1851 the city was referred to as "the Paris of the Pacific." Luxury imports from France increased; restaurants such as Marchand's, La Maison Dorée, and the Poulet d'Or (rechristened "the Poodle Dog" by the Americans) developed a taste for haute cuisine, and the Ville de Paris (original name for the City of Paris department store) a taste for haute couture.

All of these helped to establish the city's cosmopolitan reputation, a reputation enhanced by the presence of a Chinese ghetto in the center of town. In 1849, there were fewer than a thousand Chinese men and only two Chinese women in the city. By the end of 1850, the number of Chinese men had increased to 3,000, but there were only seven women. Within twenty-five years, the male Chinese population was nearly 50,000 and the female 2,000—of which 1,900 were prostitutes, girls sold into slavery. In addition, Italians, primarily from Sicily, Genoa, Turin, Lombardy, and the Piedmont, established themselves in North Beach. Portuguese immigrants, nearly all fishermen, rimmed the port. Mission Dolores became the center for the Spanish-speaking and Irish populations, and Germans set up corner groceries and then breweries throughout the city.

As mentioned earlier, Albert Benard de Russailh had come to California to seek wealth. An aristocrat, he had grown up in considerable comfort, but financial reverses left him without funds and caused him to emigrate to California. He had heard that San Francisco was short on all sorts of supplies and had brought with him assorted merchandise which he hoped to sell, flea-market style, to obtain the capital necessary to open a general store:

> Early next morning, I conquered my vanity, put on a red flannel shirt, and went down to the long wharf, where I chose a good place, and with a few old boards rigged up my open air shop. My goods were soon spread out to attract customers. I had many things of no particular value: brushes, gloves, perfumes, cutlery, colored shirts, and other articles....I sold a pair of suspenders for more than six times what I had paid for them, and a toothbrush for ten times its cost.

Benard de Russailh was astounded to find that one item he had brought along to give away to his customers, toothpicks, were a great rarity in San Francisco. He had about 6,000 of them and carefully divided them into packages of twelve, which he sold for fifty cents each. In less than a week he had sold them all and had enough capital to rent a store.

Tales of such entrepreneurs who went rapidly from rags to riches are legion in the Gold Rush days of San Francisco, but none had a longer-lasting success than that of Loeb Strauss, a Jewish refugee from Bavaria who had come to New York in 1847 to join his two older brothers who were earning their living as peddlers. As soon as he arrived, his brothers changed his name to one more familiar to Americans, Levi. When news of the Gold Rush reached the East, a brother-in-law of the Strausses went off to California and wrote back that San Francisco was in great need of tent canvas. Accordingly, the brothers acquired a consignment of brown canvas and sent young Levi with it in a ship around the Horn. By the time he arrived, the market for tent canvas was already glutted, and he could not give the stuff away. However, hearing repeated complaints from the miners that ordinary cotton or wool pants would wear out in a week, Levi conceived an inspired idea: he had a tailor make pants from his canvas stock. Thus the first Levi's—"waist high overalls" as he called them— were created; brown at first, later the familiar denim blue. They were styled in the manner of trousers worn by Genoese sailors and became known as "jeans," but the common name remained "Levi's" and before long, Levi Strauss and Company at 117 Sacramento Street was one of the city's major businesses. The firm later moved to 15-16 Battery Street, now Levi Plaza, and is presently the world's largest clothing manufacturing firm.

A similar story is told about David Robison, a young man who, on his way to the Gold Rush in 1849, cleverly bought a large consignment of green bananas while waiting for his ship in Panama. Once in San Francisco, he sold the bananas at such an enormous profit that he gave up the idea of mining and became a greengrocer instead. Sailors who delivered his produce began to bring him gifts of tropical animals—goldfish, monkeys, and exotic colorful birds—which he used to attract customers to his stand. When his customers began wanting to buy the animals, Robison phased out his fruits and vegetables and established the city's first pet shops, one on Washington Street and another on Kearny. Robison's Pet Store became a family business which eventually moved to the fashionable Maiden Lane and was operated by four generations of Robisons until it closed 140 years later. As a boom town filled with young men far from home seeking wealth rather than a place to sink roots, San Francisco suffered from a lack of community spirit and of self-discipline. Austrian travel writer Ida Pfeiffer reported in 1853:

> In the finest and most frequented parts of town, you see old clothes and rags, crockery, boots, bottles, boxes, dead dogs and cats, and enormous rats (in which the town is particularly rich) and all sorts of filth flung before the doors. Constantinople may be considered clean in comparison.

San Francisco was a town where life centered in public places rather than around a family hearth, so it was natural that saloons, restaurants, and boarding houses vastly outnumbered churches. Lonely miners were eager for distraction after weeks or months of hard labor scratching for gold. Aside from a few catch-penny circuses, the first formal entertainment took place on June 22, 1849. An English actor named Stephen C. Massett gave a one-man variety show in the town's only schoolhouse with the town's only piano. He sang popular ballads such as *When the Moon on the Lake is Beaming,* did scenes from Shakespeare, and performed "A Yankee Town Meeting," taking seven different parts, each with a different accent. Tickets were three dollars, and the first row was reserved for ladies, four of whom attended. Only three years later, Massett gave his farewell performance in the 1,200-seat concert hall of the Philharmonic Society, accompanied by a full orchestra!

The Mining Camp Becomes a City, 1854–1860

What attracts performers to a place is appreciative audiences, and San Francisco has provided those from its earliest days with strong support for the performing arts. Ballet performances have been running there since 1854, and grand opera since 1851. By the early 1850s, the finest building in town was a stone theater on the Plaza that attracted such luminaries as the Shakespearean actors Edwin and Junius Booth. But no performer could match the success of the legendary Lola Montez. This "Spanish dancer" was actually an Irish girl christened Marie Gilbert. Her beginnings were humble, but her exotic beauty and daring manner made her the toast of the continent. Although she was married, she had a string of lovers, including Franz Liszt and Alexandre Dumas. King Louis of Bavaria fell in love with her, made her Baroness Rosenthal and Countess of Landsfeld, and installed her in a palace. But the Bavarians, already fed up with their king's excessive spending, ran him and his mistress out of the country. Two years later, the sultry former Baroness-Countess was acting and dancing in San Francisco and doing one-night-stand tours of the mining camps. Tickets for her performances went for as much as sixty-five dollars each, and while her acting was rather mediocre, her "spider dance"—during which she shook whalebone spiders from her skimpy costume and stamped on them in time to a fiery Spanish tune—enhanced her already remarkable reputation. At the end of her last tour, which netted her $1,600 a week, she married a local newspaper editor and retired to Grass Valley, where she undertook the guidance of a talented child named Lotta Crabtree. Little Lotta began as a child singer and dancer in the mining camps and by the time she was grown had become the highest-paid actress in America. She never forgot her roots, however, and in 1875, at the height of her career, donated funds to erect Lotta's Fountain at Kearny and Market Streets across from the just-completed Palace Hotel, where it stands today.

By 1860 the gold dust had settled and San Francisco was turning into a city with families, schools, and law enforcement. Over three hundred million dollars in gold had been mined in California in the first ten years of the Gold Rush, and most of it ended up in the pockets of the owners of gambling parlors and bordellos, who became San Francisco's first political leaders. The vast majority of men who flocked to the hills in search of fortune never found it. They found instead that mining was hard work that paid poorly most of the time—and even when they did make a lucky strike, they rarely kept their nuggets very long.

Many of those who had been in on the very beginning of the Gold Rush came to disappointing ends. John Sutter, on whose property the first gold was discovered, saw his enterprises destroyed, first by deserting workers and then by squatters. What money he had left was spent in the courts seeking compensation for his losses, and he died in poverty. James Marshall, Sutter's foreman, who had been the first to find gold, also lost his land to squatters, became disillusioned and spent his final years doing menial work for paltry wages which he spent on liquor. The enterprising Sam Brannan, the man who let the cat out of the bag, made a fortune in San Francisco real estate and business enterprises, but his fondness for the bottle got the best of him also, and he died alone and poor in Southern California. Their stories are typical of thousands of others with whom Fortune flirted briefly before turning her back. Of the tens of thousands of men who came for the Gold Rush, most returned home with no more money than when they had arrived.

Yet it was not all failure. They returned with a sense of having participated in a major historical event: they had been in a magic place where, sometimes, a man could go from pauper to plutocrat in a single day. They had seen what the folks back home would never see, and they would have stories to tell—enough for the rest of their lives. Perhaps they, more than most of their contemporaries, were better prepared for the vast changes and upheavals in human affairs that lay ahead, for while they were off in California, two books had been published in Europe that would rattle the world's self-concept: Darwin's *The Origin of the Species* and Marx and Engel's *The Communist Manifesto*.

Many of the more optimistic argonauts remained in California, most of them in or around San Francisco, where possibly they had noticed something that was expressed by a *Scribner's Monthly* reporter in 1875, describing the city: "The air has an indefinable softness and sweetness—a tonic quality that braces the nerves to a joyous tension, making the very sense of existence a delight."

Whatever their reasons for staying, they—and the settlers who followed them—created a cosmopolitan city whose streets and waterfronts have the appearance of stage sets where an earthy *joie de vivre* persists through the generations and where what Gerald Haslam calls "the soul's search for the possible" remains the prevailing spirit—in short, a city with *cachet*. It is a place from which many of America's most talented authors have drawn inspiration and established themselves. In return, they have enriched the area by their presence.

I

The Golden Era

In the early days of San Francisco, newspapers sprang up like mushrooms to compete for the advertising dollars of local merchants. And, like mushrooms, most of them did not last long. One exception was a weekly literary journal called the *Golden Era* which managed to stay profitable from 1852 to 1893. It was certainly not much to look at—eight pages of the cheapest newsprint covered with six columns of seven-point type, so small that only the sharpest eyes could read it without the aid of a magnifying glass. Its mainstay, since there was no enforcement of copyright laws, was translations of contemporary European novels printed in serialized form. But as the city grew, an increasing number of local authors appeared in the *Era's* pages. It was, by Eastern journalistic standards, a wretched publication, but it provided an early outlet for California residents who wanted to see their words in print, and more importantly, it brought together the four authors who would form San Francisco's first literary group.

Francis Bret Harte, called "Frank," arrived in the city in 1854 at the age of seventeen with his older sister; the pair had come from New York via Nicaragua to join their mother and new stepfather. Harte had been raised in Albany, New York and had left school at thirteen to help support his family after his father died. Although his formal education was brief, he grew up in a literary environment and devoured the novels of Dickens and Dumas, writers who were to influence his writing powerfully.

The San Francisco that Bret Harte discovered was a city in transformation. The northeast corner, where the port and the downtown area were located, was comprised mostly of new stone or brick buildings abundant with columns, capitals, and statuary, aligned on cobblestone streets with broad sidewalks of redwood

Bret Harte

planks. Among these neoclassical edifices, vestiges of the boom town days remained—hastily built wooden structures, often with false fronts. Outside the commercial area, sparkling new residences stood out among the shanties lining the unpaved streets that ran through the sand hills.

Young Bret Harte set about finding his niche in life. He began by teaching school in a mining camp, but when the local veins ran out, the miners moved on and the school closed. He tried working as a tutor, an apothecary's apprentice, a stagecoach shotgun rider, and an amateur miner. Eventually he landed in the town of Union, later to be renamed Arcata, on the coast, seventy-five miles from the Oregon border. There he found employment as an apprentice printer and apprentice reporter on a local newspaper, and the eager novice developed both a sharp eye for detail and an earnest style.

It was the best job Harte had ever had, but it came to an abrupt end when the editor took a trip to San Francisco, leaving the young reporter in charge. During the editor's absence, a group of local ruffians attacked and murdered, without provocation, a small settlement of Indians living on a nearby *rancheria* on Humboldt Bay. Everyone knew who the guilty men were, but no one spoke out against fellow white men in defense of the Indians—no one except Bret Harte, who wrote an editorial condemning the massacre. It was a courageous attempt to rouse the respectable citizens of the town to seek justice, but its only result was that the young reporter had to leave town before the culprits lynched him.

So, in 1857, Harte returned to San Francisco and landed a job as a typesetter for the *Golden Era*, where he developed the practice of slipping samples of his own work into the paper, mostly humorous short pieces signed "Bret." When the editor finally noticed these stowaway items and learned that they came from one of his typesetters, he encouraged Harte to write more, but to submit them before setting them in type. By 1860, Harte had published a novella in the *Era* called "M'liss," the romantic story of a willful twelve-year-old mining camp girl and her teacher.

It was at this point that Harte came to the attention of a woman who would alter the course of his life—Jessie Benton Frémont, the wife of John C. Frémont (who had stirred up the Bear Flag Revolt). The Frémonts were indisputably California's first family at the time. Frémont served as one of California's first U.S. Senators and, when gold was discovered on his Mariposa property, became a wealthy landowner. He ran for president on the Republican ticket in 1856 but lost to James Buchanan. His wife was a no less colorful figure, who helped him enormously with his political career as well as in writing his books.

When Mrs. Frémont read "M'liss" in the *Golden Era*, she recognized raw talent and took Harte on as a protégé. She obtained for him a post at the U.S. Mint in San Francisco, a job that paid well and demanded little of his time, so that he was free to develop his literary skills. Mrs. Frémont also introduced Harte to the social circles of San Francisco, and before long he was writing a column on people and events around town for the *Era*, called "The Bohemian Feuilleton." The title came from the enormous popularity of the English version of *Scènes de la Vie de Bohème*, a novel which would quickly be forgotten once Puccini in 1896 wrote the opera based on it, *La Bohème*. From one story, "M'liss," Harte had gone from typesetter to columnist with a good salary and social standing. Moreover, he became the leader of a group of journalists and writers who were forming the city's first literary clique. They called themselves, in honor of Harte's column, "the bohemians." It is somewhat ironic to associate the word "bohemian" with Bret Harte, because in both appearance and behavior he was anything but. Once he had a steady income from the Mint, he wore nothing but the finest tailored suits and kept his long dark wavy hair carefully brushed. He was a handsome man except for the pockmarks on his face, which he kept concealed with sideburns and a large mustache.

By contrast, his closest "bohemian" friend, Prentice Mulford, looked the part. He was a short fellow with an enormous mustache like a chimney brush that nearly hid his expression of constant amusement. His suit and hat were invariably shabby and in bad need of cleaning. He was two years older than Harte and had grown up in Sag Harbor on New York's Long Island, where he had expected to devote his life to the sea. He shipped aboard a sailing ship, the *Wizard*, for a voyage around the world, but by the time it reached San Francisco, the twenty-two year old sailor was discharged as incompetent. He worked for a while sorting rotten seagull eggs from edible ones. (Fresh food was still hard to come by in San Francisco in 1856, and enterprising merchants sent whaleboats out to gather eggs in the Farallon Islands, some thirty miles out from the Golden Gate, where tens of thousands of seabirds nest). From egg-sorting he moved up to sailor; he managed to sign aboard as a cook on the whaler *Henry,* headed for Mexico. As the weather grew rough, his pots, pans, and kettles would fly off the stove and right out the galley door. He contrived to wire them up to the ceiling, with the result that they swung on and off the stove "like a complicated system of pendulums, but at least they stayed in the galley." He had auditioned for the job by preparing an Irish stew and was accepted, but the crew nearly mutinied when it turned out that Irish stew was the only dish he knew how to make. As he described it:

> There was a general and daily howl of execration from cabin to forecastle against the cook, first started by such misdeeds as coffee boiled with salt water. Misfortunes fell upon me thick and fast. I tumbled down those cabin stairs overwhelmed in the ruins of wearily prepared dinners. I left faucets running; I flung overboard spoon after spoon, hidden in the cloudy water of the washtub. When "cutting in" whales, the decks were filled with blubber, and I cooked in a sea of grease. Worse, the try pots fed by blubber scraps sent forth day and night an unceasing shower of sooty flakes, which covered and permeated

everything. A greasy, dismal, blackened cook performed greasy, dismal, blackened cookery.

Back in San Francisco, Mulford abandoned his ambitions for the sea and took up gold mining. He found it extremely difficult work that brought him only two to three dollars a day, not quite enough to meet his living expenses. Like every other miner, he was sure that his big strike lay just around the corner, and because his other attempts at employment had met with failure, he kept at it despite the meager rewards. Then, one Monday morning, after a particularly lively community drunk celebrating the arrival of the spring rains, Mulford sat beside a stream bed suffering from a hangover

Prentice Mulford

too great to permit him to operate his rocker. This was such a monumental hangover that he felt it needed to be commemorated in prose, and he wrote a tall tale description of it which appeared in the *Sonora Union Democrat* over the name "Dogberry." When the *Era* editor saw the piece, he asked Mulford to submit more such humorous work, and "Dogberry" sketches became a regular feature.

At first, like most of his fellow journalists, Mulford lived in rooming houses which were then abundant in San Francisco, but he eventually found that arrangement extravagant and purchased an old whale-boat, which he berthed away from the busy port area. He lived aboard his boat, sailing alone during the day to contemplate, write, and catch his dinner from the Bay. It was a simple life that would have won the admiration of Thoreau, and Mulford's boyhood dream of becoming a sailor had finally been realized.

A third member of Harte's bohemian group was Charles Warren Stoddard who, although he was the youngest member, had been in San Francisco since arriving with his family at the age of twelve. He had grown up there in the Gold Rush era, and had seen Lola Montez leading her pet grizzly cub on a gold chain down Kearny Street. He had been only thirty feet from the disgruntled county supervisor James Casey when he assassi-nated muckraking publisher James King of William (the "of William" was added to distin-

Charles Warren Stoddard

guish him from another prominent man named James King). Shortly thereafter, the thirteen-year-old Charley saw Casey and another accused assassin dangling from their gibbets where the second Vigilante Committee had hanged them.

Charley had shown promise in school, and his teachers encouraged him in his efforts to write poetry. He was extraordi-narily shy and submitted his first poems to the *Era* under the pseudonym "Pip Pepperpod." It was not until 1862 that he found the courage to begin signing his own name to his work. Because he lived with his parents and was thus under no financial con-straint, he drifted from job to job, unable to work up enthusiasm for any of them. He had clerked in several stores and had been dis-missed from each for his indifferent attitude. By 1860 he was working at Beach's bookstore, where he spent most of his time reading rather than attending to customers.

Although neither Mulford nor Stoddard worked for the *Golden Era*, they could often be found in the editorial offices of the paper, elaborate large rooms with red Turkish carpets, gold chandeliers, and overstuffed chairs and sofas, along with some of their journalist cronies such as Alonzo "Old Block" Delano; George "Squibob" Derby; or John Rollin "Yellow Bird" Ridge.

The first woman to join this group arrived in 1862—a tall, slender, twenty-one year old poetess who was born Josephine Donna Smith. Although she would become a close friend to Harte, Mulford, and Stoddard, none of them would ever know her real name nor the secrets of the life she had led before they met her. She was born in Nauvoo, Illinois on March 10, 1841. Her father was Don Carlos Smith, the youngest brother of Joseph Smith, founder of the Mormon Church; and her mother was Agnes Coolbrith Smith.

Agnes had converted to the Mormon faith in Boston and moved in with the Smith family, where she met and later married Don Carlos, providing him with three daughters. The Mormon Church at this time was essentially a commune made up of the Smith family and the growing numbers of converts who joined them and remained with them in their westward journeys from New York to Ohio to Missouri to Illinois, seeking refuge from the persecutions of the "gentiles." At one point in Ohio, Agnes had been forced out of her home by locals who wanted to drive the Mormons away, and had had to run three miles through the snow with her two babies to find refuge at a friend's house. At Nauvoo, the Mormons built their own city on the banks of the Mississippi, and for a while lived in peace. By the time the third daughter of Don Carlos and Agnes Smith was born, the little family of five had begun to prosper. Five months later, however, Don Carlos died of pneumonia at the age of twenty-five. Agnes was still in mourning when her eldest daughter succumbed to scarlet fever. Then the community was shaken by the loss of its leader: Joseph Smith, along with his brother Hyrum, had broken into the print shop of a newspaper that had been printing inflammatory articles about the Mormons and destroyed the paper's types. They were arrested and awaiting trial in Carthage, Illinois, when a mob broke into the jail and shot them.

Brigham Young then took over the direction of the church and convinced his followers that they would find peace only by leaving the United States and moving to an unpopulated area in what was then northern Mexico. The Smith family, rejecting Young's leadership, determined to remain in Nauvoo. Agnes eventually met and married a young printer named William Pickett who obliged her and her two daughters to swear never to reveal their Mormon background for fear of persecution. He took them to St. Louis in 1847; the following year, Agnes bore him twin sons.

When gold fever took hold in the East, the Pickett family, like everyone else, began to think about going to California. In the spring of 1851, they packed all their belongings into a covered wagon, one of seventeen that made up a small wagon train heading west. Their crossing of the plains and the Rockies was smooth, with no disease, no floods, no trouble with Indians; but when they reached the Sierras they became lost. They camped and each day some men would set out seeking a pass that the wagons could manage, but every evening they returned, unsuccessful. It was autumn and the days were getting colder. They all knew that once the snow began to fall, they would never find their way out of the mountains.

Then they discovered a mulatto mountain man lying in a crude shelter, delirious with fever. The women nursed him back to health. His name was Jim Beckwourth, and he had been constructing a trail for a toll road on a pass when he had fallen sick. He guided them through the mountains and put ten-year-old Josephine, whom everyone called "Ina," up on his horse in front of him. When they reached the summit and could look down into the valleys, he told her, "There it is. That's California, and you're the first white child to enter it on Beckwourth Pass!"

Agnes and her children stayed in Marysville, while her husband went off to try his luck panning for gold along the Feather River. The winter of 1851 was difficult for Agnes and her four children. William became snowed in at a mining camp and could not get back until spring. Agnes was obliged to do sewing for the prostitutes of Marysville to feed her children. A year in the camps convinced William that gold mining was not going to pay off and that he would do better to practice one of his two professions—law or printing—in San Francisco. He moved his family there, opened a law office, and borrowed enough money to build a house in the Mission District.

At the time, San Francisco was filled with unemployed men who had had no luck in the gold country. Some, in desperation, turned to crime. One of these broke into the Pickett home; to cover his burglary, he set fire to the house. Pickett remained in San Francisco long enough to pay off his mortgage and then moved his family to a less dangerous location.

He chose Los Angeles which in 1855 was a little town of 2,000 people of whom

Ina Coolbrith

roughly half were Mexicans and the other half Indians. There were a few English-speaking families, however, and their number was growing. Eventually a school was started, and it was there that Ina received the only formal education she ever had—three years in a tiny two-room schoolhouse. Ina and her sister spent their adolescence in the pueblo of Los Angeles and found diversion from the rather bleak life there in the cotillions and fandangos of the Californios. At sixteen, Ina opened a grand ball on the arm of California's last Mexican governor, Pio Pico.

During her adolescence, Ina began writing poems. They were conventional and sentimental verses, but sufficiently well-crafted to be printed in the local English language newspaper, the *Los Angeles Star*. This early recognition encouraged her to submit her work to a larger market, the *California Home Journal*, a San Francisco Sunday newspaper with wide circulation. The editor, Joseph Duncan, not only accepted her poems but encouraged her to send him more. Then the sixteen-year-old poetess caught the eye of a young Los Angeles businessman named Robert Carsley, who owned a growing iron works company. He also had musical talent, and worked in a minstrel show that went on occasional tours around the state. Carsley courted her, and they were married a few weeks before Ina's seventeenth birthday, and moved into a small house near the ironworks. The following April, just as Fort Sumter was fired on and the Civil War began, Ina discovered that she was expecting a child.

Her joy was short-lived, however. A few months later, Carsley returned from a minstrel engagement in San Francisco. He came by Ina's parents' house to take her home. For some reason, he was in a fit of jealous rage. He accused Ina, without justification, of infidelity and threatened her life. He dragged his pregnant wife into the street, waving his pistol about and shouting threats. At that moment, Ina's stepfather returned home. He saw Carsley and ordered him to release Ina. Carsley, startled, turned toward Pickett and Ina was able to break away and run toward the house. Carsley fired at her as she ran, narrowly missing both Ina and her mother. Pickett fired and struck his son-in-law in the right hand, shattering it. Carsley's hand had to be amputated, ending his career as an ironworker as well as that of a minstrel. Ina obtained a rapid divorce, but the loss of what had seemed to her an ideal marriage paled beside the subsequent loss of her child, born dead, probably from the trauma of its father's wild escapade.

Ina could not go on living in the small town of Los Angeles, especially with all of the scandal reported in the same newspaper that had published her poems. She decided to move to San Francisco and take a new name. Using her mother's maiden name, Josephine Donna Smith Pickett Carsley became Ina Coolbrith. Her stepfather determined that his twin sons would have greater opportunity in a large city, so the family moved with her.

When she arrived in San Francisco, Ina looked up Joseph Duncan, only to find that he had given up the editor's chair at the *California Home Journal* to open Duncan's Bazaar on Sacramento Street, an emporium of fine furniture and art works to serve the needs of the city's growing *nouveaux riche.* It was Duncan who introduced her to Charley Stoddard and who helped her find a job teaching at a private elementary school at the corner of Mason and Jackson, within walking distance from the Russian Hill house where she lived with her mother, stepfather and her two half-brothers. Before long, Ina Coolbrith's poems became familiar to

Era readers, and the tragic events that had occurred in Los Angeles slipped to the back of her memory. She was busy with her teaching, and she was accepted as a friend and a colleague by San Francisco's most promising writers. Although she did not yet realize it, she was forming relationships that would prove to be the deepest and most enduring of her life.

II.

The Bohemians

Any doubts about the status of Francis Bret Harte as San Francisco's most famous author were dispelled in 1863 when the *Atlantic Monthly* printed his story "The Legend of Monte Diablo," a finely-wrought allegorical tale about the confrontation between a Spanish missionary priest and Satan on top of Mount Diablo. No other writer west of the Mississippi had ever appeared in that most prestigious of literary magazines, and the recognition extended to Harte by the Eastern press was unprecedented. His little band of "bohemians" grew as journalists and aspiring writers sought to associate themselves with him. All of these were men except Ina Coolbrith and Mary Tingsley, a young woman who specialized in short stories that appeared regularly in the *Era*.

Mary Tingley and Ina Coolbrith were often escorted to theatrical performances by Harte, Mulford, and Stoddard. One Saturday evening, when San Francisco was abuzz over the opening of *Mazeppa* starring Adah Isaacs Menken, the five of them were sitting in the orchestra at Mcguire's Opera House. The play was based on Byron's poem of the same name, a long narrative in which a seventeenth-century nobleman is killed by a jealous husband. The advance publicity on the play indicated that San Francisco had never before seen anything so audacious as this on a stage, and the theater was sold out.

The house lights went down, the curtains parted, and the play began. When Adah Isaacs Menken walked onstage, the crowd burst into enthusiastic applause even before she spoke her first line. She was playing the lead, the Tartar prince, and with her prominent nose, heavy eyebrows, and close-cropped curly hair, she looked very much like a handsome young nobleman. The play itself was not particularly moving—a lot of stomping about on the stage with long, histrionic speeches—but the climax was the source of all the excitement: in Byron's poem, Mazeppa's captors tie him naked to a wild horse, which they then chase into the wilderness of the steppes.

The audience was stunned when, at the end of the play, a glistening white stallion galloped across the stage with the star, quite nude, tied on her back on top of him. As the horse zigzagged up a ramp among painted mountain sets, the crowd exploded into thunderous applause and cheering.

Harte insisted that his friends accompany him backstage to pay their respects to the actress. She received them in her dressing room, and, to their amazement, accepted Harte's invitation to join them at a café down the street from the theater. With Adah was her husband, John Heenan, known as "the Benicia Boy," an unofficial heavyweight boxing champion of the United States. He was a big, smiling, agreeable fellow who seemed to understand nothing of what was being said around the café table. Before long, the writers could see that Miss Menken had accepted Harte's invitation for a purpose. She wrote poetry, and she very much wanted to see her work appear in the *Era*. Although she was no longer in costume, she had left her stage makeup on and was the undisputed center of attention, talking at length and controlling the conversation, making sure it did not stray far from herself as the principal topic. Before long, her fascinated hosts had learned that she had started her career as a dancer in New Orleans; had traveled broadly, studying painting and sculpture; was fluent in Hebrew, French, and Spanish; acted in everything from Shakespeare to vaudeville; had seen her poetry published in the *New York Sunday Mercury*; and was well known at Pfaff's, the center of bohemianism in New York. Now she was going to make her home in San Francisco with her new husband, and she was anxious to establish herself here as a writer as well as a performer.

Harte and the others were amused to see how absolutely smitten Charley Stoddard was by the actress. After he managed to get her autograph on a menu, he stared at her with an expression of awe and admiration. Finally, at one of the rare pauses in Adah's conversation, he blurted out, "I can't tell you how much I admire your courage and your dedication to your art, appearing undressed like that on the horse in front of all those people." Adah turned her lovely features on him and fixed him with a gaze from her dazzling blue eyes that caused him to turn beet red. "That's very well put, my young friend," she said in her deep, husky voice. "I *appear* naked. Actually, I wear a garment, something like a stocking, but flesh-colored, and it goes from the neck to the ankles."

Adah Isaacs Menken

"Like a silk union suit," Prentice Mulford suggested. Adah turned her double-barreled look on him. "Like silk long underwear perhaps. You would never catch me in anything called a *union* suit!"

There was a general murmur of disapproval at this slur against the government. The war was far away, but Harte and his friends were ardent supporters of Lincoln and the Union cause. "Don't get me wrong," Adah continued, unperturbed by their rebuke. "I do not support slavery for one moment. It has no place in this country. It must be eradicated, but that must be done by the South. I support the Confederacy. I support the right of states to secede, and I believe Jefferson Davis is one of the greatest men who ever lived."

She waited for rebuttal, but no one wanted to take her on. Finally Harte said, "I completely disagree with you on that subject, Miss Menken, but I respect your right to your opinions. Let's not get into a political argument. When can we see some of your poetry?"

She smiled at him and replied, "When you *see* it is up to you, Mr. Harte, but you can *hear* it whenever you like. Right now if you wish."

They were all astounded that she could recite her own poems without notes, but she did, in a full stage voice that stopped every conversation in the café and fixed every eye on her:

> Let us follow the heavy hearse that bore our old dream
> Out past the white-horned Daylight of Love.
> Let thy pale Dead come up from their furrows of
>   winding sheets
> To mock thy prayers with what the days might have
>   been.
> Let the living come back and point at the shadows
> That swept over the disk of the morning air...

Her hosts listened, fascinated. There was no rhyme, no discernible rhythm; it was blank verse, a series of mournful images, but the lines were delivered with such skill and intensity that everyone in the café was spellbound. There was a heavy luxuriance in her verse that brought to mind intricate oriental carpets. After ten minutes, Adah ended her performance, looked directly at Harte, and said in a velvet voice, "What do you think, Mr. Harte? Does some of this merit the attention of the *Golden Era*?"

He was obviously confounded by Adah's presumptuous approach, and sputtered something about being sure that the editor would be proud to print poetry by such an accomplished person as Miss Menken. The actress stood up abruptly, without warning, causing all of the men to push their chairs back hastily and rise. She announced, "Then I would consider it an act of friendship if you would call on me tomorrow in the early afternoon. I will give you some manuscripts, and I will be forever in your debt if you will go over them with the editor. Johnny, give Mr. Harte a card, please." She swept the group with her electric glance. "It has been a delightful evening, and I hope that you will excuse me. I am very tired and must retire. Good night." She gave them a stunning smile and turned and walked out of the café with them calling "Good night" after her. John Heenan handed Harte a card and followed his wife out the door.

The men sat down again. Harte said, "Look at this. She only recently arrived here, and look." He showed them the card which read:

ADAH ISAACS MENKEN
Artiste
The Lick House   San Francisco

"Look at the back," Harte said. They turned the card over and saw a photograph of Adah's face printed there. "How do they do that?" Mary Tingley asked, and Stoddard said, "Oh, everyone in New York is getting calling cards with their pictures on them these days. Watkins over on Montgomery Street is making them now. I think I'm going to have a set made."

They all teased him a little, saying that photo calling cards were a bit pretentious, but every one of them was wondering what it would cost and if they would have the courage to use them. In later years, Charley Stoddard would recall the experience of seeing Adah perform: "Every curve of her limbs was as appealing as a line in a Persian love song. She was...a living and breathing poem that set the heart to music and throbbed rhythmically to a passion that was as splendid as it was pure."

III

The Circle Grows

Not long after Ina Coolbrith's arrival, a young reporter for the Virginia City, Nevada *Territorial Enterprise* began making regular visits to San Francisco and eventually fell in with the bohemians. His name was Sam Clemens, and he was somewhat more rowdy than the others, with his shock of red hair and his raucous voice. He spoke in a broad Midwestern drawl peppered with rough slang and profanity, which he tried to curb a bit when Ina and Mary were in his company. Despite his contrast in appearance and behavior to Bret Harte, the two of them got along very well. Harte wrote of him, "He had the curly hair, the aquiline nose, and even the aquiline eye—an eye so eagle-like that a second lid would not have surprised me—of an unusual and dominant nature. His eyebrows were thick and bushy. His dress was careless, and his general manner was one of supreme indifference to surroundings and circumstances." As their friendship deepened, Sam's visits to the city grew longer and more frequent.

Sam Clemens had grown up on the banks of the Mississippi River in rural Missouri—an idyllic boyhood until his father died and Sam was obliged to quit school and go to work as a printer's devil. He finished his adolescence as an itinerant printer but then realized his youthful ambition and became a Mississippi riverboat pilot. He very probably would have spent the rest of his life guiding those majestic boats up and down the river if the Civil War had not come along and put a stop to riverboat traffic. He joined the Confederate Missouri Volunteers, but after three weeks found military life not to his liking and deserted. His older brother Orion had been appointed secretary to the Governor of the Nevada Territory, and Sam accompanied him West by stagecoach to Carson City. He tried silver mining for a while but found the work too unpleasant and the rewards too meager. Then he managed to land the job as reporter for the *Virginia City Territorial Enterprise*. In a remote town of 15,000 men and a handful of women, with everyone either mining or servicing miners' needs, there was not much news to report. The *Enterprise* not only allowed but encouraged its reporters to practice "creative journalism," extravagant exaggerations, obvious hoaxes, mock feuds, and outrageous satire. The young Missourian was in his element here and rapidly became the leading practitioner of this type of frontier entertainment. Of an unpopular law, he wrote that it was an "act born out of wedlock—the bastard offspring of an emasculated governor and four impotent Legislative officers!" Of the passing of another act of which he approved, he wrote "Great excitement exists. Half the population is drunk—the balance will be before midnight." As his popularity increased, he began signing his work, using the pen-name "Mark Twain," a river term indicating the depth of the water at two fathoms, twelve feet, a safe depth for a riverboat's passage. As his salary increased and he saw some profits from wildcat mining stocks, Sam could afford to take trips to San Francisco to enjoy the city's high life. He liked staying at the best hotels, dining in the finest restaurants, patronizing a much more elegant brothel than Virginia City had to offer. "I fell in love with the most cordial and sociable city in the Union," he wrote to his family. His most frequent companion on these trips was a printer named Steve Gillis, a short wiry fellow with a penchant for getting into saloon brawls.

Once Sam had made the acquaintance of Harte, it was not long before his articles began to appear in the *Era*. Virginia City residents loved to read stories that poked fun at the pretentiousness and affectations of San Franciscans, and Sam gave them plenty to laugh over. The pieces he wrote for the *Era* gave San Franciscans the opportunity to laugh at themselves.

In May of 1864, Sam and Gillis found it expedient to leave Virginia City and relocate in San Francisco. Both of them were practical jokers, and when their joking was done in company with over-indulgence in sour mash whiskey, the results were often less than humorous. While the Civil War raged "in the States," Union supporters in the Territory of Nevada competed to see who could raise the most money for the Sanitary Fund, a forerunner of the Red Cross. A fancy dress ball in Carson City raised $3,000 for the Fund, and Sam, while drunk, wrote a sarcastic article about the ball, implying that the money was actually going to a "miscegenation society." The article was a spoof, never intended for publication, but a copy boy inadvertently picked it up and delivered it to the printers. The next morning, the *Enterprise* appeared carrying the article, and the leading citizens of Carson City were up in arms against the brash reporter. At the same time, Sam had written a column for his paper accusing the publisher of the rival *Virginia City Union* of failing to honor his pledged contributions to the Sanitary Fund. The publisher responded with a column of his own, and the attacks began to escalate. Joshing quarrels between rival frontier papers were common, but this battle in ink was a serious and bitter one, getting to the point where the *Union* publisher wrote that Sam had "proved himself an unmitigated liar, a poltroon, and a puppy!" These were fighting words, dueling words, and Sam had two good reasons to avoid a duel. First, dueling was illegal in the Territory, and second, Sam was a very poor pistol shot. All in all, it seemed to Sam and Gillis that the time was right for a move, and the logical destination was San Francisco. As a journeyman printer, Gillis had no trouble finding employment, but Sam found himself obliged to take a position with the *Morning Call*. His San Francisco friends warned him that the "one-bit washerwoman's rag" would wear him out, but Sam had no choice. Until his various mining stocks paid off, he needed income to keep him in whiskey, cigars, and the other necessities of life.

For forty dollars a week, Sam was expected to begin his day early at the police court to write up the misbehavior of the town's low life the previous night, a very popular feature for the *Call's* readers. Then he would go to the county court to write up the misdeeds of a more refined class of criminals. His afternoons were spent covering fires, accidents, ship arrivals, public meetings, ceremonies for the openings of new buildings, and the stock exchange. Every evening he would run from theater to theater for a sample of whatever plays, concerts, lectures, or minstrel shows were taking place. Finally, he would return to the newspaper office and turn all of his notes into copy, rarely finishing before one o'clock in the morning. It was, as he put it, "awful slavery for a lazy man."

He sustained himself through this drudgery with daydreams of a triumphant return to Missouri as a man of prosperity. The value of his stocks was rising every day, and, as tempting as it was to take the profit in hand, he resisted. All around the city mansions were being erected by men who had made huge fortunes from Comstock Lode stocks; but Sam was determined to live from his wages and leave his investments untouched until they had grown to a sizable fortune. One hundred thousand dollars was his goal. The day they reached that, he would sell out and turn his back on the West. As he sat in fetid courtrooms or at tedious meetings, he visualized himself in a fine white house, somewhere near St. Louis perhaps, with a sweeping view of the Mississippi. He would have his own billiard room where he could pass the time with his cronies. And of course there would be a Mrs. Clemens, a gentle quiet person who would chide him harmlessly about his cigars and whiskey and profanity. Sometimes at the stock exchange his heart would skip a few beats when he saw that the value of his stocks had dipped, but they always came back and began to rise again within a few days.

The only good thing about his job was that the *Call* offices were in the same building as the Mint annex, so he had the opportunity of seeing Bret Harte regularly. Harte never seemed to have much to do at the Mint, and Sam arranged whenever he could to be at the office at lunch time. The two of them would go off to the Bank Exchange Saloon in the Montgomery Block where, for the price of a couple of mugs of steam beer, they could stuff themselves with delicacies from the free lunch counter laden with fresh shrimp, oysters, and clams as well as generous slices of corned beef, ham, turkey, and smoked salmon surrounded by sauces, crab salad, boiled eggs, and pickled vegetables, all under the huge painting of a naked voluptuous Delilah shearing the locks of a sleeping Samson.

Sam complained to Harte about the hours he had to work and the frustration of having his best articles censored. When he reported on San Francisco policemen brutally beating Chinese vendors for no good reason, his editor pointed out that "our readers are not interested in the welfare of John Chinaman." And every time he would try to slip in a bit of the caustic wit or sarcasm that had made his writing so popular in Nevada, the editor would cut it right out. It was then that Harte encouraged him to write some of his articles twice; once in the bland style the *Call* wanted and then again with the freewheeling exaggerations that the *Territorial Enterprise* preferred. "You could send those up to Virginia City as 'Letters from San Francisco'," Frank suggested. "You know how they love to print anything that ridicules us here."

Mark Twain

Sam sipped his beer pensively. "It's true enough that the boys up at the mines do love to read Frisco scandals. And it would give me a chance to get in a few licks on those bastards on the police force." After that, despite his schedule, Sam began writing second versions of his *Call* articles, mocking every aspect of the city: the police, ladies' fashions, the *nouveau riche*, the latest fads, and the weather. He would bring these pieces to Harte before sending them off, and Harte, who was as meticulous in his style as he was in his dress, went through them, excising all that was crude or awkward and making Sam's prose even more biting and effective.

As Sam was refining his satirical style, the bohemian group was joined by its first married couple, Cincinnatus Hiner Miller and his bride Minnie Myrtle Miller, who had come down from Oregon to San Francisco to astound the city with their poetry. Cincinnatus was born in 1837 and raised in frontier Indiana, the son of a Quaker school teacher with a penchant for moving West and losing money. The Miller family's westward migration ended on a homestead hardscrabble farm on the banks of the Willamette

River. At seventeen, bored with unremunerative farming, Cincinnatus drifted down to Northern California where he took on a variety of jobs. One of these was as cook for a mining operation. When the mine owner refused, after many requests, to pay Miller the wages he had coming, the young cook took a team of pack horses into the town of Deadwood for supplies. Instead of buying beans and bacon, Miller sold the pack team, pocketed the wages owed to him, and then returned the remainder of the

Joaquin Miller

proceeds of the sale to the owner along with his resignation. The mine owner was livid and reported him as a thief to the local sheriff. When the lawman apprehended him and threatened him with a cocked pistol if he did not stop, Miller put a rifle bullet through the sheriff's shoulder and rode calmly on his way. To avoid arrest, he spent several years living with the Wintu Indians on the McCloud River near Mount Shasta. There he cohabited with a Wintu woman; she bore him a daughter whom he named Calle-Shasta.

Eventually he wandered back to Oregon, graduated from Columbia College (after three month's attendance), and continued his succession of various jobs: teaching school, practicing law, and riding for the pony express. By 1863, he was the editor of the *Democratic Register* in Eugene, no small accomplishment for a man who never could spell correctly. While he had been an express rider in Idaho, Miller had read some poems by a young girl living in a remote fishing village on the Oregon coast, Minnie Myrtle Dyer, and had begun a correspondence with her. In Eugene, he continued the correspondence and eventually came calling on her. He arrived on a Tuesday and they were married the following Sunday. Miller, an amateur poet himself, announced they would relocate in San Francisco and live from their pens or starve.

Cincinnatus Miller was over six feet tall, with a most impressive face. He had bright blue eyes that glared from a heavy scowling brow and gave him a constant look of great intensity, heightened by his expansive forehead under a tumult of blond wavy hair. He wore a mustache and goatee, but his clean-shaven cheeks revealed high cheekbones that gave him a dramatic look. Minnie had a mass of long dark hair that fell on her shoulders and back in a cascade of ringlets and framed a sweet, pretty face. She was enthralled by her dashing husband and her new life in San Francisco. They rented a cottage at First and Folsom and devoted themselves to writing. Both had poems printed in the *Era,* but without remuneration. Miller was convinced that the key to literary success was perseverance—the important thing was not to give up and take a job that would steal one's energy, but to keep writing and to keep making contacts with prospective publishers. For a little while it looked as if his conviction might be rewarded; the *Police Gazette* accepted his story "The Devil's Castle," to be published as a serial. They did not pay much, but it was Miller's first income since the couple had arrived in San Francisco, and it was definitely an encouragement. Miller did his best to court Bret Harte's good opinion, but Harte, having read some of his poems as well as Minnie's, wanted nothing to do with them. Charley Stoddard and Prentice Mulford, however, befriended the couple and encouraged them, impressed by their dedication.

At the time, Harte was spending less time with his bohemian cronies since making the acquaintance of Anna Griswold, a fellow member of the First Unitarian Church. She was five years older than he and not particularly attractive either in looks or personality. What attracted Harte to her was a mystery to his friends. Miss Griswold was a rather obsessively respectable woman who felt that achieving and maintaining social status were the purpose of life. They married and settled in the residential suburbs of San Francisco, and Harte's "Bohemian Feuilleton" began to dwell on subjects such as gardening and the pleasures of parenthood rather than on city night life. Mrs. Harte felt that her husband should devote more time to his position at the Mint and less to his "writing hobby."

IV

The Californian

As San Franciscans celebrated the New Year of 1865, they knew that the war was nearly over. Atlanta and Savannah had fallen to Sherman, the long battle of Nashville had ended in a Union victory, and Grant now had his headquarters in Petersburg, Virginia. The Confederacy was writhing in a death agony, unwilling to acknowledge that all hope of ever expelling Federal troops from the South had vanished. Talk of military campaigns had shifted to discussions of how the peace would be administered. Should the rebel states be reinstated to the Union? What should be done with all the former slaves? Would Robert E. Lee and Jefferson Davis be tried for treason? On April 9, the news was telegraphed that Lee had surrendered the Army of Northern Virginia to Grant at Appomattox. San Francisco broke out in a frenzy of celebration. Nearly every house and business establishment displayed an American flag or red, white, and blue banners. Schools and shops were closed as the city commemorated victory and peace with continuous parades, speeches, and marching bands. Then, just five days after the surrender, came the word that President Lincoln had been assassinated. The city fell immediately from joyous celebration into deep mourning. By early afternoon a mob had gathered at Union Square. They were harangued by one speaker after another, urging retribution against "copperhead" newspapers that had supported the South all through the war. Before night fell, offices and press rooms of the *Democratic Press, Monitor, Occidental Newsletter, L'Union Franco-Américain,* and *Écho du Pacifique* had been demolished. The police were unable to quell the riot until aided by the military. Four days later, a memorial service to the fallen President was held at Union Square with 14,000 citizens in attendance.

After that, the hostilities between the supporters of the North and those of the South subsided, and the city turned its attention back to its rapid growth, its increasing sophistication, and the progress of the transcontinental railroad that would bring an end to California as a part of the frontier. Although the war had been far away, it had affected the city considerably. More than 100,000 people emigrated to California as refugees from the battles or from conscription, most of them settling in or near San Francisco. Moreover, when the war cut off shipments of goods to the West, local industries started up to fill in the gap, and there were more than eight hundred factories and foundries in the city at the end of the war. San Francisco was already sprucing itself up. Open gambling and prostitution were no longer visible, though neither vice was difficult to locate, and the rough clothes of the miners was giving way to tall silk hats, broadcloth suits, and morning coats for the gentlemen and increasingly larger hoop skirts for the ladies.

Cincinnatus and Minnie Myrtle Miller departed even before the war had ended. Unable to make a living by writing and unwilling to compromise, Miller took his bride back to Oregon where he took a succession of jobs until he was finally appointed Judge of Grant County, a position he held for several years despite the fact that, because of his completely illegible handwriting, no one, including himself, could read his decisions. To San Francisco he left a parting shot:

> Gay Frisco! To one who was reared in the mountains,
> Your beauties are dim and your pleasures are spare;
> Though maybe to those who are born in commotion,
> My forests were ever as irksome and bare;
> Yet a day with my mountains and billows and
> fountains,
> Were dearer to me than a century there.

For his part, Bret Harte now had a son at home, and although he greatly enjoyed his role as a father, his relations with Mrs. Harte grew increasingly strained. He had received two promotions at the Mint, and his income was sufficient to provide his family with a comfortable home, but to his wife's displeasure he persisted in frequenting writers and journalists. One of Harte's colleagues from the *Era* established a new literary weekly, the *Californian*. He felt, justifiably, that the *Golden Era* was too old-fashioned, too deeply rooted in Gold Rush nostalgia, and lacked the sophistication to reflect a growing urban center like San Francisco. Harte encouraged this enterprise, agreeing to serve as an unofficial editor and to convince his bohemian friends to submit their work to the new paper. It was advertised as "The Best Journal on the Pacific Coast, and the Equal of any on the Continent." High-flown self-praise perhaps, but in appearance at least it was true. It was printed on white imperial stock with three columns of large, clear print, sixteen pages each week; five dollars for an annual subscription. Before long, Frank had all of his friends submitting manuscripts, and the *Californian* ran poems by Ina Coolbrith and Charles Warren Stoddard and sketches and articles by "Mark Twain," Prentice Mulford, and Mary Tingley.

The poems that Charley Stoddard published from time to time were rewarding to his self-confidence but brought him very little money. He was tired of the succession of clerking jobs that always seemed to lead to boredom and indifference before finally ending in a polite dismissal. The opening of the College of California in Oakland inspired him to attempt higher education, and he enrolled in one of its first classes. He was still living with his family in San Francisco and would rise early and take the horse trolley down to the foot of Market Street and the ferry building. It was a long brown structure that faced a huge wood-planked plaza where coaches, carriages, and trolleys stopped to unload passengers before turning around for a return trip. Then he would take a cup of strong coffee which always seemed to taste better in the invigorating salt air on the deck of the five-cent steam ferry that carried him across the Bay toward the sun rising over the Oakland Hills. In Oakland he would catch another horse trolley that took him to the College of California building at 13th and Franklin. The commute took as long as two hours each way, and by the time he arrived home, his family had eaten their supper already, and his mother would warm a plate for him. Initially, he found the routine so exhausting that he avoided late-night out-ings with his friends on weekends. But after a few months he could no longer resist the temptation of nights at the theaters and cafés, and he fell into his old habits.

He had entered the college with the confidence that he would do well, as he had always done in school before. But even before the first semester was over, he had to face the fact that he was not doing well at all. The only subject that could hold his interest was English, and even there he could not manage to get himself to write compositions on assigned topics that were of no interest to him. He continued to rise early every day and cross the Bay with a firm resolve that he would attend every class and make a sincere effort to focus his attention on every lecture and complete every assignment. Once he arrived at the college, however, his resolve would melt away. A kind of illness would overtake him. He would become nervous and his knees would go weak, as if he were going to faint. His mind would race with self-doubts: *You don't belong in that classroom. If you go in, you won't understand anything; the professor will question you, and you'll make a fool of yourself.* So to calm down, he would go to the library, select a book that had nothing to do with his courses, and wander off into the foothills to spend the day reading, writing verses, or just daydreaming. As final examinations drew closer and Charley realized that there was no longer any chance of making up for the time he had wasted, he grew despondent. He faced the fact that he was no better at schol-arship than he had been at business, and the self-loathing that his lack of discipline brought on deepened to the point of a nervous breakdown. His distraught parents sought to take his mind off his depression with an ocean voyage, and sent him to Hawaii to visit his sister, who had married a well-to-do plantation owner. A long vacation in the tropics, they hoped, would calm the mind of their sensitive and high-strung son.

V

Famous But Broke

While Charley Stoddard recuperated in Hawaii, Sam Clemens was watching the stock market nervously. Statehood had been proposed for the Territory of Nevada, and Sam, like most of the people who were knowledgeable in Nevada affairs, was convinced that the government regulation that statehood would entail would bring a hasty end to the flush times there. He feared for his mining stocks and had a difficult time resisting the temptation to sell out before the vote was taken on the state constitution. He was in sight of his $100,000 goal, and, sure that the voters would reject statehood, he held on nervously. But the measure passed. His stocks, instead of dropping, began to rise rapidly, and silver stock speculation became frenzied. Each day as he went to the stock market on California Street, wondering if this was the day to unload, Sam saw his fortune increased and the share prices still rising. "One more day" became a ritual, until one day he arrived to find the market overrun with a sea of bobbing silk hats—men were shouting, even screaming. It was not unusual to hear the shouts of curbstone brokers in the street outside the big board, but this day, all the brokers, including the ones who generally sat behind ornate desks in quiet offices, were out there, hollering and pushing along with the rest like frightened animals. The anticipated effect of Nevada statehood had finally occurred and the bottom *had* dropped out. Sam's Hale and Norcross stocks were worth only a fraction of what he had paid for them. He had lost everything.

All that did not make his present circumstances any easier. He was sitting in the office of George Barnes, the *Call's* editor, and he knew he had not been called in for a commendation nor a promotion.

"I like you, Sam," Barnes was saying. He rose from his roll-top desk and paced the wooden floor of his office, chewing his cigar. "I really do. But the fact is, you have no real interest in this job. It's clear to me that you've been spending more and more time on your letters to the *Enterprise* and less on your work for us. And you know as well as I do you're more interested in being clever than in reporting the facts, even with something as serious as the earthquake last month, for God's sake! Sam, our readers want news, not jokes."

Sam made no reply. There was no point in denying the obvious.

"I've gotta have a city beat reporter with ambition and drive," Barnes continued, "and I'm afraid you just don't fit that description. You're too...you're not aggressive enough, that's the thing. I think too much of you to dismiss you, Sam, so I'm asking you, as a gentleman, to tender your resignation, to give me two weeks' notice. I'm sorry, but I have to do what's best for the paper."

Sam stood up. "I understand. You shall have it in the morning." He turned and left the editor's office, heading straight for the stairs that led to Harte's office below.

"You'll see. This is the best thing that could have happened to you." Harte was doing his best to console his friend, but Sam was skeptical. "Sam, you were tied down working for the *Call*. Now you're free. You can write the kind of pieces you want to. The *Californian* will pay you twelve dollars for every sketch they print. And if you continue sending pieces to the *Era* and the *Enterprise*, that'll augment your income. The *Daily Dramatic Chronicle* is always after me to write reviews for them. I'll recommend you to them, and that will be another source."

"I don't know, Bret. Hell, I've had a reg'lar job of some kind ever since I was twelve years old. The idea of going without a steady salary is damned frightening."

Harte tried to sound confident. "Oh well, it may be tight for a while, but just hang on. Once the circulation of the *Californian* builds up, they'll need a staff of writers. You'll be the first choice. Don't be discouraged. Now you're free to make a name for yourself, you'll see."

"Maybe. On the other hand, now that the boats are running

on the Mississippi again, I could go back to my old river pilot job. It's jest that I powerfully hate to go back home broke. It damages my vanity."

"Exactly so," Harte replied cheerfully. "You can always go home broke. You've nothing to lose by staying. You still have a chance to make good here. You're a journalist, not a sailor."

So Sam gave up his room at the Occidental and moved in with his friend Steve Gillis, who had taken up residence in a Mission District boarding house. Gillis promised Sam he would tide him over the rough spots until he had a good income again, and Sam threw himself assiduously into writing for every publication that might accept his work. He showed up at the Mint almost every day, and Harte would patiently go through his work, indicating what was awkward or unclear and how to improve it. Before long, most issues of the *Californian* carried a piece signed "Mark Twain."

His parodies, burlesques, and tall tales concerning life in San Francisco that were so popular among Virginia City readers began to appear in the *Californian* as well. In a city with a rapidly-growing wealthy class that took itself very seriously, the society columns had become an important part of the newspapers, and every social gathering was described in glowing, even gushing terms. They were a natural target for Sam's mockery:

> Mrs. W. M. was attired in an elegant *pâté de fois gras*, made especially for her, and was greatly admired. The queenly Mrs. L. B. was attractively attired in her new false teeth, and the *bon jour* effect they naturally produced was heightened by her enchanting and well-sustained smile.

> Miss C. L. B. had her fine nose elegantly enameled, and the easy grace with which she blew it from time to time, marked her as a cultivated and accomplished woman of the world.

The hoop skirt was in full fashion at the time and provided Sam with broad opportunity:

To critically examine these hoops—to get the best effect—one should stand on the corner of Montgomery and look up a steep street like Clay or Washington. As the ladies loop their dresses till they lie in folds on the spreading hoops, the effect presented by a furtive glance up a steep street is very charming.

Although the *Californian's* readers were shocked by such outright salacious material, it boosted the paper's popularity, and Sam gave them more, such as his example of "Nature's Eternal Law of Compensation:"

Behold, the same gust of wind that blows a lady's dress aside and exposes her ankle, fills your eye so full of sand that you can't see it.

While his articles maintained a style of buffoonery, he never failed to get his digs in at the brutality and corruption of the San Francisco police. All the frustration he had felt at having his articles censored while writing for the *Call* now came out, and his ridicule of the police became even more daring. He reported acidly and accurately on how policemen severely enforced the law on the poor but looked the other way when crimes were committed by those affluent enough to pay them off. Finally, Chief of Police Burke brought a libel suit against the editor of the *Territorial Enterprise* where Sam's most biting satires had appeared. The litigation intimidated neither Sam nor his editor. In fact, Sam's barbs at the police increased in frequency and in rancor. On one occasion, seeing an overweight policeman on a bench downtown, minding his beat by taking a sonorous nap, Sam stepped over to a Chinese vegetable cart, took a leaf from a large cabbage and, holding it in both hands, proceeded to fan the dozing officer slowly and ceremoniously. Before long, a small crowd of passers-by had stopped to watch and snicker at the scene. When the cop finally woke up, he found himself with a cabbage leaf on his lap and a couple of dozen people surrounding him, laughing. From the corner of his eye, he saw Sam Clemens disappearing down the street, waving at him.

Despite these antics, Sam was not happy in San Francisco. He was working hard and just earning enough to pay his food and rent. He had no prospects and could not shake the depression that the loss of his mining stocks had brought on. It was in these circumstances that he went with Steve Gillis to Gillis' brother's cabin on Jackass Hill near Angel's Camp. Legend has it that Sam and Steve left San Francisco hurriedly because Gillis was jumping bail over a saloon brawl, but the truth is simply that the two men were bored and hoping for a chance to strike it rich. "Pocket mining," the type of gold mining in practice around Angel's Camp, involved shoveling and washing dirt from a hillside to try to locate traces of gold and then to discover the pattern of the traces to determine the source from which they had washed down, the rich deposit that would yield a fortune. As Sam described the process:

> Your breath comes short and quick, you are feverish with excitement; the dinner bell may ring its clapper off, you pay no attention; friends may die, weddings transpire, houses burn down, they are nothing to you; you sweat and dig and delve with a frantic interest and all at once you strike it! Up comes a spadeful of earth and quartz that is all lovely with soiled lumps and leaves and sprays of gold.

It did not take long for Sam to discover that pocket mining was hard work and that the excitement in it seemed to be always in what one might discover rather than in what one actually discovered. He grew tired of it and began to spend more and more time jawing with the boys who hung around the saloon in Angel's Camp. One of these was a bald ex-corporal named Ben Coon who loved to spin yarns in an infuriating manner: he would ramble, interrupt himself, go off on tangents, wander back to his story for a few seconds and then take off on another side-track. On one occasion, Ben Coon told a story about a man who claimed that his pet frog could out-jump any other frog in the world and who would challenge his cronies to find a frog that his couldn't beat.

The story, hardly more than a joke, gave Sam an idea. When he had still been in Virginia City writing for the *Enterprise*, Sam had made the acquaintance of the humorist Artemus Ward who was in town on a lecture tour. The two men had hit it off and became friends. Shortly before Sam's departure from San Francisco, he had received a letter from Ward who was in New York putting together a book of "frontier humor." He asked if Sam had anything he wanted to contribute. Sam had not responded because, in the first place, he could not think of anything he had written that would be appropriate, and in the second place, he considered that writing humor was beneath the dignity that he hoped to acquire. But this frog story inspired him, and he wrote it up as a letter to Artemus Ward. The tale of the champion jumping frog defeated by being filled with bird shot was narrated by "garrulous old Simon Wheeler" in the same meandering style in which Sam had first heard it. He sent it off to Ward, only to learn that Ward's book had already gone to press. Ward liked the story, however, and convinced the editor of the *New York Saturday Press* to publish it. It was to appear that month in what, unfortunately again, was to be the final edition of that paper, the owners having filed bankruptcy. Sam was sure that no one would ever notice his story in the last issue of a dying weekly newspaper.

It turned out that he was quite wrong. "The Celebrated Jumping Frog of Calaveras County" was reprinted in nearly every newspaper in America. All the praise and publicity were gratifying and encouraging, but he received not a penny in royalties from the reprints. Anything that appeared in one newspaper was considered fair game for all other papers.

Back in San Francisco, Sam took up journalism again writing pieces for the *Californian,* the *Golden Era,* the *Virginia City Enterprise,* and writing theater reviews, sometimes of very bad but completely imaginary plays, for the *Dramatic Chronicle.* His usual "desk" was in a window well in the Montgomery Block building above the Bank Exchange saloon. There he would perch with his back against the well and his knees up supporting his writing pad.

It was at this point, early in 1866, that Sam saw the chance of regaining the fortune he had lost on the stock market, and his spirits rose to new heights. Five years before Sam was born, his father had purchased, for $400, a plot of land in Tennessee comprising many thousand acres. The elder Clemens had died before amassing the capital needed to exploit the property, and it had remained the great opportunity for the family if they could ever find a buyer who would pay a good price for it. Several times, faced with burdensome taxes on the property, the widow Clemens had wanted to let it go for whatever she could get, but Sam and his older brother Orion convinced her to hold on; some day it would be their salvation. Now it appeared to Sam that that day had arrived. He had made the acquaintance of a speculator named Herman Camp who was on his way to New York. Sam had shown Camp a letter from a prominent Eastern wine grower stating that the Tennessee land was ideal for the cultivation of grapes. Camp agreed to help Sam find a buyer. Once in New York, Camp wired that he had decided to buy the land himself, import immigrants from the wine-growing districts of Italy and France, and create his own winery. He offered the Clemens family two hundred thousand dollars. Sam, ecstatic, sent the contract to his brother Orion in Nevada for his signature. Now, at last, Sam would be able to return home wealthy and successful. He had found his fortune in the West—but not at all in the manner he had expected.

It is not hard to imagine Sam's disappointment when Orion returned the contract unsigned saying that he would not consider letting the family property be used for the evil purpose of producing spirits. The deal was dead, and once again the property was no more than a tax burden. Sam went so far as to put a pistol to his head, but, as he later related, "I wasn't man enough to pull the trigger." Instead he set off for the low dives of Pacific Street where he got so drunk that when the police arrested him, he lay down on the ground and obliged the officers to drag him by the legs to the paddy wagon. After a night in the drunk tank, Justice of the Peace Alfred Barstow passed sentence on him for public drunkenness, with the usual fine. Sam claimed he had nothing in his pocket "but a plug of tobacco and a broken jackknife," and Barstow dismissed him. Once more, Sam returned reluctantly to the daily routine of journalism.

VI

Outcroppings

When Charley Stoddard returned to San Francisco from Hawaii in 1866, his bohemian friends were pleased to see that he was in much better shape than when he had left, pale, nervous, and unable to sleep. Now, he was tanned, exuberant, and bubbling over with enthusiasm for the glories of the tropics. He had been immediately charmed by the easy, gracious ways of the Hawaiians and chose to spend his time among them rather than with the friends of his sister and brother-in-law who were, to his mind, stuffy and prudish colonials. He became a prototype beach bum, fishing and swimming, drinking in the beauty of a lush paradise where no one really needed to work to survive, and discovering that he was a kindred spirit with those who never associated shame with sexuality. Moreover, he had fallen in with a theatrical troupe returning to San Francisco on the same ship, and they had convinced him that the proper career for him was on the stage. Accordingly, he had signed up to do a tour that was to start production in a few weeks in Sacramento.

Although he had been away for less than a year, Charley could see many changes in San Francisco. Vestiges of the thrown-together town of the Gold Rush were fast disappearing, as more and more fashionable shops and restaurants replaced saloons and gambling halls. Bret Harte had been promoted to a more responsible position at the Mint but had not neglected his writing. Each issue of the *Californian* carried something of his, a poem, a humorous sketch, or a parody. His wife had given birth to a second son, and he was trying—without much success—to spend more time with his family. Ina Coolbrith was seeing her poems appear regularly in the *Californian*, and Prentice Mulford, still living alone on his old boat, had become editor of the *Golden Era* and was deepening his serious study of spiritualism. His friends laughed off the fad of table-rapping and ghostly voices from "the other side," but Mulford patiently explained to them, whenever he could get them to listen, that the existence of frauds and charlatans in the spiritualist camp did not mean that *all* spiritualism was fake. He could speak convincingly of early Christianity as a highly spiritual and mystical cult that had been perverted after it had been taken over by the Romans and turned into a practical and aggressive hierarchy.

Charley's acting career was not long-lived. After a few weeks of trying to memorize vast quantities of dialogue and attending endless hours of rehearsals during which the director insulted him constantly, he abandoned the stage and returned to his parents' house, disappointed and depressed once again over his failure to stick to something until he succeeded. It was not long, however, before rumors began to circulate that lifted his spirits and gave him new hope. Bret Harte was editing a book, the first anthology of poems by Californians. Surely Frank would select at least one of Charley's poems and perhaps rekindle his muse.

The project Frank was working on was to be called *Outcroppings,* and his task was an enormous one. He would have to sift through the thousands of poems that had appeared in the numerous journals and newspapers of California and select those of the highest merit and quality. Given the general sentimentality and imitative nature of most of the West Coast poets, it was hardly an enviable task, but he had been talked into it by his persuasive old friend, Anton Roman.

Roman had come to California from Germany in 1851 and began prospecting in the Shasta County area. By the time the snows started to fall, he had collected a respectable amount of gold and headed for San Francisco for the winter. Unlike most, he shunned the gambling dens and saloons, and when spring arrived, he set off for the mining camps with a mule and wagonload of books. The miners were starved for reading material, and by 1857, after peddling books through the camps of Shasta, Trinity, and Siskiyou Counties, Roman had enough capital to open a small bookstore in San Francisco. Two years later, he moved to a larger and more prestigious location at 617 Montgomery Street which quickly became a gathering place for people of literary taste. Success at selling books was not enough for Roman; he wanted to publish them as well. He had begun with practical titles: *Geometrical Stair-Builder, Process of Silver and Gold Extraction, Confucius and the Chinese Classics, Russian and English Phrase Books.* These were bread-and-butter works, but Roman's real love was literature, and now he was ready to participate. *Outcroppings* would be his first literary publication.

Roman started publicizing the book even before Harte had finished editing it, and he swore Harte to absolute secrecy about its contents. No one was to know whose poems had been selected until the book was in print. Ina and Charley were confident that their work would be included; surely their old friend would not leave them out—would he? Considerable speculation went on over the book, and people came to realize that Harte was in the process of determining who the worthwhile poets of California were. Every Californian who had ever had some verse published was holding his or her breath. Although Harte was well-versed in the classics, he had apparently forgotten the lesson of Paris, assigned to be the judge of a beauty contest with Hera, Athena, and Aphrodite as contestants: beware the vengeance of those who don't win.

When the small quarto in purple and gilt finally appeared, selling for one dollar, just in time for the Christmas trade, people crowded Roman's bookstore for a week to see who had "made it." Harte had selected forty-two poems by nineteen different authors, and he was astounded by the violent reaction of those whose poems had not been selected. A reviewer, with tongue in cheek, wrote a review of the book in the *Californian:*

> The population of California is now divided into two classes: those who contributed to *Outcroppings* and those who did not. The latter have decidedly the advantage as numbers are concerned. Merit, I think, is pretty evenly divided.

And, in the San Francisco *Newsletter*, another reviewer, not to be outdone, wrote:

Within two hours after *Outcroppings* was known to be in town, a mob of poets, consisting of one thousand persons of various ages and colors, and of both sexes, besieged Roman's bookstore, all eager to ascertain if they had been immortalized by Harte. By Thursday the news had been circulated throughout the state, and the "country poets" were in a state of fearful excitement. Yesterday it was rumored that three to four hundred of these were coming down on the Sacramento boat in a "fine phrensy" and were swearing vengeance on Harte. That gentleman, by the advice of his friends, immediately repaired to the Station House to be locked up for protection.

Harte did not actually have to seek refuge in the jail, but he did stay close to his office in the Mint for several weeks until the furor died down. Roman was delighted to see his newest publishing effort sell out by the New Year. And Ina and Charley were relieved that some of their poems had been included—Frank had anointed them. The eastern press looked on *Outcroppings* as something of a curiosity. Westerners writing poetry was, to them, something akin to a dog trained to play the piano. There was among them, however, grudging admiration for Ina Coolbrith's work. The *Nation* wrote: "Miss Coolbrith is one of the real poets among the poetic masqueraders in the volume."

VII

Realizations

Having finished his window-seat scribbling for the day, Sam Clemens descended to the saloon below for a mid-afternoon beer. The bar was crowded with businessmen, journalists, gamblers, stock brokers, process servers, and newcomers—the latter easily identified by their astonished admiration of the voluptuous Delilah in the painting over the bar. Sam moved casually among the line of men drinking there, each one with one foot on the gleaming brass rail, and each one taking advantage of the brass cuspidors on the sawdust-covered floor. Sam was well known to all the regulars, and he listened to the various conversations, looking for a joke or an item or a bit of news that he could turn into a squib to write up.

When he had traveled the length of the bar, he stepped to the entrance. On the sidewalk in front of the saloon was a veritable Chinese marketplace. Vendors in blue cotton pajamas were hawking lottery tickets, live fowl, cooked meat, and fresh shrimp and crab meat at ten cents a pound. Sam stepped out among them and a chorus of sing-song pleas to buy assaulted him. He approached a peddler with two large baskets of licorice-flavored cigars tied in bundles of one hundred.

"How much?" he asked.

"Two dollah," the vendor replied.

"I don't want a whole bundle. How much fer ten?"

They haggled over the price and the vendor's reluctance to break up a bundle, and eventually Sam walked away with twenty-five cigars in his pockets. He knew they contained significant amounts of sawdust, firecracker paper, and who-knew-what-else, but they were all he could afford, and he could hardly be expected to get through the day without at least a dozen cigars.

With his jerky gait, he ambled down Montgomery Street past the city's most elegant hotels, the Russ House, the Lick House, and the Occidental, recalling the days when he had first arrived in California and had stayed in those luxurious temples waiting for his mining stocks to bring him fortune. Now he was reduced to sharing a room with Gillis in a boarding house that forever smelled of cooked cabbage. He turned up the hill. Kearny Street would have taken him directly to the North Beach saloons where he was headed, but it was too filled with fancy shops that mocked his poverty. He continued uphill one more block to Dupont Street, the heart of Chinatown. It was like turning a corner and stepping into a different continent. Blue-clad peddlers were everywhere, each with a long bamboo pole over his shoulder with a basket at each end. They would enter the village, replenish their baskets with fruit, vegetables, fish, or some other wares, and then set off again at a trot, their queues and woven bamboo hats bobbing as they jogged along the crowded street.

On the wooden sidewalks, Chinese merchants strolled, looking very self-satisfied in their silk trousers and brocade jackets, some followed by wives whose feet had been bound as infants and who could walk only with the assistance of a servant. The store fronts were a riot of gaudy colors, displaying their strange goods in a succession of tiny shops that, along with the stands of cobblers, tinsmiths, chair-makers, and barbers, formed a six-block long bazaar. As Sam walked along, he was enveloped in a confusion of aromas: incense, fresh fish, sandalwood, spices, roasting ducks, and occasionally—as one of the evil-looking doors leading to an underground room opened to admit a client—a whiff of opium. There were nearly thirty thousand Chinese jammed into this bustling ghetto, and it always seemed to Sam when he entered it that they were all talking at the same time. It amused him to be in the midst of so much communication and not to be obliged to listen to any of it. From the theaters along the street came the cacophonous sounds of the cymbals, flutes, and fiddles of Chinese opera, and from the rooms over the restaurants, he could hear the shrill songs of concubines entertaining customers.

In isolation from the people and activity around him, Sam walked along, thoroughly absorbed in the irony of his situation.

His jumping frog story had made the name "Mark Twain" known throughout the country. He was famous, but he could not afford a decent suit, a decent meal, not even a decent cigar. There had to be some way to cash in on that blasted frog's phenomenal success. As he shuffled across Broadway, the exotic surroundings led his mind to Charley Stoddard's vivid descriptions of Hawaii. He thought to himself bitterly that a visit to the Hawaiian Islands was one more item to add to his list of things he had been planning to do once his stocks had paid off. But there was something...something in his head he was trying to realize. The Islands...why not, while his pen name was still popular, convince some newspaper to stake him to a trip to Hawaii in exchange for a series of letters? Yes! A series of fascinating humorous letters about his adventures in the land of the Kanakas!

It took him a while to find a newspaper willing to underwrite him, but eventually, he convinced the editor of the *Sacramento Union* that his letters would increase their circulation. Accordingly, Sam, accompanied to the dock by a band of bohemian well-wishers pressing gifts of cigars and brandy on him, set sail for Honolulu aboard the *Ajax* on March 6, 1866. He had instructions to stay a month and "ransack the islands, the great cataracts, and volcanoes completely, and write twenty or thirty letters" for twenty dollars apiece.

Charley Stoddard, having given up the stage after a career of four weeks, was still seeking his niche in the world. Seeing his poems included in *Outcroppings* had boosted his confidence, and he decided to approach Anton Roman with a proposal while Roman was still basking in the success of his first literary publication. Charley showed up at Roman's office one day with a large packet of poems he had written in the past few years, many of them composed under the oak trees in Oakland when he was supposed to be in class at the college. What he had in mind was an anthology, *The Poems of Charles Warren Stoddard*.

Roman was cool to the idea at first, but when he saw Charley's ace-in-the-hole, he changed his attitude. Charley had been an avid autograph collector since childhood. Many of the

famous and infamous characters who had passed through San
Francisco had scribbled their names in one of his autograph
books, but in recent years he had hunted larger game by writing
questions to famous people in the hope that they would send him
a reply with a signature, as many of them did, including Charles
Darwin and then vice-president Andrew Johnson. In the past
year, he had taken to sending proof sheets of a few of his poems
to well-known writers requesting their comments and criticism.
His efforts were not wasted. He had encouraging letters from
George Eliot, Longfellow, Emerson, and Whitman. Even the not-
so-complimentary letters from John Stuart Mill and Oliver
Wendell Holmes could have extracts taken from them, and Roman
realized that Charley had inadvertently come up with some
remarkably good material for advertising a book that could be sold
through a subscription list. Roman's mind began to work rapidly.
He had recently been impressed by the work of a young artist,
William Keith, who could surely provide appropriate illustrations.
Keith's rising reputation would help sell the book. Roman envi-
sioned a calf-bound decorative book printed by Bosqui on the very
best quality paper. His imagination was fired up, and he told
Charley to talk his friend Bret Harte into editing the poems. If
Harte agreed, Roman would publish the book.

The next few months saw Charley in a state of increasing
excitement as Harte and Roman proceeded with the project. He
became such a pest that they talked him into going to Yosemite for
the last few weeks before publication. The final result was a beautiful piece of work, the most elegant book ever published in San
Francisco, and Charley was justifiably proud of it. The local
reviews were mixed, but Charley was more concerned with what
the Eastern critics would say. If they liked it, he would be established.

They did not like it. They praised the quality of the illustrations, binding and printing, rather surprised that such fine work
could be done in an outpost of civilization, but found that the contents of the book were imitative, juvenile, and—cruelest of all—
effeminate. As the reviews appeared in the eastern newspapers
and magazines, Charley became increasingly despondent. He
underwent a second period of deep depression and sought help

from every source available. Eventually, he received counseling from a Catholic priest that lifted his spirits and helped him overcome his melancholy. He found solace in the pageantry, the beauty, and the forgiveness of the church, and decided to convert. He was baptized at Saint Mary's Church with Peter Burnett, another convert to Catholicism and California's first American governor, as his godfather.

VIII

Magnificent Fireworks

Sam had not been in Hawaii long before he realized that one month would not give him nearly enough time to complete his tour of the islands. The leisurely pace of the natives from "tropical indolence" as well as his own natural distaste for hurrying made his progress agreeably slow, and the one month stretched to four. The *Union* did not complain about his additional expenses since his letters were, as he had predicted, stimulating the Sacramento paper's circulation. The *Californian* and the *Golden Era* began reprinting them for the benefit of San Francisco readers. Taking a cue from the success of his frog story, Sam invented a companion whom he called Brown, a vulgar, uneducated, crass character who despised sentiment and romanticism and through whom Sam could express his broadest jokes and most biting satire, all the while pretending to be shocked at Brown's unrefined comments.

In his own voice, he sprinkled his descriptions of the islands with colorful phrases, observing "smoke-dried children clothed in nothing but sunshine." and "dusky saddle-colored native women sweeping by, free as the wind, astride fleet horses with gaudy riding sashes streaming like banners behind them." On the one hand, he credited the missionaries, with whom he stayed when traveling in the countryside, with having elevated the Hawaiians from cannibalism, but at the same time, he could not resist poking fun, sometimes viciously, at their insincerity and hypocrisy. "How sad it is," he wrote in one letter, "to think of the multitudes who have gone to their graves in these beautiful islands and never knew, before the missionaries came, there was a hell." Each letter contained preposterous descriptions that Sam knew would be popular quotes among his readers: his interview with the king of the islands who, at the time, happened to be sitting on a barrel on the wharf, fishing; or "at noon I observed a bevy of native young women bathing nude in the sea, and I quickly went and sat down on their clothes...to keep them from being stolen."

Back in San Francisco, he found the name Mark Twain even better known than when he had left, but he still had no money and no job. He conceived a plan for a lecture on his Hawaiian adventures, wrote a sketchy outline, and presented the idea to Harte and Stoddard for their opinion. Charley Stoddard, remembering his own embarrassing experience behind the footlights, was skeptical. Harte was bluntly opposed to the idea, convinced that Sam would not draw a large enough audience to pay for the rent of a hall. Sam continued to seek advice until he heard what he wanted. Colonel John McComb, editor of the *Alta,* who had passed up the opportunity to sponsor Sam's trip, was still regretting that mistake. He slapped Sam on the back and told him to rent the largest hall in town and charge a dollar a ticket. So Sam approached his friend Tommy McGuire who had recently completed his 2,000-seat Academy of Music. "One night, fifty dollars," McGuire told him. "And you have to sell advance tickets. I want the money at least three days before the performance." Sam convinced some of his printer friends to make tickets and posters on credit, and he was on his way.

He glued his posters all over town, and they soon had the citizens buzzing. In addition to informing the public that Mark Twain (Honolulu Correspondent of the *Sacramento Union*) would deliver a lecture on the Hawaiian Islands on Tuesday, October 2, 1866, the notices proclaimed:

A SPLENDID ORCHESTRA
is in town but has not been engaged

A DEN OF FEROCIOUS WILD BEASTS
will be on exhibition in the next block

MAGNIFICENT FIREWORKS
were in contemplation for this occasion,
but the idea has been abandoned

A GRAND TORCHLIGHT PROCESSION

may be expected; in fact, the public are
privileged to expect whatever they please

DRESS CIRCLE $1.00   **FAMILY CIRCLE 50¢**

DOORS OPEN AT 7 O'CLOCK   **THE TROUBLE TO BEGIN
                                    AT 8 O'CLOCK**

As the evening of the performance approached, Sam grew more and more nervous. He had been able to sell two hundred tickets to his friends and acquaintances, so he had already paid for the theater, but he owed the printers much more than he had left. What if no one else came? What a humiliation! What if he made a fool of himself in front of all those people? Would they throw things at him and drive him off the stage? He began to think about all the bad reviews he had written and all the people who would love to get even with him. The more he practiced his speech, the more dreary it seemed to him, and, severely depressed, he told his friends in the Bank Exchange that he was going to have a coffin in the wings so that if the lecture went as badly as he thought it would, he would quickly turn the whole affair into a funeral. In the final days of September, he became even more nervous and disconsolate and started giving away tickets to saloon moochers in exchange for their promise to laugh uproariously at his jokes.

On Tuesday evening, Sam's closest friends were sitting in the front row: Steve Gillis, Charley Stoddard, Bret Harte, Ina Coolbrith, Mary Tingley, Prentice Mulford, and James Bowman, the new editor of the *Californian*, and his wife. As soon as they entered it was obvious that Sam was not going to lose money on the venture. By 7:45 the theater was full, and there were men standing along the walls.

At eight o'clock the house gaslights were dimmed, the footlights turned up, and Sam, dressed in a "claw hammer coat," strode jerkily to the podium. A gratifying round of applause greeted him. He looked out and drawled, "Good evening, ladies and gentlemen." Then he drew from his coat pocket a large sheaf of wrapping-paper sheets with notes scribbled on them. He set them on the podium and began, in apparent confusion, to shuffle through them, dropping one to the floor from time to time. The audience began to giggle, and he kept up his "organization" until he had them laughing. Then he looked up and said, "Before I begin, I want to say something about the orchestra my handbills mentioned. As a matter of fact, I did hire a fella to play the trombone tonight. He had a gorgeous instrument, and I was convinced that if he played it from time to time, it would help to keep you all awake. But when I found out that this trombonist required a half-dozen other scattermouche musicians to assist him, and I would have to pay them as well, why I jest told him if he thought he could bilk me like that, he had the wrong coon up a tree."

Sam's friends began to fidget. Was he going to stand there for an hour and a half cracking jokes as if he were entertaining his cronies at a saloon? People had paid good money to hear a lecture on Hawaii, not a lot of tomfoolery. Finally they heard him say that he was about to "disgorge as much truth about the islands as I can without damaging my constitution." His narration was punctuated by quick, unexpected jokes delivered with a stony expression, and each time the audience laughed, he would look up at them in mock astonishment causing them to laugh all the more. He ended a passage in which he lyrically described the graceful coconut palms swaying softly in the breeze, outlined by the sunset sky, by saying that, to tell the truth, they looked rather like feather dusters that had been struck by lightning. Each time he carried his praise of the beauty of the tropics to the point where he felt that his listeners' attention might begin to wander, he would throw in a joke: "Hawaiian women have a profound respect for chastity...in other people." "The natives are very fond of fish— they eat the article raw, and alive! Let us change the subject." "The Sandwich Islanders have no chairs; they simply squat on their hams, in true native fashion. Who knows but what they may be the original 'ham sandwiches'?" These remarks were so unexpected and delivered so seriously that before long, the audience was in tears of laughter, barely able to control themselves enough to hear the serious parts of his talk. It was not that what he said was all that funny, but his droll delivery and deliberate, mock-solemn style, created a sense of the ludicrous that convulsed them.

He was rolling now. The crowd was completely in his hands, and he had to shout to make himself heard as he held forth on his observations of Hawaiian lawmakers:

> Their legislature is like all legislatures. Some wood-en-head gets up and proposes an utterly absurd some-thing-or-other, and he and a half-dozen other wooden-heads discuss it with windy vehemence for an hour, and then some sensible man shows the foolishness of the matter in five sentences; a vote is taken and the matter is tabled. Do not do an unjust thing now and imagine Kanaka legislatures stupider things than other similar bodies. Rather blush to remember that, here in our country, when a Wisconsin Legislature had the affixing of a penalty for the crime of arson under consideration, one member got up and serious-ly suggested that when a man committed the damning crime of arson, they ought either hang him or make him marry the girl! The mental caliber of the Hawaiian Legislature is up to the average of such bod-ies the world over—I wish it were a compliment to say it, but it is hardly so. I have seen a number of legisla-tures, and there was a comfortable majority in each of them that knew just about enough to come in when it rained, and that was all. Few men of first class ability can afford to let their affairs go to ruin while they fool away their time in a legislature, but your solemn ass from the cow counties, who don't know the Constitution from the Lord's Prayer, enjoys it.

As he drew near the end of his talk, Sam grew increasingly eloquent. He described a trip aboard the *Emeline* sailing to the island of Hawaii. He told of stepping out on the deck in the bright moonlight "to see the broad sails straining in the gale, the ship keeled over on her side, the angry foam hissing past her lee bul'arks, and sparkling sheets of spray dashing high over her

brows and raining upon her decks." He completed his lecture
with a description of his trip to the crater of the still-active vol-
cano of Kileuea:

> The greater part of the vast floor a thousand feet
> below us and ten miles in circumference was as black
> as ink and apparently as smooth and level; but over a
> mile square of it was ringed and streaked and striped
> with a thousand branching streams of liquid and gor-
> geously brilliant fire! It looked like a colossal railroad
> map of the state of Massachusetts done in chain light-
> ning on a midnight sky. Imagine it—imagine a coal-
> black sky shivered into a tangled network of angry
> fire!

Then, with his audience breathless, hanging on his words, he
concluded the evening with, "The smell of sulphur is very strong,
but not unpleasant to a sinner like me."

Six times they called him back to take another bow, and there
was no doubt in anyone's mind that Sam Clemens had a new
career. For his part, Sam was greatly relieved that it had gone over
so well, but even more important, once all his bills were paid, he
had four hundred dollars in profit. Four hundred dollars in one
night!

The reviews in all the local papers were enthusiastic. Sam had
inspired the reviewers to ardent praise. A particularly perceptive
one wrote:

> After you have listened to his wild extravagances
> for over an hour, you are astonished to perceive that
> he has given you new and valuable views of the sub-
> ject. Every sentence may be burlesque, but the result
> is fact. And what insures his success as a teacher is
> that his manner is so irresistibly droll that it conquers
> at the first moment the natural revolt of the human
> mind against instruction.

IX

The Overland Monthly

Sam took his lecture on the road, traveling up and down the mining towns of California and Nevada: Sacramento, Marysville, Grass Valley, Nevada City, Red Dog, You Bet, Virginia City, Carson City, Gold Hill. He pumped up his advertising with new posters which announced his lecture as "Mark Twain Takes a Bite Out of the Sandwich Islands." At each town, a local character was recruited to introduce him. One introduction was, "Ladies and gentlemen, this here is the celebrated Mark Twain from the celebrated city of San Francisco with his celebrated lecture about the celebrated Sandwich Islands." At another, a grizzled old miner stepped up on the stage and said simply, "I'm to introduce Mark Twain. To tell the truth, I only know two things about him: he ain't in jail, and I don't know why not."

The *Alta California* contracted to pay his way to Europe and the Holy Land in exchange for a series of letters, and Sam ended his lecture tour with a final performance in San Francisco, an "impromptu farewell address, gotten up last week, especially for this occasion." In the course of this speech, he predicted great things for San Francisco, which would become "a vast metropolis" when California's "deserted hills and valleys shall yield bread and wine for unnumbered thousands." On December 15, 1866, he departed for New York, "leaving more friends behind...than any other newspaperman who ever sailed out of the Golden Gate."

Sam Clemens was almost immediately replaced, in several senses, by a strikingly handsome twenty-four-year-old Union Army veteran who arrived in San Francisco just as Sam departed. Ambrose Gwinett Bierce had enlisted at eighteen as a private in Company C, North Indiana Infantry, the second man to enlist after Fort Sumter was fired on. He spent the next four years in active combat. Captured, he then escaped, was seriously wounded, and was cited for his courage several times. One man in three of his brigade was killed in action. Assigned to a group of topographical engineers whose job it was to scout and map enemy positions, he was quickly promoted to lieutenant and finished the war as a brevet major. He came to San Francisco mainly to avoid going back to the

Ambrose Bierce

drudgery of farming. He obtained a position at the United States Treasury Department and began making new friends. Most of these were journalists, and before long, poems and articles, mostly satirical, by A. G. Bierce were appearing in the *Golden Era* and the *Californian*. He met and befriended Bret Harte, Ina Coolbrith, Charley Stoddard, and Prentice Mulford, and quickly became one of the bohemian regulars. His literary hero was Edgar Allan Poe, and he yearned to create similar stories of macabre and grotesque fascination. He was still a novice, but he was in the right place and traveling with the right crowd.

Francis Bret Harte took a seat in a large red leather chair in the office that Anton Roman kept over his bookstore. Roman's prosperity, Harte noted, was evident: a merino suit encased his short and rather corpulent figure, his hair and Van Dyke beard were turning from brown to a distinguished silver. Frank accepted a proffered cigar, and the two men lit up, puffing a bit more than was necessary to get the cigars going. It was an awkward moment. Obviously Roman had some proposition to make or he would not have invited Harte to lunch at Ricci's in North Beach. They had not dined in the noisy sawdust-covered street floor but had gone to a private room above and enjoyed the house specialty, six different pasta dishes with a bottle of dark red wine. During the meal, Roman had chatted with him pleasantly but had given him no hint of the purpose of this meeting. Now, as they sat smoking in Roman's office, Harte prepared himself warily, remembering the mess he had gotten into in editing *Outcroppings* for Roman. In the past year, Harte had published *The Lost Galleon*, a book of his own poems, with Roman's competitor, Towne & Bacon, and *Condensed Novels and Other Sketches* with Carleton's in New York. He assumed that his host was going to try to convince him that A. Roman & Co. should be the publisher of his next book, and he was mentally rehearsing some polite ways of avoiding any promises. Roman unbuttoned his vest and relaxed. They were discussing the rumor that the *Californian* was going under. "You see," Roman said, "a newspaper is the wrong format for literary works and serious essays. A weekly is fine for reporting news, but with a weekly, you are always concerned with production and deadlines." He turned and looked at Harte, his index finger raised. "With a monthly, on the other hand, you have enough time to reflect, to select carefully, to edit properly..."

"Like a magazine, you mean," Harte suggested.

That was precisely what Roman meant. He was proposing to start a West Coast literary and general-interest magazine, to take advantage of the tremendous concentration of talent in and around San Francisco—not just literary talent, but scientists, engineers, philosophers, and historians as well. Harte was skeptical. Did Roman really think he could get enough advertising business to support such a magazine? Roman smiled; he already had $900 in commitments for advertising in his magazine though it was still little more than an idea. Harte wondered if there was enough local talent to sustain a magazine over the long haul. Roman showed him stacks of manuscripts he had received, good writing looking for a publication outlet. Roman referred frequently to the *Atlantic Monthly,* the most respected magazine in America. "What do you think is the reason for their success?" he asked.

"Well, the quality of the writing, of course."

"And who is responsible for maintaining that quality?"

"The editor."

"Exactly. And what James Russell Lowell has done for the *Atlantic Monthly*, you can do for me."

Harte began enumerating reasons why he could not possibly undertake the editing of a new magazine, but Roman brushed them away. He walked over to a world map that was tacked to his wall. The two hemispheres were shown in circles. Like a teacher with a recalcitrant student, he pointed to San Francisco. "Look where we are. For years, California has been like a colony, a two-month trip away from its mother country. But in less than a year, the railroad will link us to the East. People and goods will be able to get here in a matter of days. All *this* part of the world," his hand swept across Asia and the Pacific, "will begin to trade through the port of San Francisco. The Pacific Mail Steamship Company will no longer carry passengers and freight from the East. What do you think they'll do with all those ships, burn them? They've already begun expanding their trade across the Pacific. They will, in effect, extend the railroad right to Manila, Tokyo, and Hong Kong. Our population is nearly half a million now, but that's nothing to the growth that the railroad will bring! We are on the verge of becoming a great city, my friend. The Gold Rush was nothing but an overture."

Despite himself, Frank felt his wariness slipping away. "If you're planning a puffer magazine to promote growth, Anton, then I'm not the fellow you want. I—"

"Promote growth!" Roman exclaimed, his voice rising and his face flushed with emotion. "I don't need to promote the inevitable. Mankind has been moving westward since the beginning of civilization. The transcontinental railroad is the final surge of a movement that's been going on for thousands of years. And it ends right here! After that, the story will be the filling in of the spaces between here and the Mississippi, which will become the largest farming area in the world. This town doesn't need me to promote its commercial growth. What it needs is for you and me to ensure that a *cultural* growth goes along with it. And I'm convinced that this magazine is just the right device for that."

Roman knew very well that the major obstacle to getting Harte to work for him was Mrs. Harte. She had no interest in her husband's literary pursuits and resented his contact with artists and journalists. It was for those reasons that she had obliged her husband to move their residence from San Francisco to San Rafael across the Bay. But Roman also knew that Mrs. Harte liked nothing better than staying at resorts where she could be waited on all day and forget domestic responsibilities. He suggested that Harte bring his wife and sons for a two-week stay with the Romans at a resort in Santa Cruz. That would give them time to discuss the idea without distractions.

The two weeks at the seaside resort of Santa Cruz stretched into four months, as Mrs. Roman managed to keep Mrs. Harte away from their husbands as much as possible and filled her mind with the promise of considerable income for the editor of a successful magazine. The title that Roman had chosen for his venture was *The Overland Monthly*. As the railroad progressed, the word overland was becoming synonymous with progress and prosperity. Roman had always used a snarling grizzly bear as a logo for his publishing company. Harte suggested placing the bear on a pair of railroad tracks, thus symbolizing the confrontation between the frontier and the "engine of civilization." There was no question as to which of these two conflicting elements Harte favored. He detested the efforts of the California Society of Pioneers and others to romanticize the Gold Rush days and to portray themselves as heroic argonauts. "Nonsense," he would snort. "The Forty-niners were largely a thieving, selfish gang of ruffians and cut-throats bent on pillaging the land and one another. They should be left to obscurity, not glorified."

But Roman reminded him that the Gold Rush was the event that had catapulted California into statehood, and that there had been more change and development in the past twenty-five years than most places see in a century. It did not need romanticizing, but it *did* need recognition that it was the foundation on which their institutions stood. The legends of the Gold Rush, he told Harte, should be for them what the tales of Homer and Virgil were for the Greeks and Romans.

By the time they returned from Santa Cruz, Harte had agreed to accept the editor's chair at *The Overland Monthly* and was already working on his first mining camp story, convinced that it would serve as an antidote to the idealized versions of the Gold Rush with which Californians were convincing themselves that their state had been founded by stalwart and admirable pioneers. He had talked Roman into hiring two assistant editors to do the time-consuming tasks, leaving him free to function as editor-in-chief. He knew that Ina Coolbrith and Charley Stoddard would jump at the chance. Ina would earn as much as she did teaching in Mibièle's private school and would have more time to write poetry—for the *Overland,* of course. As for Charley, still going from one clerking job to the next, this position would be a godsend.

X

Author And Lecturer

In the spring of 1868, Ina Coolbrith and Charley Stoddard were working full time in a small room that Roman had provided above his bookstore for the staff of his new magazine. Harte would report each morning to the Mint, take care of whatever minor tasks he had to perform there, and then join Ina and Charley for the more interesting work of bringing the *Overland* to life. Generally the three would spend their afternoons at Ina's house. Their office at Roman's was tiny, and there was no table there to spread out their papers. It was a short walk up to the Pickett house, where Ina's mother permitted them to use the dining room table until it was time to set the places for supper.

While Harte, Ina, and Charley labored to get the *Overland* launched, news arrived that Sam Clemens was on his way back to California. He had stopped in New York while waiting for the *Quaker City* to depart for its five-month cruise of Europe and the Holy Land, and decided to try out his Sandwich Island lecture there. He went whole hog and rented the largest hall in Manhattan, the Peter Cooper Institute—which he insisted on calling the "Keeter Pooper Institution"—for one night. He sold it out and cleared three hundred dollars. Obviously, he was no longer just a frontier humorist.

A few nights later, he spent the night in jail instead of his room at the Westminster Hotel. It was all a misunderstanding, of course. He and his companion came upon two men who were fighting. They tried to break it up, and when the police came, all four of them were arrested. He took advantage of his night in the Police Court lockup to interview the prostitutes and derelicts with whom he was sharing quarters—"a pretty good sort of people...though a little under the weather as to respectability." He reported his adventures in New York with frequent humorous letters to Charley Stoddard. On the envelopes of these, above Stoddard's address, he would write, in reference to the conflicts between settlers and the Plains tribes that were taking place:

> To Postmaster—Dear Sir: Per Steamer–d—n the
> Overland—too many Injuns.

Once his voyage was under way, his letters to the *Alta California* were even more irreverent and popular than his letters from Hawaii had been. He wrote that he had expected to spend the voyage "singing, dancing, and making love," only to discover that the captain and other passengers were "abominably religious" and their idea of entertainment did not extend beyond prayer meetings and hymn-fests.

The Quaker City docked at Marseille and gave the passengers a chance to take the train to Paris, where the World Exposition of 1868 was under way. Sam discovered that fellow San Francisco bohemian Lillie Hitchcock was staying at the same hotel. He escorted her in touring the city, and if some of his unpublished bragging can be believed, took his morning café-au-lait with her, in bed. Now that the trip was over, Sam had decided to rewrite his European letters into a book he intended to call *The Innocents Abroad,* and he was coming to San Francisco to work out an agreement with the *Alta* for the rights.

In mid-April, the bohemians were once again gathered at a North Beach café with Sam Clemens as their center of attention. Prentice Mulford was saying to him, "So, Sam, what's Paris like?"

"Waal, Dogberry," Sam said, "the Parisians simply opened their eyes and stared when I spoke French at 'em. I never could succeed in making those idiots understand their own language, but then I'll allow there might be a difference between Parisian French and Missoura French."

"Yes, but tell us—insofar as you can in mixed company— about those infamous Parisian *grisettes*," Mulford said.

"In two words: vastly overrated," Sam replied. "They're ugly as sin, smell of garlic, and it would be base flattery to call them immoral. But I must tell you all that my tom-catting days are finished. No, no. You needn't to laugh; it's true. I have seriously fallen in love, seriously, with a person and a place."

"Who's the unlucky girl?" Mulford asked.

"Her name is Olivia Langdon, and she lives in upstate New York. There is no question in my mind that we were fated fer each other. Her brother was on the tour with me, and he happened to show me a picture of his sister. I looked at it, and I announced to him then and there, 'That's the girl I'm going to marry.' He thought I was fooling, of course, but when I visited the family when we got back, and I met her in person, I was even more convinced that she was the one fer me. Her family—they're quality folk—always assumed she'd marry some respectable God-fearing man, but they'll get reconciled to having me fer a son-in-law. I'll see to it."

"What's she like, Sam?" Ina asked

"She's a perfect angel. What she sees in me, I'd give worlds to know, but I believe I have captured her heart. I'm not worthy of her, of course; but then, I wouldn't have any girl I was worthy of."

Charley asked, "What's the place you've taken to, Sam?"

"Connecticut, the area around Hartford. That's where I hope to settle down and raise a litter of little Clemenses. Shucks, I'm thirty-two years old, and I've been an apprentice printer, apprentice riverboat pilot, apprentice miner, apprentice journalist, and apprentice lecturer. I'm flat tired of apprenticin'. There's no profit in it. If my book does well, I expect to scrape together enough money to invest in some thriving business. Then I'm going to put a brick in my hat, settle down in one place, and spend the rest of my days as a convincing imitation of a Christian."

Harte said, "Then you're determined to go back East, to leave San Francisco for good?"

"Yaas, I am. I love this place, and I've had good times and good friends here, but you all know that real success has to be accomplished back there. I've had some tempting offers here. They asked me to be San Francisco's postmaster, did you know that? And Sam Brannan offered me a job to run his Society of California Pioneers..."

Harte interrupted angrily. "You'd best stay away from Brannan, my friend. His money's tainted."

"That's true," Sam said thoughtfully. "It's twice-tainted, Bret...'tain't yers and 'tain't mine." He recalled to his friends the day that Adah Isaacs Menken had handed Harte one of her cards with her picture on the back; and then he passed around one of his own. He had had them made at Bradley & Rulofson's, San Francisco's best photographic gallery. His picture was on one side. On the other it read:

Mark Twain
Author and Lecturer

It circulated around the table and Ina remarked on Sam's grim expression in the photo, saying he looked more like a tax-collector than a humorist.

"Waal, Ina, publishing's a hard business," he said. "I figgered I'd better show my mean side." He told them more about Adah Isaacs Menken. They all knew that she had died in Paris, but they were unaware of the elaborate funeral accorded to her. "The Parisians put her in Père Lachaise, their four-star cemetery where all the best folks are planted. There's Chopin, Molière, Eloise and Abelard, and why, Adam and Eve fer all I know. Anyways, she's in much better company under the ground in Paris than she ever was on top of it here in California. They set great store by American *artistes* there. Seems strange, don't it?"

The junior member of the group, Ambrose Bierce spoke up. "If that's the case, perhaps we should all plan to die there."

Sam reminded them of his forthcoming lecture at Platt's Hall, "Mark Twain's Sermon on Pilgrim Life." They all assured him that they would be there except for Harte who said, "I'll attend your lecture and applaud vigorously, on one condition: that you give me an excerpt from your forthcoming book to print in our new magazine. What do you say?"

"I'll see you and raise you one," Sam replied. "You come to the lecture and make some racket at the appropriate moments, and you promise to go over my manuscript and edit out 'infelicities,' and I'll give you two pieces fer yer magazine."

Harte stood up and shook Sam's hand. "All right, partner. That's a bargain."

That Saturday, Platt's Hall was sold out and people were turned away at the box office. At eight-thirty, Sam strode out on the stage, stopped at the lectern, and peered out at the crowded theater. "Ladies an' gentlemen, I have the honor of announcing that the lecture this evenin' will be delivered by Samuel L. Clemens...a gentleman whose high character an' unimpeachable integrity are only equaled by his comeliness of person and grace of manner...and I am that man!" He paused while the audience laughed and settled down. "I would like to inform you that this lecture will be repeated one week from tonight, in Oakland. Now, I'll allow that I was a bit surprised to learn that there was a sufficient population of intelligent people over there to warrant a lecture. I must admit that I've always thought of Oakland as the edge of the frontier. But Geeminy! I may have to forfeit my poor opinion of the place. I hear now they've got gas street lamps over there, and by and by they're even going to have a membership library. Waal, so mote it be." Another long pause. "Y'know, I used to be quite partial to libraries, but now that I'm publishing my own book, I'm having some second thoughts. See, if the library buys one copy, that means a'couple a dozen folks can read my book without buying it! Now that won't do! No, I've decided that libraries are fundamentally an evil influence because they encourage young people into the dangerous habit of borrowing things. As fer me, waal, I'd never borrow any book...unless of course it was Mr. Rothschild's pocketbook!"

With his audience warmed up, he began leisurely and without notes, to describe his trip. "Wherever we went, in Europe, Asia, or Africa, we made a sensation. None of us had ever been anywheres before; we all hailed from the interior; travel was a wild novelty to us, and we conducted ourselves accordingly. We always took care to make it understood that we were Americans—AMERICANS! We talked loudly at table and looked out fer expenses, getting the most we could from every franc or whatever. And we never once failed to remind them foreigners of America's greatness."

He went on to describe Paris, where he was able to "study those subjects of which Paris folks are fond—art, literature, history, and adultery." He held forth eloquently on the Cathedral of Notre Dame, recounting the historical events that its carved saints had witnessed in the past seven hundred years. He told them of the sidewalk cafés, of strolling through the Bois de Boulogne and seeing Napoleon III pass by in his carriage.

He told of his first-hand experience with the notorious *can-can* that was the rage in the dance halls. "A handsome girl before me tripped forward to meet her partner, tripped back again, grasped her dress vigorously on both sides, raised it to a considerable elevation, danced an extraordinary jig that had more activity and exposure in it than any jig I ever saw before, and then, drawing her skirts still higher, she advanced gaily to the center and launched a vicious kick at her partner's face that would have infallibly removed his nose if he had been nine feet tall. It was a mercy he was only six. That's the *can-can*. The idea of it is to dance as wildly, as noisily, as furiously as you can; and—if you are a woman—to expose yourself as much as possible!"

He spoke in an informal manner, maintaining his habit of looking up with a surprised expression, solemn as an owl, whenever the audience broke into laughter. He guided them through Europe, praising the cathedral of Milan with its 7,148 statues, but remarking that Lake Como "ain't a patching to Lake Tahoe" and, for a man who had known the Mississippi, the Arno of Florence was merely "a great historical creek."

He left the lectern and walked back and forth on the stage for a while as if in deep thought. Then he looked up and asked, "Have you ever noticed the picture that's on a package of Connecticut Pipe Tobacca? It shows a pasha sitting cross-legged in apparent bliss in a Turkish bath, smoking his narghili in a water pipe an' enjoying his Turkish coffee. Waal, I can tell you right out that it's all *humbug*! For years I dreamed of the wonders of the Turkish bath. Many times in my fancy I was in the marble bath breathing fragrances of Eastern spices, gently bathed by naked savages and then, swathed in fine fabrics, conveyed to a princely room and laid on a bed of eider down where eunuchs in gorgeous costumes fanned me while I sipped delicious Turkish coffee, smoked soothing Turkish tobacca, and listened to the music of fountains in the courtyard like the pattering of summer rain. HAH! If I were the sort of man who cursed, I would tell you it is all a damned lie!"

Then he described his actual Turkish bath experience—the bath lined with rusty old mattresses, the cadaverous attendants, the aromas not of oriental spices but more reminiscent of an Arkansas County Hospital. The water pipe, he said, contained the vilest tobacco he had ever known, second only to the taste of the thousands of infidel tongues that remained on its mouthpiece. "And then, an unclean starveling dressed in a gaudy tablecloth brought me the world-renowned Turkish coffee. I seized upon it as the last hope of my old dreams of Eastern luxury...Ugh! Of all the unchristian beverages that ever passed my lips, Turkish coffee is the worst! The cup is small. It is smeared with grounds. The coffee is black, thick, unsavory of smell, and execrable in taste. The bottom of the cup has a sediment in it half an inch thick. I can tell you, this Turkish bath business is a malignant swindle, and I've half a mind to bring a lawsuit against the Connecticut Pipe Tobacco Company!"

In Russia, the *Quaker City* passengers had been invited to meet Czar Alexander II and his family, who were vacationing at Yalta. The passengers had commissioned Sam to compose a formal address to the Emperor which was read by the American Consul in Odessa as the passengers were introduced to the royal family.

"The whole tribe turned out to greet us," Sam recounted. "Emperor, Empress, the eldest daughter—a pretty girl of fourteen—her brother the little Grand Duke, the Emperor's brother Grand Duke Mikhail, and a platoon of Admirals, Princes, and Peers of the Empire. They were as nice to us as they could be; gave us a tour of the palace and threw a champagne blow-out and ball fer us. I spent the evening dancing with the most beautiful girl that ever lived, and we talked incessantly, laughing all the while since neither of us had the slightest idea of what the other was jabbering about. Now the Grand Duke Mikhail, he's a rare brick. He invited us all to his palace fer breakfast, and what a rich and elegant place it is! When we left, I told him if he was ever in Missoura he should not fail to drop by the Clemens' residence fer a return of the favor. So, any time any of you all out there need someone to help you entertain royalty, you jest call on me. I've got the hang of it. Not only do I have a natural talent fer it, I've got experience to boot!"

The *Quaker City* had then taken the tourists to the high point of the trip, the Holy Land. The ship deposited the passengers at Beirut where they traveled across the desert by mule to Damascus, and then into Palestine to visit the Sea of Galilee, Nazareth, the Dead Sea, Jerusalem, and Bethlehem. He vigorously described the Biblical territory as a horrible, rocky desert, "worse than Nevada," filled with squalid villages of mud huts and camel dung—"a land of dust, rags, vermin, hunger, and wretchedness inhabited by ignorant, depraved, superstitious, thieving tatterdemalions." He was well aware that ministers across the country were condemning him as a blasphemous son of the devil for describing the Holy Land in this manner in his letters, but he had no intention of toning down his remarks now. Jerusalem, he said, was "a mournful, dreary, lifeless place, offering only more poverty, dirt, and gloom." At Bethlehem, in the Church of the Nativity, he painted a picture of the American tourists "encompassed by beggars, cripples, and greasy monks, all insistently demanding 'bucksheesh.'" He raised his index finger over his head and declared, "If there is a Second Coming, my friends, I can assure you it will not occur in Palestine. For Jesus Christ, having already seen the place, would never, ever want to set foot there again!"

He was less severe with Egypt, and took the audience through Alexandria down the Nile Valley to Cairo, then to the top of the pyramids at Ghizeh. On the long and uneventful trip home across the Atlantic, he said, he had time to reflect on his frantic travels, and worked out an itinerary for his concept of the ideal cruise: forty days in London, five months in the Sandwich Islands, six months in Egypt, forever in France, and two hours and a half in the Holy Land.

Sam had his pocket watch on the lectern, and he saw that he had been talking for over two hours. He was tired, but he was exhilarated too by the response of his audience throughout his rambling discourse. "There was not a single passenger aboard the *Quaker City*," he said, building up to a grand finish, "who did not feel that this trip had been one of the most edifying experiences of his life. But I can tell you, in all sincerity, that as our ship came into New York harbor and we saw our flag go up the Peak in salute to our arrival, that staid bunch of old fogies went wild, and we all embraced each other and cried for joy to be home! And then, at that moment, the captain's son sprang to the rail and recited these lines from 'The American Flag,' and you can bet yer boots there wasn't a dry eye among all those on board:

> Flag of the free heart's hope and home,
> By angel hands to valor given;
> Thy stars have lit the welkin dome,
> And all thy hues were born in Heaven.
> Forever float that standard sheet,
> Where breathes the foe but falls before us?
> With Freedom's soil beneath our feet
> And Freedom's banner floating o'er us."

For ten minutes, Sam stood on the stage, bowing and waving his white handkerchief to acknowledge the cheers and whistles and applause. It was a triumphant moment, and he was filled with love for the people of San Francisco who were welcoming him back so enthusiastically—but at the same time his mind was calculating. After all his expenses, he would clear $1,600 for this evening's performance, more than he would have earned in two years as a reporter. He could not help but think, *if the book don't pan out, I can sure as hell make my way doing lectures.*

XI

The Golden Gate Trinity

After repeating his performance in Oakland, Sam took it on tour, revisiting familiar places where he was greeted and fêted by his old cronies as a prodigal son. His tour complete, he returned to San Francisco and took a room at the Occidental. For a full month he devoted himself to transforming his *Alta* letters into *The Innocents Abroad.* As he finished each chapter, he would take the scrawled sheets to Harte for editing and revision. It was only two blocks from the Occidental to Roman's bookstore, and if he got there before noon, Sam would be sure to find Ina and Charley there, working on the first issue of the *Overland.* By the first of July, Harte had completed Sam's revisions, and on the day after Independence Day, Sam was on his way East to supervise the publication of his book. He was saying goodbye to his friends who had come to see him off—Harte, Charley, Ina, Prentice, and Steve Gillis. "They gave me free passage on the ship," he confided to them as he boarded. "They said it was something they did fer traveling celebrities. What do you think of that?"

Harte slapped him on the back and replied, "Maybe the railroad will do the same when it's finished, and you can come back and see us."

"I don't think so," Sam said. "I'm going East to settle down. I think it's up to you all to come and visit me. But you must remember not to let on to folks back there what you know of me. They're still under the impression that I'm a reputable fella."

As the steamship pulled away from the dock, Gillis shouted, "You'd better send me a check every month, Sam, else I'll come back there and fill folks' ears with yarns about what a dissolute rounder you really are!"

"I'm not worried," Sam shouted back. "They don't allow drunkards into Connecticut!"

A week later, the first issue of the *Overland Monthly* appeared. Harte had been desperately trying to bring his first "California mythology" story to completion in time for the premier edition, but he had spent so much time on Sam's manuscript that he had not finished, and he refused to print it until he was satisfied that it was as good as he could make it. He substituted one of his poems, "San Francisco from the Sea." Charley also had a poem in the first issue, "In the Sierras," as did Ina. Hers was called "Longing." In one stanza she expressed her feelings about her release from the routine of teaching and her excitement over her new job:

> O foolish wisdom sought in books!
> O aimless fret of household tasks!
> O chains that bind the hand and mind—
> A fuller life my spirit asks!

Another stanza boldly proclaimed her romantic attachment to nature:

> And I could kiss with longing wild,
> Earth's dear brown bosom, loved so much.
> A grass-blade fanned across my hand
> Would thrill me like a lover's touch.

Harte finished his story in time for the August issue. It was titled "The Luck of Roaring Camp." It concerned the changes brought about in a group of rough miners who find themselves in charge of a new-born infant whose mother, a mining-camp harlot, died giving birth. The orphan child, in honor of improved diggings that coincided with his birth, is named "Luck." Thus Frank used the concept of Luck as the *leitmotif* of the '49ers just as Fate had been the theme of classical myths. As the second issue was being put together, a young woman employed as a proof-reader marched stiffly, with pursed lips, into Anton Roman's office with a proof copy of "The Luck of Roaring Camp" in her hand.

"Mr. Roman," she said in a determined tone, "I know that my job is to look for errors and not to comment on the content of what I read, but I simply must protest this story. I am very much afraid that if you print it as it is, your new magazine will get a reputation as coarse and vulgar!" Roman looked surprised and asked her what she had found objectionable in the story.

"To begin with, this character, Cherokee Sal is a...a prostitute. I don't believe your readers really want to read about such women. Moreover, Mr. Harte has the men laying bets about whether this woman is going to survive childbirth. In my opinion, the subject of obstetrics should be restricted to medical books. And I think that most people would agree that expressions like this have no place in a family magazine!" She pointed out to her employer the offending sentence, which was "The d—d little cuss!" Roman promised her he would discuss the matter with Harte, but even as he did, he knew that Harte would not consider changing a word. The story ran in its original form, was enthusiastically received by the public, and caused no objections.

Roman had hoped to achieve a circulation of 3,000 copies by the end of the first year, but shortly after Harte's story appeared, the *Overland's* circulation had exceeded that number and continued to rise steadily. Roman was delighted. The magazine was becoming everything he had dreamed it would. Harte was getting contributions from the best writers in the area. Sam Clemens had delivered the two travel articles he had promised; Prentice Mulford contributed humorous reminiscences of mining camp life, as well as vivid descriptions of his adventures as a seaman; and Ambrose Bierce provided a horror story, "The Haunted Valley." Each issue contained at least one poem by Harte, Ina, or Charley, and sometimes one by each of them. Before long, San Francisco was referring to them as the "Golden Gate Trinity." Roman, grateful for the success their hard work had brought him, rented a large office for them on Clay Street, facing Portsmouth Square. He handed each of them a key to their new office and proclaimed that they were now completely independent of his publishing business.

Harte had warned Roman that he would be no part of a "booster" magazine whose primary purpose was to promote

California business and attract new residents, and even though Roman had insisted on a sub-title for the *Overland,* "Devoted to the Development of the Country," editor Harte remained firm. When he published Henry George's article in the fifth issue, "What the Railroad Will Bring Us," many San Francisco brokers and businessmen were understandably upset. The article predicted that the completion of the transcontinental railroad would bring prosperity only to the already-prosperous—those who were speculating in real estate—and would bring hard times to the rest of the population. George's article predicted that, if Californians were not vigilant, the connection with the rest of the country would destroy the cosmopolitan, open-handed spirit that prevailed in their state, and replace it with the grinding poverty and exploitation common to eastern cities. Such talk did not set well with Montgomery Street entrepreneurs, but Roman made no effort to interfere with Harte's editorial policies. The *Overland* was growing in circulation and reputation, and it filled the publisher with pride to overhear comments such as, "Why, it's every bit as good as the *Atlantic Monthly.*"

XII

The Dispersement

In May of 1869, the Golden Spike was driven, completing the railroad link between California and the Eastern states. Even though the Western terminus of the Central Pacific was Sacramento, San Francisco celebrated in grand style, just as if the tracks ran all the way to Market Street. American flags hung from every window, and a huge parade of military units, fire brigades, and just about every other organization in the city, got under way at ten o'clock in the morning, taking four hours to pass any one point. Harte, Ina, and Charley watched it go by from their office window, marveling at the idea that people would now be able to get from New York to San Francisco in less than two weeks.

Harte had written two more of his mining camp stories, "The Outcasts of Poker Flat" and "Tennessee's Partner." People were calling him "the American Dickens" now, and his popularity in the East was soaring. Ina and Charley were well aware, however, that Mrs. Harte was not impressed. She had stormed into the office one day, unexpected and unannounced, demanding that her husband go shopping with her. He had taken her to one end of the room and tried to explain to her in a low voice that he was occupied at the moment and could not just break away. But she was loudly adamant, and he had to make his excuses and leave hurriedly to avoid any further embarrassment.

"Well, I've finally met Mrs. Harte—sort of," Ina said to Charley.

"She's not always like that," he replied. "Usually, she's very nice." Charley was obviously embarrassed also, so Ina did not discuss the incident further, but she could not help but wonder how Frank's wife could be so inconsiderate and so unappreciative of her husband's accomplishments.

When Sam's book, *The Innocents Abroad*, finally appeared, Harte wrote a glowing review. It outsold every other book ever published in America except for *Uncle Tom's Cabin*. At the same time, but almost completely unnoticed, a slim volume of self-published poems by Cincinnatus Hiner Miller appeared. Charley received a copy in the mail along with a letter from Miller, now Judge Miller in Canyon City, Oregon, announcing that he had finally returned to his destined career, Poet.

He called his book *Joaquin et al* after the first poem, a highly romanticized version of the adventures of the Mexican bandit, Joaquin Murietta. It was filled with bombast, impossibilities, and hyperbolic images such as his description of a starry sky as "Diana's maid hanging her mistress' garments on the ridge of the Sierras after washing them in liquid moonlight." He told Charley that he and Minnie had two children now, but their marriage was in rough water. He was hoping for an appointment to the Oregon Supreme Court but, if he did not get it, he planned to go to seek his fortune in Europe. Charley managed to get Frank to review Miller's book, but the review was so devastating that Ina insisted on rewriting it in gentler tones. Harte wrote that Miller's work showed "poetic instinct," but he criticized him soundly for his "theatrical tendencies, feverish exaltations, crudeness, and dubious taste." Nonetheless, Miller wrote to Charley and thanked him for having talked Harte into doing the review. He was clever enough to know that a poor review was better than no review at all.

For his part, Charley had been growing increasingly dissatisfied with his own writing. During its first year of publication, the *Overland* published seventeen poems, all but one by Harte or Ina or Charley. But Charley was aware that his poems were not nearly as good as those of his two colleagues, and he was anxious to find a way to make a better contribution. He showed Harte the manuscript of one of his experiments, a story of the South Seas called "Chumming With a Savage." Harte liked it and ran it in the next issue, and Charley began a series of exotic South Seas tales with both humor and pathos that were very well received.

Anton Roman had good reason to be proud of his magazine. Circulation was well over 10,000 by the end its first year of publication, and that made it especially difficult for him to give it up, but poor health gave him no choice. His doctor told him if he did not move to a warmer and drier climate, respiratory illness would surely claim his life. Reluctantly, he sold the *Overland* to publisher John Carmany for the ridiculous sum of $7,500. He knew that other investors would have paid more for such a successful venture, but he wanted to be sure that the new owner would retain its quality.

"The key to the success of this magazine," Roman told Carmany, "is Bret Harte. Without him as editor, it'll surely flounder. You mustn't let him get away. I know that other magazines are after him, and he is a vain man—susceptible to flattery. Take care." Carmany, aware that Harte did not have the same esteem for him that he had for Roman, immediately raised the editor's salary to $2,000 a year plus premium payments for each story or poem he contributed. Harte was able to resign his position at the Mint and devote all his time to editing and writing.

After Roman left, Harte was working with Ina and Charley on the next edition and found that they needed several pages more material. He had been working on something which could be used as a filler, but he was not sure if it was appropriate. What did they think? He showed them a long narrative poem he had nearly completed. "We could stretch it out with an illustration if you think it's all right to use. It's just nonsense—doggerel verse, but perhaps it will do." It was called "Plain Language from Truthful James," a ten-stanza humorous poem in limerick rhythm, concerning two miners who undertake to teach an apparently naive Chinese named Ah Sin how to gamble. Despite their efforts to cheat him, Ah Sin keeps winning until the miners discover that he has twenty-four decks of cards concealed in his voluminous sleeves. The poem ended with Truthful James' declaration:

> Which is why I remark,
> And my language is plain,
> That for ways that are dark
> And for tricks that are vain,
> The heathen Chinee is peculiar—
> Which the same I am free to maintain.

Ina and Charley found the poem hilarious and convinced Harte to include it. He wanted to print it anonymously to avoid sullying his reputation as a serious poet, but they encouraged him to put his name on it. When that issue of the *Overland* came out, "Plain Language" was on everyone's lips. The time was just right for its publication because, as thousands of coolies were pouring into San Francisco from the camps where they had been laying the track for the transcontinental railroad, local demagogues were firing up crowds of unemployed white men with talk of the "Yellow Peril" and ruin from "cheap Chinese labor." Harte's poem, ridiculing the two white card sharks who complain when they are outwitted by the impassive Ah Sin, was an obvious satire on those who sought to make scapegoats of the Chinese for current economic difficulties. It was a device that dated to the *fabliaux* of the Middle Ages, the wily servant who outwits his master, and like Sam's jumping frog, Ah Sin caught the public imagination. Harte's poem was reprinted in newspapers throughout the country. People cut the poem out and tacked it up in trolley cars in every city, and Francis Bret Harte, a name that was well-known to every literary person in America, became familiar among the not-so-literary as well.

"Tahiti! But why? And for how long? What about your job here?" Ina was reacting to Charley's surprise announcement that he was departing for Tahiti that weekend. "I've run dry, Ina," he replied. "My South Sea tales have been the best work I've ever done, but I'm out of ideas; I need some new material. And I've just met a young fellow who's on his way from France to take a post there. André—that's his name—has convinced me to come along. I know it's spur of the moment, but you know me—that's how I am."

"But Charley, we need you here. You can't just run off for an indefinite time and expect Bret to hold your position open."

"I know, I know. Since I have no idea how long I'll be gone, it's perfectly proper for him to replace me. It's all right. My best contribution to the *Overland* would be more stories, and I need to go back to the source. I'll work everything out; you'll see."

Ina took his hand. "I wish you wouldn't be so impetuous. You worry me."

"I know. But as long as I have you to worry about me, I'll be fine. I'll write to you and tell you all my adventures. And...I, ah...could you do me a favor?"

"What do you need?"

"Well...Cincinnatus Miller wrote to me recently. It seems that while he was running for Oregon Supreme Court Justice, Minnie divorced him, charging him with infidelity and failing to support his family. That cost him the election, so he's decided to go to England to try his luck over there."

"And?"

"Well, you see, I agreed to sort of look after him for the few days he'll be in San Francisco prior to departing for Europe. He wants to be reintroduced to the old gang, to renew his publishing connections, you know. I feel a bit remiss, leaving when I'd promised to host him..."

"You want *me* to entertain that savage man?" Ina said incredulously.

"Oh, he's not all that bad," Charley responded. "He's all talk and bravado. He'll be a perfect gentleman with you. Please, Ina. It's just for a couple of days. Be a good sport. Ah, you're a true friend. You won't be sorry. Thank you, dear Ina."

Miller arrived just before Charley was leaving and was quite pleased to be turned over to Ina. She took him first to her house to impress upon him that she was a member of a respectable family since he had previously seen her only in cafés and theaters. Then, in a cab he hired, she took him to every publisher and newspaper office in the city, introducing him to the editors as "the author of a new book of poems, *Joaquin et al*, who is on his way to England." Miller conducted himself admirably and was genuinely grateful to Ina for her efforts on his behalf. He told her that he had enough money to survive for six months in England, and that he was determined to make his mark there. "Walt Whitman's gittin' popular over there, an' I jes' have a feelin' that I can make a hit with the limeys. I'm gonna give it a good try." The following day he proposed that they stop at Edouart and Cobb's photographic parlor and have their pictures made to include with a long letter that Miller was sending to Charley in Tahiti. In the process, Miller happened to mention that his first stop in England would be at Hucknall Torkard, to visit Byron's grave.

Ina was filled with envy. Visit Byron's grave! What spot on earth could be holier? She asked Miller if he would be willing to take a small laurel wreath in his suitcase to lay on the poet's last resting place, and he readily agreed. The following day they took a ferry to the little fishing village of Sausalito on the other side of the Golden Gate and picked branches from the bay laurels that grew there. On the evening ferry back, as she wove the branches in a circle, Ina suggested that Miller adopt a new name when he went to England. Somehow, "Cincinnatus Hiner" did not have a particularly poetic ring to it. He had spelled his middle name "Heine" in *Joaquin et al*, hoping to associate himself with the German poet Heinrich Heine, but Ina suggested he use a name associated with America, with the frontier. Why not use the title of his book and go to Europe as "Joaquin" Miller?

He thought for a moment, leaning on the rail of the ferry and watching the gray-green water, and then turned to her and proclaimed, to the astonishment of the other passengers, "Sweet Jesus, Ina, that's pure inspiration! From this day forward, I am JOAQUIN Miller!"

With Charley off in Tahiti "pursuing moonbeams," as Harte put it, he and Ina were spending more time in the *Overland* office. Carmany, the new owner, was desperately afraid that one or both of them might leave the magazine for greener pastures, so he raised Harte's salary again to two hundred dollars a month plus four times the going rate for each of his stories and poems. Ina's salary was raised to fifty dollars a month and an additional twenty for each poem. Carmany had little to worry about where Ina was concerned; she could not imagine a better job. But Harte was restless. His mining camp stories were renowned throughout the country. The most recent one, "The Iliad of Sandy Bar," had received outstanding reviews in the major magazines. His Ah Sin character had begun to show up in vaudeville sketches, and Harte knew that there was a fortune in this popularity if he could just find the time to work on such a project.

Carmany's fears of losing his editor were not unfounded. The College of California had moved from Oakland to Berkeley and become the University of California. Henry Durant, the University President, had offered Harte the position of Chief Librarian and Professor of Recent Literature, a singular honor for a man who had never set foot in a college classroom. Even more tempting was an offer from a group of businessmen in Chicago who wanted to start a new magazine. They would pay him $5,000 a year, twice his present salary, if he would come to Chicago and edit their venture. Harte resisted these temptations, but then another came along in 1870 that no writer could have resisted. The *Atlantic Monthly* offered him $10,000 to go to Boston and provide them with twelve stories, one a month for a year. It was the highest salary ever offered to an author anywhere. And to have twelve stories in the *Atlantic* in one year was unprecedented.

So, Francis Bret Harte prepared to take his wife and two sons to Boston. Knowing that he would be associating with publishers in the East, he offered to take a portfolio of Ina's poems with him to see if he could interest one of them in producing a collection. She selected thirty of what she considered her best work, saying, "Take good care of these and send them back to me." Ina was deeply saddened by his departure—not only was she losing a close friend, but she also realized that this was the end of the Golden Gate Trinity.

XIII

The Bohemian Club

Charley Stoddard's friendship with the young Frenchman who had talked him into going along to Tahiti ended even before the ship arrived in Papeete. Charley had arrived with a small sum of money, which quickly ran out. Unable to find work but determined to stay in his tropical paradise, he "went native" and lived the life of a beachcomber among the natives in one village after another. When the weather turned bad, he crept back to Papeete and took up residence in a chicken coop. In desperation, the white citizens of the town took up a collection to rid themselves of this embarrassment. Although he was a steerage passenger on charity, Charley boarded the ship with ten times the luggage of any first-class passenger. Among his affairs were outlandish gifts of native crafts given to him by island friends from Tautira to Papetoai, but his most important possessions were the journals that contained stories, descriptions, character sketches, and notes of general impressions.

Once again installed in the home of his forbearing parents, Charley turned his journals into a collection of exotic tales which he called *South Sea Idyls,* filled with images of a simple, happy people who devoted themselves to physical pleasure, *joie de vivre,* and gregarious affection. In Charley's tales, rendered in a languorous, adjective-rich prose that evoked tropical heat and lushness, island life shimmered between fancy and reality and stirred the imagination of his readers. The book sold well and he could once again hold his head high—running off to Tahiti had been a good idea after all.

While Charley had been researching in the islands, Ina Coolbrith had tried to hold the *Overland* together. Once Harte left, a series of editors followed, each less competent than the one before. Circulation dropped, and the magazine's office was filled with tension and hostility. Finally, in frustration, Ina resigned her Assistant Editor's position and devoted herself to writing poems and submitting them directly to the owner, John Carmany. Her poems were appearing in several publications now, and each one brought her at least fifty dollars. Moreover, she was often asked to write ceremonial verses which paid even better. She regretted the loss of the pleasant times she had known working with Harte and Charley, but those days were gone.

Shortly before Charley returned from Tahiti, Ina had received a thick envelope from London. It was a letter from "Joaquin" Miller. He had found a cheap boarding house at 11 Museum Street, just half a block from the British Museum, and he was going to all the city's publishers with his poems. He had not found any takers yet, but he was undaunted and confident that some editor would soon have the sense to recognize his genius. Along with the letter were several newspaper clippings concerning the laurel wreath that Ina had made for him to place on Byron's grave. Miller had adopted the practice of preparing an ode for each of the famous artists whose final resting place he visited. When he arrived, he would read his ode in a loud voice, to the consternation of whatever English folk were in earshot. The ostentatious wreath-placing for Byron aroused the ire of the vicar of Hucknall Church, who wrote a letter to the local paper objecting to foreigners coming in and ceremoniously honoring someone who had publicly broken all ten of the commandments. Miller had then replied with his own letter, decrying the neglect of one of England's finest poets, and a controversy was under way which eventually reached the ears of King George I of Greece. The monarch was furious and proclaimed that the English did not deserve to keep the remains of such a great hero who had died in the cause of liberty. He sent a wreath of his own and arranged through the archbishop to have his wreath and Ina's placed in a glass case on Byron's grave. The publicity from this caused an outpouring of donations sufficient to rebuild the dilapidated church of Hucknall Torkard. Ina could not repress a thrill at seeing her name, "the California poet, Ina Coolbrith," in the London papers, and was moved to write a poem, "With a Wreath of Laurel," which contained the stanzas:

> Unfelt the venomed arrow-thrust
>> Unheard the lips that hiss disgrace,
> While the sad heart is dust, and dust
>> The beautiful face!

> For him I pluck the laurel crown!
>> It ripened in the western breeze,
> Where Sausalito's hills look down
>> Upon the golden seas.

While Charley had still been an editor on the *Overland Monthly*, he had fallen in with a group of journalists, writers, and artists who gathered frequently for late-night beer and sandwiches, discussions, and song. Charley was a favorite among them because he could play the piano. They met generally at the home of James and Margaret Bowman, where Sunday brunches were held every week for the group and where evening fests often lasted until the early hours of the morning. James Bowman had been the last editor of the *Californian* and continued in one job or another in journalism. He was a convivial man who deeply enjoyed the company of talented men and women, conversation, and imbibing. Mrs. Bowman was the soul of patience, having virtually turned her house over to her husband's friends. They were her friends too, but eventually she grew tired of the notes and sketches all over her white tablecloths, and a smoke-filled dining room just about every night. It was time to make this group into a club, collect some dues, and rent a hall.

Suitable space was found at the Astor House on Sacramento Street, and the Bohemian Club was born in March, 1872. It was to be an organization of creative and talented men—no stuffed shirts. Pompous politicians and self-aggrandizing businessmen were banned. "Weaving Spiders Come Not Here" was their motto, and the owl, bird of night and wisdom, their symbol. Membership in the club, of course, was for men only, but Margaret Bowman and Ina Coolbrith, having sewn the curtains for the new quarters, were made honorary members, as were Bret Harte and Sam Clemens, even though they had both already departed for the East. The club developed the practice of presenting literary entertainment from time to time, called "High Jinks," with scripts written and performed by the members. Wives and lady friends could be invited for these special occasions.

John Muir

All this had taken place while Charley was in Tahiti, and when he returned, he took up with his old friends in their new location. He spent his days working on his South Pacific stories and his evenings at the club, telling tales of life among the savages or "the good old days" in San Francisco. It was here that he met and befriended a new Bohemian Club member, a man a bit younger than he with long russet hair and a full beard, dressed in a rather threadbare suit and worn shoes—a genuine bohemian named Johnny Muir.

Muir had come from Scotland to a farm in Wisconsin at the age of eleven. His early inventions won him a scholarship to the University of Wisconsin where he majored in botany and went on solitary field trips to study nature. Eventually his walking trips left no time for classes, and he tramped all the way to Florida. From there he sailed an indirect route to California and arrived in San Francisco in 1868 where he set off on foot for Yosemite Valley. He fell in love with the Sierra Nevada range and devoted himself to the exploration of the mountains, supporting himself as a shepherd, bronco buster, and sawmill foreman. As he studied the mountains, he evolved the theory that the great Yosemite Valley had been created by glacial action. His idea was met with derision by the state geologist, Josiah D. Whitney, who had determined that the Valley was the result of some cataclysmic natural event. Whitney was unimpressed with the theories of a self-educated working man and dismissed them as nonsense.

That rejection had brought Muir down to the city. He was determined to put his geological findings into the marketplace until they could be proven. Through connections at the Bohemian Club, he was able to convince *Overland Monthly* editors to print his articles. To the average *Overland* reader, the question of how Yosemite was formed was not a burning issue, but Muir's prose captivated them and obliged them, in spite of themselves, to take an interest in geology:

> The mighty Sierra, miles in height, reposing
> like a smooth cumulous cloud in the sunny sky, and
> so gloriously colored, and so luminous, it seems not
> to be clothed in light, but wholly composed of it,
> is like the wall of some celestial city. Along the
> top and extending a good way down, you see a pale,
> pearl-gray belt of snow; and below it a belt of blue
> and dark purple, marking the extension of the forests;
> and along the base of the range a broad belt of rose-
> purple and yellow, where lie the miner's gold fields
> and the foothill gardens. All these colored belts
> blending smoothly make a wall of light ineffably fine,
> and as beautiful as a rainbow, yet firm as adamant.

One of the topics of conversation that Charley and Muir encountered frequently at the Bohemian Club was distressing news about the man whom the members considered as their founder, at least in spirit. People were saying that Bret Harte had taken the ten thousand dollars from the *Atlantic Monthly* but had failed to provide them with one story per month, as his contract called for. He had installed his wife and children in New Jersey with some of Mrs. Harte's relatives, and had convinced Sam Clemens to collaborate with him on a humorous play featuring his crafty Chinese character, Ah Sin. They worked together in Connecticut, but started quarreling; by the time the play was in production, they were not speaking to each other. With neither playwright willing to work on the script after its initial off-Broadway performances, it quickly folded. Desperate for money, Harte tried the lecture circuit, but painfully discovered that he was no good as a public speaker. Now rumors were circulating that he was borrowing money from everyone he could and not paying it back. In a little more than a year, he had gone from America's highest-paid author to a man everyone tried to avoid.

XIV

11 Museum Street

In London, Joaquin Miller was running out of money as well. None of the English publishers would even consider his manuscripts, but Miller's faith in himself bordered on the irrational. In desperation he pawned his watch, sold his return ticket, and had one hundred copies of a slim volume he called *Pacific Poems* printed and bound. These he began to pass out to every editor and journalist he had met. The scheme produced no results at first, but finally led to a dinner party invitation where a number of influential people would be present. While everyone else at the party was in formal clothes, Miller appeared in a long sealskin coat which he did not remove—he could not because he had only a shirt under it. Down to his last few dollars, he had not been eating very regularly, and after a few glasses of wine, he began to regale the guests with exuberant tall tales of his adventures on the frontier. His tipsy antics made them laugh, and by the end of the evening, he had two more dinner invitations. Before long, no London society party was complete without the outrageous wild poet from San Francisco. In a theatrical costume shop he acquired riding boots, a red flannel shirt, and a Mexican sombrero, which he wore wherever he went. He knew that he was invited more as a buffoon entertainer than as a guest, but he did not mind. Eventually he came to the attention of a group of aesthetes, painters, and poets who called themselves the "Pre-Raphaelite Brotherhood." One of them, William Michael Rossetti, took a liking to him and initiated him into the brotherhood. Miller met and amused Algernon Swinburne, William Morris, Christina Rossetti, and Dante Gabriel Rossetti. As a lark, some of the group took to editing Miller's poems, improving the meter and spelling, and the idea evolved of having them published by a major London firm.

With a glowing introduction by William Michael Rossetti, *Songs of the Sierras* was published by Longman's, a publishing house with no use for Miller but not willing to offend some of its most successful writers. With the Pre-Raphaelites' promotion and Miller's penchant for publicity, the book became a best-seller. The critics hailed him as a "diamond in the rough," "a true and original singer," "the most remarkable poet that America has yet produced." Miller was invited to all the best London clubs; he met Tennyson and Matthew Arnold, had tea with Robert Browning, and began to hobnob with English aristocracy.

At the height of his success, he learned that his sister had died and one of his brothers was mortally ill. He went as quickly as possible back to Oregon to console his parents who were, by the time he got there, grieving for two of their children. Still in his frontier garb, he returned to San Francisco anticipating a hero's welcome. He was sadly disappointed. What the locals knew of his antics and writings in London led them to call him a fool and a charlatan. Understandably, he decided to return to England where his genius was properly appreciated. Before he left, however, he had an obligation to discharge. The daughter he had fathered while living with the Wintus, Calle-Shasta, was now thirteen, and the Wintu tribe was dying out. The kind of life she had grown up in was rapidly disappearing, and the girl needed someone to prepare her for a life in the white man's world.

So, Miller managed to convince Ina Coolbrith and her mother to take Calle-Shasta in, introduce her to urban life, and teach her domestic arts. He assured them he would send money regularly to cover her expenses. Two weeks later, a shy, dark little girl with a sweet face and lovely frightened black eyes arrived at the Taylor Street residence of Ina and her parents. They called her "Callie" and enrolled her in the local elementary school and began the gradual process of including her as a member of the family.

Although the San Francisco critics were harsh with Miller, his old friends introduced him to the Bohemian Club, where he became a member and spent a good deal of time describing his unorthodox methods of self-promotion. Prentice Mulford was intrigued by Miller's stories and his obvious prosperity, and let himself be talked into applying to local businessmen for subsidies to go to England "to advance trade by writing and speaking on the good and glory of California." To his astonishment, under Miller's guidance, Mulford quickly collected five hundred dollars and an agreement from the *San Francisco Bulletin* to publish his travel letters.

"You see, Prentice?" Miller confided to him. "The secret to literary success is *boldness.* You cannot overdo it. The choice is between bein' bold and theatrical or bein' obscure." Miller told him of a contract he had made with a London publisher for a book to be called *My Life Amongst the Modocs.* The Modoc tribe in Northern California was resisting the efforts of federal troops to force them onto a reservation, and their efforts were gaining the attention of the world's press. When Mulford pointed out that Miller had never lived with the Modocs, Miller dismissed the point as irrelevant by replying that the English would have no way of knowing the difference between the Modocs and the Wintus.

In London, Miller secured a basement room for Mulford in his boarding house at 11 Museum Street. Here Mulford met the odd assortment of characters among whom Miller had been living. The landlady was so long-winded that her tenants scrupulously avoided any contact with her other than at mealtime; Mulford, however, was a captive audience since his room was next to the one where she kept photographs of all her deceased friends and relatives, and which the tenants referred to as "the crypt." An exiled Polish count lived on the top floor, the very prototype of impoverished aristocracy. Also on the top floor was Josie Allen. Miller explained that he had found this child of the streets peddling flowers in the theater district. Taking pity on her, he had brought her home, obtained a room for her, and found her a job in a milliner's shop. It was his intention to adopt her. Mulford was rather astonished at this last piece of news, since Josie was eighteen at the time. Josie was an outrageous flirt, the sort of girl who threw herself at every man who looked at her—and since she was uncommonly pretty, every man looked at her.

At first Mulford accompanied Miller on his forays into London society, but he soon declined these invitations; he could not stand the embarrassment he felt at Miller's behavior. Joaquin would enter a drawing room with a bearskin rug over his shoulders, smoking two cigars at once and bellowing Indian war whoops to assure that he was the center of attention. He shocked his hostesses by plucking goldfish from their tanks and swallowing them whole. He would pour rose petals over the head of any attractive debutante and kiss her hands and fondle her face. The evening that Mulford watched him crawl across the floor and bite his hostess' daughter on the ankles was the last time he attended a dinner party with him. The British gentry, it seemed to Mulford, had a bottomless tolerance for eccentricity.

As for his own career, Mulford was not doing well in London. His lectures on the glories of California—ostensibly to encourage capitalists to invest in Pacific Coast ventures and to lure skilled workers to emigrate—were dull and poorly attended, and the articles on London he sent back to San Francisco were so gloomy that the *Bulletin* editor politely suggested that if he could not brighten them up he should stop sending them. His five-hundred-dollar grubstake was gone, and Mulford was obliged to get Miller to pay his rent in exchange for editing the lurid manuscript of *My Life Amongst the Modocs.* In addition, he scraped together scarce shillings by printing and peddling tracts on spiritualism.

Miller and Mulford were soon reunited with their old friend Sam Clemens, who was in London on a lecture tour. His second book, *Roughing It,* was out, and he was promoting it very effectively. Sam visited his bohemian companions in their humble Museum Street quarters, but did not reside there; he was staying at the best hotels. He had accepted the invitation to take his Europe/Holy Land lecture on the road in England because he had in mind doing a satire on the pompous and stuffy English, but he was so graciously treated there that he abandoned that idea and arranged for a longer second tour. Mrs. Clemens had no desire to remain in London, for she felt that London society people looked down their noses at her, so Sam escorted his wife and their baby daughter Suzy back to Connecticut and then returned hastily to London. Back in San Francisco, Charley Stoddard could not bear the thought that three of his old pals were living it up in London while he was still stuck on the West Coast. He managed to talk the editor of the *Chronicle* into a fifteen-dollar-a-week roving reporter commission and left for New York in the fall of 1873. When he arrived in London, he proceeded directly to 11 Museum Street, only to find that Miller, Mulford, and Clemens were all out of town. No matter; the landlady introduced him to Josie Allen.

> I turned toward the little imp. There stood a child with a round baby face, full of curious inquiry; exquisitely sensitive lips of the brightest scarlet glowed in brilliant contrast to the milky whiteness of the skin; brown, drowsy eyes, under the shadow of those half-awakened lids that one looks for in childhood only....Yet Josie was no child...the jaunty sailor jacket, with its broad flannel collar trimmed with big anchors, could not hide the full and graceful curves of the exceedingly feminine figure.
>
> Josie and I, alone with ourselves, were at once familiar. Josie had heard all about me from the personal recollections of Joaquin....The fire had gone out. Josie was the first to notice it, and she insisted on rekindling it herself, although I was quite warm enough without it. It was as pretty as a picture to see those two little hands fishing out the big black lumps of coal, and when she took hold of a hot piece, now and then, she dropped it with the dearest little scream that made me shiver with horror. It was great fun!

When Miller and Mulford returned, Charley learned that Miller had abandoned Josie and taken his affections to greener fields. He had met and captured the heart of the daughter of the archivist Sir Thomas Hardy. Iza Hardy was twenty-six, beautiful, romantic, cultured, intelligent, and (poor thing) hopelessly in love with the dashing American poet. Miller announced their engagement and made no effort to conceal from his friends that he was fully aware that a marriage to the daughter of one of England's most famous families would assure him of a comfortable living for the rest of his life. Josie dealt with her rejection by attempting to intensify her relationship with Charley, but finally gave up when he convinced her that friendship was all he could offer her.

Four of San Francisco's major writers were now gathered in London, and they were soon joined by a fifth, Ambrose Bierce. Bierce had established himself in San Francisco when he took over the "Town Crier" column of the *News Letter*, a weekly journal specializing in irreverent satire and gruesome humor. In his column, Bierce honed his skill at mockery. He specialized in derisive accounts of crime and suicide as well as contempt and ridicule for dishonest politicians, greedy businessmen, and hypocritical clergymen. His jibes became extremely popular, and he dreamed of achieving greater heights. In spite of the fact that he had written that "love was a mental illness, generally cured by marriage," Bierce married. And in spite of the fact that he had written concerning Sam Clemens' marriage that "the most attractive thing about Olivia Langdon to Sam Clemens is her father's bankbook," he married Mollie Day, the daughter of an Irish immigrant who had struck it rich in the mines and who, by way of a wedding gift, offered the newlyweds a honeymoon trip to England. Bierce suffered from asthma and found the atmosphere of London too sooty and foggy for his health, so he settled in the historic Roman town of Bath. From there, he could take the train to London, meet with his old friends, and engage in the sort of activities of which his bride would not approve. He loved the sophistication and urbanity of England and decided to try to remain there. Not only San Francisco, but all of America was too provincial for him. He was determined to become England's new Jonathan Swift. He cultivated literary acquaintances and managed to get three of his books reissued by London publishers. Miller introduced him to Tom Hood, the editor of a humor magazine called *Fun,* and Hood gave Bierce a part-time job as assistant editor. He began to take on the airs of an English gentleman to the extent that his California friends referred to him as "Lord Ambrose," but just when the possibility of earning a comfortable living in England appeared within reach, disaster occurred. His mother-in-law, impatient with his continued prolonging of his honeymoon, came to England and moved in with him and her daughter. That was more than he could bear. He had no choice but to swallow his pride and return to San Francisco, where he accepted the editorship of a muckraking weekly, the *Wasp,* saying it was his intention "to purify journalism in this town by instructing such writers as it is worthwhile to instruct and assassinating those that it is not."

It was also time for Sam Clemens to return reluctantly home. He had been hailed as a genius in Britain, never before so well-treated, and he could easily have spent the rest of his days there, but he had family and obligations in Connecticut. All thoughts of a satirical book on the English had vanished, and he was working instead on a satire of Americans, *The Gilded Age,* a novel of greed, speculation, and political and moral corruption.

While Sam had been lecturing, Charley Stoddard had acted as his secretary, handling his correspondence, arranging his reviews and clippings into scrapbooks, and organizing his scattered scraps of notes for his projected books. With his employment over, Charley explored the English countryside, managing while in Statford-upon-Avon to spend the night in Shakespeare's bed. He was preparing to return home when he received an invitation from Joaquin Miller to come and join him in Rome. Miller's engagement to Iza Hardy had fizzled, and to console himself he had set off on a tour of Italy. Charley arrived to find the flamboyant Joaquin as wild as ever. He was involved with an Italian countess whose husband, in a jealous rage, had challenged Miller to a duel with swords. Miller, on receiving the challenge, simply punched the count in the stomach, and the affair of honor was concluded. Charley took advantage of being in Rome to gain an audience with Pope Pius IX and to discuss seriously with several Cardinals the prospects of joining a monastery. While Charley investigated a life of chastity, Miller did just the opposite. He lost all interest in his countess the day he met Miriam Leslie.

Of the numerous women who had shared Miller's bed, none but she could match him for scandalous behavior. Born in New Orleans to impoverished Creole parents, she had married a jeweler in New York at eighteen and divorced him shortly thereafter. Her brother had fallen in love with Lola Montez and followed her to California, where he became her lover and her manager for a tour to Australia. On the return trip, he was so mad with jealousy over Lola's attentions to other men that he threw himself in the ocean and drowned. Lola, overcome with remorse, had gone immediately to visit Miriam and her mother to share their grief. By way of compensation, she hired Miriam as an actress in her next tour, and before the tour was over, Miriam had married again, this time to Ephraim G. Squier, an older man who wrote articles for the Leslie magazine chain. Miriam began to write also, and soon became the editor of America's first illustrated woman's magazine. Frank Leslie, a millionaire who published a dozen successful magazines, divorced his wife and moved in with the Squiers. Then he and Miriam conspired to get Squier into a bordello with five girls. Miriam quickly filed for divorce using the testimony of the five prostitutes for evidence of her husband's infidelity. She and Leslie married and set off for a honeymoon in Rome. It was at that point that they met Joaquin Miller. Frank Leslie accepted several of Miller's pieces for his magazines and apparently accepted as well that his bride was spending most of her nights in Miller's room rather than his.

The Leslies returned to New York, and Stoddard and Miller headed back to London. When they arrived at 11 Museum Street, they were horrified to learn that Prentice Mulford had married Josie Allen and taken her on a frugal honeymoon weekend trip to Paris. Their stupefaction was augmented when he returned and told them he had decided to take his bride back to his birthplace, Sag Harbor on Long Island, where he intended to start his own newspaper. He had no money, was now encumbered with a coquette for a wife, and he intended to start a newspaper in New York! Charley and Joaquin could only shake their heads in sympathy.

As the Museum Street gang drifted back across the Atlantic, only Charley returned to San Francisco. He found that a remarkable change had taken place. Previously, the tops of the city's steepest hills, so difficult to ascend, had been inhabited mainly by squatters who, although they had to work hard to reach their abodes, enjoyed free rent and the best of views. Andrew Halladie's project, the cable car, had changed all that. Once he had a car running up and down Clay Street, and once San Franciscans were convinced that riding in the funny little contraption was not likely to prove fatal, the tops of Russian and Nob Hill became prime property, and mansions of the wealthy were under construction.

Charley also found that his old friend Ina Coolbrith had fallen on hard times. In 1874, for reasons known only to himself, William Pickett, Ina's stepfather, abandoned his family and went off to Mexico. He sent no money and the family never heard from him again. His twin sons were independent and out of the nest, so the household consisted of Ina; her mother, aged 63; Joaquin Miller's half-Indian daughter Calle-Shasta, 15; Ina's nephew Henry, 14; and her niece Little Ina, 7. With her stepfather gone, Ina suddenly became the sole support of this large family. Her friends at the Bohemian Club were sympathetic and conducted an auction on her behalf that raised six hundred dollars. She was embarrassed to accept the money, but had no choice. With the help of one of the club's members, she obtained a post as Oakland's first city librarian at a salary of eighty dollars a month. It was California's second free public library (the first one was in Eureka) and consisted of the second floor of a building that had been detached and moved to a vacant lot next to the City Hall at Fourteenth and Washington Streets. Ina moved her family to a house nearby in Oakland which, by that time, had grown to a city with a population of ten thousand. It was difficult for her to assume the role of head of a household so abruptly. Her mother was so shaken by being abandoned that she aged quickly and sank into infirmity, and Ina, who worked in the library from nine o'clock in the morning to nine at night six days a week, had little time for poetry.

Ina was not the only person suffering from difficulties. Henry George's predictions about the economic effects of the transcontinental railroad had turned out to be quite accurate: the new link with the East had brought increased wealth to the affluent, but a large influx of work-seekers caused high unemployment, aggravated by a general business recession. Small businesses failed while larger ones grew. The distribution of wealth had become heavy at each end of the social spectrum and light in the middle. The working class, for the first time in San Francisco's history, was experiencing general poverty, while those engaged in commerce or who had good investments flaunted their riches. James

Flood, the former bartender who had made a fortune simply by listening to the conversations of his customers and investing wisely, had a $30,000 brass fence erected around his mansion at the top of Nob Hill to keep the unemployed from entering his property. The fence surrounded two square blocks, and a man was hired to do nothing else each day but polish it. John Carmany reluctantly ceased publication of the *Overland Monthly*. It had been losing money for some time, and he could no longer afford to subsidize it. Hailed a few years earlier as the finest magazine west of the Mississippi, it had begun to suffer from the day that Francis Bret Harte left the editor's chair.

XV

A Perfect Day

Once John Carmany had laid the *Overland Monthly* to rest, he devoted himself to a new project, a collection of Ina Coolbrith's poems. He had written to Harte about the scrapbook of poems that Ina had loaned him to take back east. Harte claimed to have left it with a publisher, but no one at the publishing house could recall ever having seen it. Carmany painstakingly went through old copies of the *Golden Era*, the *Alta,* the *Californian,* and other newspapers and magazines, collecting all of Ina's work and turning it over to her to make the final selection. The lead poem was "A Perfect Day," and the book was given the same title. In the course of their working together, Carmany finally made up his mind to ask Ina to marry him. He had been smitten with her since their first meeting, when he bought the *Overland,* and he had been envious of the easy camaraderie that Harte and Charley shared with her. A cautious and conservative man, he had never declared his feelings, but now he was ready. Ina was aware that she was being courted, and at thirty-eight, with a family to care for, she knew it would be foolish to turn down a prosperous businessman. She did not love him, but she admired and respected him, and was confident that love would grow in such a marriage. When Carmany was ready to propose he consulted his brother and sister, with whom he was very close. His brother thought it would be an excellent match, but his sister pointed out that Ina Coolbrith was an accomplished poet, a genuine artist—and artists were, after all, generally not well suited for domestic life. Moreover, Ina had kept company with a number of literary men and journalists. She was used to night life, theaters, restaurants, and cafés. Now, trapped in a demanding job that paid very modestly, of course she would jump at the chance to marry a well-to-do gentleman—but would she make a good wife? Wasn't it possible that she was a little too headstrong, a shade less than thoroughly respectable, and that John might regret marrying her? Carmany apparently found his sister's warnings convincing, and never proposed. Although Ina was always profoundly grateful to him for getting her book into print, she never knew what had caused him to discontinue his obvious courtship. *A Perfect Day* received critical praise in magazines and newspapers throughout the country. Even the curmudgeon Bierce wrote that it was a "pleasant rill of song in a desert cursed by fantastic mirages." For Bierce, that was a rave review.

Another compensation for Ina was a deepening friendship with John Muir. His *Overland* articles had motivated publishers to ask him for a book on the natural wonders of California, and he had moved from Yosemite down to Oakland to work on the manuscript, spending much of his time in Ina's small library. His other reason for descending from the Sierras was a young woman named Louise Strenzel of Martinez, whom he planned to marry once his book was completed. As a betrothed man, he could speak frankly to Ina without danger of her misunderstanding his intentions. He felt that she had imprisoned herself in a career which demanded all of her time. "You're a poet," he told her. "You should be writing books, not shelving them." To help her escape, Muir would show up at the library regularly with some eligible bachelor who "just happened" to be coming in at the same time and appreciated very much the opportunity of being introduced to the handsome tall woman with gray eyes moving briskly about the large oak reading tables. Muir decided that one of these candidates, a schoolmaster named Brown, would be an ideal husband for Ina. He started showing up daily with Brown, concocting projects to bring them together until finally Ina, in desperation, sat down and wrote him a seventy-five line doggerel poem which began:

> Up from her catalogues she sprung,
> And this is the song she wildly sung,
> O Johnny Muir! O Johnny Muir!
> How could you leave your mountains pure,

Your meadow breadths, and forests free,
A wily matchmaker to be?

And it ended with:

Sail him across the placid Bay
And sun him up the smiles of MAY
Or tow him up to Martinez
There to abide with fair Louise
Or clasp him to your pitying breast,
And bear him to some glacial nest,
There tuck him in and let him rest.
But O of this I pray there be
No more, John, 'an' thou lovest me!'
Or if you smile or if you frown
I DO NOT WANT YOUR MR. BROWN.

For his part, Charley Stoddard was flush for the first time in his life with royalties from both the American and the English editions of *South Sea Idyls*. He was pleased to find that the Bohemian Club had moved to larger and more sumptuous quarters at the corner of Post and what had previously been Dupont Street. Because of the numerous brothels and opium dens in the Chinatown section of the street, Dupont had become synonymous with the infamous crib-house girls, so merchants on the respectable end of the street managed to get the street renamed for the general who became President, and Dupont Street became Grant Avenue. A railroad had been established to take San Franciscans up to the Russian River sixty miles north of the city, where there were resorts for dancing, swimming, and indulging in huge meals. The Bohemian Club, prospering from a growing membership and increased dues, bought a huge tract of redwood forest along the river as its private playground, calling it the Bohemian Grove.

Charley began writing a weekly column for the *Argonaut*, which added a bit to his income. He had always been slender to the point of frailty, but now his frame had thickened and he looked a bit more substantial; the top of his head was completely bald, and these signs of approaching middle age made him realize that it was time for him to have his own place. A conventional apartment would not do: he had to have plenty of room for the huge collection of South Sea artifacts that had been encumbering his parents' basement for several years. After considerable searching, he found his nest on top of Rincon Hill. The hill (later be leveled for the western abutment of the San Francisco-Oakland Bay Bridge) was a twin to Telegraph Hill. Because it was somewhat sheltered from the wind and fog and had sweeping views of the city and the Bay, it was one of the early locations for large, fashionable houses, and in the fifties and sixties was San Francisco's most elegant residential section. When Second Street, which ran over the hundred foot-high hill, was excavated to make a flat access road between the Pacific Mail docks and the factories below Market Street, the project undermined the streets above and, one by one, the stately houses sagged and crumbled to the ground. Among these, Charley found a banker's mansion and rented it. The east wing of the house had been removed so that it would not pull the rest of the house down the crumbling hillside. What remained was intact, though slightly askew. The garden surrounding the property, once the site of tea parties, musicales, and catered receptions, was now an overgrown jungle of ivy and blackberry vines. The front porch had departed with the east wing, and the only access from the street was through a former side door. For Charley it was ideal. The rent was cheap, the rooms large—if somewhat tilted—and the views magnificent. He installed himself and decorated his new quarters with his Polynesian bric-a-brac. Spears, straw shields, oars, and primitive masks hung on the walls amid dark European oil paintings. Shark's teeth, war clubs, carved idols, patterned baskets, and coconut-shell bowls were displayed on shelves and table tops amid Italian crucifixes, satin Sacred Hearts, and plaster statuettes of saints. From assorted pots that sat near huge faded oriental carpets, indoor creeping plants grew profusely, their tendrils climbing among the jumbled bookshelves and mingling with those of outdoor vines that had found their way indoors through cracks around the windows.

From his disintegrating hilltop mansion, Charley could watch the completion of the Palace Hotel rising above the two-story buildings around it down on Market Street. It was an imposing project. Visitors' first impressions of a city were generally formed by the hotel to which they went on their arrival, and financier William Ralston was making sure that visitors to San Francisco would be properly impressed by the largest hotel in any American city: seven stories high, occupying a full city block, with at its center a glass-roofed Palm Court, six stories high, into which carriages could drive and deposit hotel guests. It was the only hotel in San Francisco with a hundred and fifty-foot dining room, bathrooms in every room, and electric lights. Across Market, Charley could also watch the construction of "Lotta's Fountain," a cast-iron column that formed a public fountain, donated by the actress Lotta Crabtree in appreciation for the city where she had launched her career. Frequently, as Charley returned home from a late-night celebration at the Bohemian Club, he would look across the Bay and see the sky beginning to lighten behind the Oakland hills and realize sadly that over there, Ina was already up and preparing for another twelve-hour day in the library. He would sigh and promise himself to go and call on her the following Sunday.

On one of the Sundays when he kept his promise, he brought Ina news that was bad but hardly unexpected: Prentice Mulford's marriage had fallen apart. When Mulford had taken his bride from London to Sag Harbor, he could find no one willing to back him in starting a newspaper and had been obliged to work as a stringer for various papers doing hack work. One day, on his way back to the dingy little apartment where he and Josie lived, he stepped into a saloon to get some matches for his pipe. There he noticed a customer opening a cheap package of cigarettes and drawing from it a printed picture of a naked girl. As much as he did not want to believe his eyes, he could not avoid realizing that the girl in the picture was his wife. He confronted her, and she admitted defiantly that, yes, she had been posing *au naturel* for various artists in the area. Mulford was furious that she had exposed herself so freely, but Josie countered that she was tired of living on next to nothing and had a right to supplement the meager sums he gave her to run the household. The argument ended in separation. Mulford left New York and became a hermit in the New Jersey woods. Like Thoreau, he built a simple cabin and lived alone, contemplating nature, thinking, and writing. Now he was writing five-cent tracts on spiritualism which he took to New York City once a month to have printed and distributed, calling his publications the White Cross Library. Later, in his autobiography *The Swamp Angel,* he would write:

> I was twelve years in California where I dug a little gold and a good deal of dirt. I have taught school, tended bar, kept a grocery, run for the legislature, been a post officer, started a hog ranch and failed, kept an express office, prospected for silver in Nevada, laid out towns which are laid out yet, run a farm to weeds, lectured, and written a good deal for the papers...I have seen Cape Horn, London, Paris, Vienna, a whale in a "flurry," a ship's crew in mutiny, a woman who did not want a new bonnet (but she was dead). And I have an ex-mother-in-law.

Also in the East, Bret Harte, deeply in debt, was casting about, desperately looking for any position that would enable him to get back on his feet, all the while keeping at arm's length a wife who "had told him so" about trying to make a career in literature. An acquaintance in the Hayes administration finally secured a position for him in the American Consulate at Krefeld, an industrial town near the Rhine in northwestern Germany. It was a dull, paper-shuffling job in a gray city of smug bourgeois people, but it gave him an income and put distance between him and his creditors. He told Mrs. Harte that she would be better off to stay in New Jersey for the weather in Krefeld was unhealthy and the children needed to finish their education. When he could get away, Frank went to London. He did not know anyone there except for—of all people—Joaquin Miller, who was back at Museum Street. As much as he detested Miller's cheap theatrics, he swallowed his pride and let Miller take him around and introduce him. The situation lay heavily on Frank's mind. Not so very long ago

America's highest paid author, he was reduced to meeting England's literary society through a man he had written off as a third-rate poet and bragging mountebank. It was as ironic as a Bret Harte story.

For his part, Miller was ready to come home. He had inflated his reputation sufficiently in Europe, he felt, to go to New York and hold his own with the best of them. He had published a book of poems, *Songs of Italy,* which re-established his reputation in London. In New York, Miller adapted one of his early novels, *First Families,* into a play called *The Danites in the Sierras,* a melo-drama in which two Danites (Mormons) appear as murderous vil-lains. Although it had a successful run on Broadway, and his renewed liaison with Miriam Leslie assured frequent publication in the Leslie magazines, he found New York publishers and crit-ics much less sympathetic than those in London. His affair with Miriam Leslie came to an abrupt halt when he attended an elocu-tion performance by Abigail Leland; he was so smitten by her that he insisted on seeing her backstage. Miss Leland was the daugh-ter of the owner of a chain of New York hotels that included the Rossmore, the Sturtevant House, the Metropolitan, and the Grand Union. Like many others before her, the young woman fell head over heels for the flamboyant poet whose long blond hair now showed streaks of gray. They married shortly after their meeting, and although Miller already had three children by Minnie Miller as well as Calle-Shasta—none of whom he was supporting—he fathered another daughter, Juanita Joaquina Miller.

XVI

The Penniless Scotsman

While Miller escorted Bret Harte through London, a romantic love story that would rival that of Robert and Elizabeth Barrett Browning and that would culminate in San Francisco, was beginning in the artists' colony town of Grez, fifty miles south of Paris. Fanny Osbourne of Oakland was having dinner in her *pension* with her family. At sixteen Fanny had married a young man who, after his service in the Civil War, brought her West where he unsuccessfully tried mining before finally settling down as a court reporter in San Francisco. Sam Osbourne bought a little cottage in Oakland for Fanny and their children. To say that Sam settled down is not quite accurate, since he had difficulty remembering to sleep in his own bed. Because of his continuing infidelities, Fanny, who had been taking art classes along with her daughter at Virgil Williams' San Francisco Art Institute, decided to take her three children off to France and continue their studies there. Her daughter Isobel was seventeen, and her son Lloyd was eight; her youngest, a boy of six, contracted a fatal case of tuberculosis in Paris. Sam Osbourne had come to France for his son's funeral and was preparing to return to San Francisco.

On that warm evening in Grez in 1876, two young Scotsmen wandered by the *pension* and peered in the open upper half of the Dutch door that opened to the dining room. They were cousins with the same name, Robert Stevenson. The older one was called Bob, and the younger one used his middle name, Louis. Louis looked in at Fanny, with her eyes, he said, "like those of a man sighting down a pistol," and fell in love just as if he had fallen into an open well.

Though no one would have known it to look at him, Robert Louis Stevenson was the only child of a highly respectable middle-class Edinburgh family. His father, Thomas Stevenson, was Scotland's foremost lighthouse engineer and the son of Scotland's previous foremost lighthouse engineer. Naturally, Thomas had hoped that his son would carry on the family tradition, but he had to give up that hope early in the boy's life. Little Louis was a sickly child who suffered from respiratory ailments every winter and spent much of his life in bed. He seemed indifferent to mathematics and physics and was much more at home with fantasy and romance. His father resigned himself to sending Louis to law school. Despite spending most of his time in Edinburgh taverns and brothels, Louis passed the bar and received a thousand pounds from his father to start his law practice. He took the money and went immediately with his cousin to France where the two of them wandered about freely, unencumbered by any sort of luggage. When their shirts became too dirty and frayed to wear any longer, they would throw them away and buy new ones.

After Louis first glimpsed Fanny, the two young men took rooms at Grez, and Bob flirted with the daughter to distract her attention from Louis' earnest pursuit of her mother. Fanny and Isobel were studying in an art school established by the painter Millet and greatly influenced by Impressionism. The students did not work in a studio but rather outdoors in the beautiful countryside along the meandering Loing River. Louis would accompany Fanny, reclining at her feet while she painted, talking and smoking his thin, hand-rolled cigarettes. She scarcely knew what to make of this strange suitor, with his emaciated, spindly figure that was all sharp angles; scraggly long hair and mustache that gave his face a rakish air, and constant cough that revealed his shaky health. As for the young bohemian, working on his first book (*An Inland Voyage,* the reflective account of his canoeing through the canals of France), he could hardly have found a less likely match than Fanny Osbourne, a married American woman ten years his senior with two children, and still in mourning for her third child. But their relationship took hold; they became lovers and spent an idyllic summer together. Then Sam Osbourne sent an ultimatum. He had been patient and indulgent long enough, and he would send no more money. Reluctantly, Fanny took her children back to Oakland. The interlude was over. Louis immediately threw himself into work, wandering alone through the Cévennes mountains of southern France, camping out and keeping a journal that would become *Travels with a Donkey.*

Then, in July of 1879, Fanny sent Louis a telegram. No one else ever knew what it said, but whatever it was, it made him leave immediately for California. He was ill, nearly out of funds, with but meager prospects awaiting him; and pursuing Fanny meant complete estrangement from his family. Yet he went, booking second-class passage on the *S. S. Devonia,* which was filled with refugees from the potato famine in Ireland, and then taking a wooden seat on the train from New York to San Francisco. His health worsened, and the long hot eleven-day trip across the plains nearly did him in. But he finally awoke one day to find himself in California and wrote to a friend in England:

> I had one glimpse of a pine-forested ravine on my left, a foaming river, and a sky already covered with the fire of dawn. I am usually very calm at the displays of nature, but you will scarcely believe how my heart leaped at this! I had come home again—home from unsightly deserts, to the green and habitable corners of the earth. Every spire of pine along the hilltop, every troutly pool along that mountain river was more dear to me than a blood relation. The sun no longer oppressed us with its heat—it only shone laughingly along the mountainside. At every turn we could see further into the land and our own happy futures. At every town, the cocks were tossing their clear notes into the golden air and crowing for the new day and the new country.

Another train took him to Monterey where he arrived deathly thin, as shabby as a pauper, sick, and thoroughly exhausted. Fanny was boarding with a Mexican family there, ostensibly serving as a chaperone to her sister Nellie, who was engaged to a Monterey resident, Adolfo Sanchez. The two sisters and Fanny's children spent weekdays in Monterey but returned to Oakland on weekends. Fanny, it seemed, had reconciled with her husband;

Robert Louis Stevenson

Louis' presence was embarrassing her. He found lodging in a Mexican rooming house, but as the skin irritation that had plagued him all across the continent grew worse, his landlady invited him to go elsewhere: he was frightening off the other guests. Twice rejected and suffering from the damp fogs of Monterey, Louis rented a horse and set out for Carmel ten miles away, where he had heard that the weather was warmer and drier. He was so weak that he collapsed and lay in the woods, unable to get up, for three days. It looked very much as if this promising young writer was going to die alone in a remote area and become dinner for the buzzards. No one would ever know what happened to him. But by chance, a goat farmer and his Indian helper discovered him and took him back to their goat farm where they nursed him back to sufficient health to transport him to Monterey to be treated for pleurisy.

At this point Louis took up residence at the inn of a Frenchman, Jules Simoneau, who ruled the kitchen as well as the intellectual life of Monterey. The diners at Simoneau's were an international and polyglot group. Louis would later write, "There were rarely more than two of the same race together; though we were rich in pairs with two Frenchmen, two Portuguese, and two Ligurians. Among Spanish, English, and French, the sound of our talk was like a little Babel. But whatever tongue might be the speaker's fancy for the moment, the oaths that shone among his sentences were always English."

Simoneau felt pity for this scarecrow of a Scotsman who had risked his life and heritage for *une affaire du coeur*. He quietly arranged for the local newspaper to "hire" Louis, his two-dollar weekly salary actually coming from donations that Simoneau collected from his regular customers.

Things picked up for Louis. A story he had sent to his friend William Ernest Henley, "A Pavilion on the Links," was published in *Cornhill* magazine, and Fanny finally made up her mind to obtain a divorce from Sam Osbourne. Louis moved to San Francisco to be closer to her. He found an inexpensive room at the home of a kindly Irish woman, Mary Carson, at 608 Bush Street, and devoted the time between Fanny's furtive visits to writing and wandering around exploring the city, "a woodyard of unusual extent and complication," fascinated by its cosmopolitan atmosphere:

> Here are airs of Marseille and of Pekin. The shops along the streets are like the consulates of different nations....For we are here in a city of gold to which adventurers congregated out of all the winds of heaven; we are in a land that till the other day was ruled and peopled by the countrymen of Cortés; and the sea that laves the piers of San Francisco is the ocean of the East and of the isles of summer. There goes the Mexican, unmistakable; there the blue-clad Chinaman with his white slippers; there the soft-spoken brown Kanaka, or perhaps a waif from far away Malaya. You hear French, German, Italian, Spanish, and English indifferently. You taste the food of all nations in the various restaurants; passing from a French *prix fixe* where everyone is French, to a roaring German ordinary where everyone is German; ending, perhaps, in a cool and silent Chinese tea-house. For every man, for every race and nation, the city is a foreign city; humming with foreign tongues and customs; and yet each and all have made themselves at home.

He found Chinatown the best place for a newcomer to loiter, where:

> The very barber of the Arabian Nights shall be at work before him, shaving heads; and he shall see Aladdin playing on the streets. Who knows but among

these nameless vegetables the fruit of the rose-tree itself may be exposed for sale? And the interest is heightened with a chill of horror. Below, you hear, the cellars are alive with mystery; opium dens, where the smokers lie, one above the other, shelf above shelf, close-packed and groveling in a dead stupor; the seats of unknown vices and cruelties, the prisons of unacknowledged slaves and the secret lazarettos of disease.

He took a cable car to the top of Nob Hill, looked down at the expanse of parallel streets in what was by then the fourteenth largest city in America. He could spy in the distance the Stock Exchange:

The heart of San Francisco: a great pump we might call it, continually pumping up the savings of the lower quarters into the pockets of the millionaires up on the hill.

Charles Warren Stoddard stepped out of the side door of his crumbling mansion. It was noon and he had just arisen and dressed. He was on his way to a neighborhood Mexican restaurant for lunch. When he saw the shabbily-dressed, emaciated young man sitting on a low wall across the street, he had a moment of misgiving about leaving the house since his door had no lock, but he was hungry and continued on down the hill. Returning an hour later, he saw that the suspicious-looking character was still there. The morning fog had receded, and the young man had removed his long ulster, revealing a worn and frayed dark blue velvet jacket. Charley approached him to determine just what his business there was. When he discovered that the disreputable figure was simply a fellow writer involved in an irrational adventure of love, he invited him in and set about making a pot of tea in the fireplace. Louis wandered around the rooms, fascinated by all the South Pacific artifacts and listening eagerly to Charley's stories of life in the islands.

"You've no kitchen," Louis remarked.

"No, it departed with the east wing," Charley said, lighting a stick of incense. "Anyway, I never could cook."

"You take all your meals in restaurants, then?"

"Yes, it's less wasteful than throwing out the food that I've tried to prepare."

Charley gave him an autographed copy of *South Sea Idyls* and loaned him his copies of Melville's *Omoo* and *Typee*. The two men became good friends, and Charley arranged for Louis to have library privileges at the Bohemian Club, where his shabby clothes were looked upon with some askance. The club was undergoing a gentrification, and there were more "weaving spider" business-men now among its members than struggling artists. The young Scotsman sitting in one of the leather armchairs raised eyebrows at the club; he looked a bit *too* bohemian. Charley had plenty of free time and spent it showing his new friend parts of the city that Louis had not yet discovered: Ocean Beach, the Cliff House, and a huge expanse of sand dunes in the south-west corner of the city that was being transformed into Golden Gate Park. On one occasion, Stevenson, having searched for Charley all day at the Bohemian Club, his favorite restaurants, and twice at his residence, sat down and left him a note in the form of a poem pinned to the door. The last stanza read:

I scatter curses by the row,
I cease from swearing never;
For men may come and men may go,
But Stoddard's out forever.

As their friendship deepened, they began writing humorous verse to one another regularly. Once Stevenson wrote a long poem in broad Scottish dialect, in the style of Robert Burns, that ended:

Far had I rode an' muckle seen,
But ne'er was fairly doddered
Till I was trystit as a frien'
Wi' Charlie Warren Stoddard.

Louis was writing furiously, sending stories and articles to his friends in England, desperately trying to obtain some funds. He was unaware that his friends were making no effort to get his pieces published, hoping that a lack of money would oblige him to come to his senses and return home. He was surviving on a seventy-cent daily food budget: a ten-cent breakfast at the Pine Street Coffee House, a fifty-cent lunch at Donadieu's French restaurant, and a cup of coffee for dinner. Then Sam Osbourne lost his job and could no longer support his family. The burden fell to Louis, and he cut his daily outlay from seventy to forty-five cents. He might never have survived if it had not been for his friendship with the painter Jules Tavernier, another Bohemian Club member. Tavernier made his living painting murals for the mansions on Nob Hill, but his studio at 728 Montgomery, which was also his home, was devoted to creating huge dream-like paintings that were his real joy, even if no one bought them. The studio, a huge third-floor skylighted room with a clutter of canvases, easels, mannequins, sketches taped to the walls, and assorted furniture, was a perpetual open house for artists, journalists, and theatrical people who congregated for lengthy conversations while helping Tavernier consume his cheap wine and his bottomless stewpot.

The winter of 1879-80 was particularly cold and wet in San Francisco, and an epidemic of influenza spread across the city. Louis stayed in bed as much as he could, trying to stay warm and writing constantly, trying not to think about the hunger that gnawed at his stomach and the panic that grabbed at his heart at those moments when he pondered the consequences of his rash actions concerning Fanny. Her divorce was under way, and she was putting herself and her family in the care of a man who was virtually penniless and too sickly to work, even if he could find employment.

In March, Mary Carson went to visit her tenant who had been severely ill for the past week and who had not left his room. She discovered him delirious and hemorrhaging, the bed covered with blood. She called a local doctor who examined him and diagnosed "consumption"—tuberculosis. There was no treatment, no cure. "He should be in a warmer climate," was the doctor's only recommendation. Mrs. Carson got word to Fanny, who came immediately. She obtained a room for Louis at the Tubbs Hotel near her cottage in Oakland, and went there every day with soups and custards in hope of rebuilding his strength. Instead, he grew weaker; prospects for his recovery were bleak. Fanny's position was hardly better. Her divorce from Sam was under way, her family disapproved of her relationship with Louis as much as his did, and now it seemed that her romantic adventure was about to end in death, scandal, and poverty. Nevertheless, without concern for neighborhood gossips, she moved Louis into her cottage in a last desperate attempt to restore his health.

Fanny Osbourne

It worked. Little by little, the bleeding and coughing subsided, and Louis rallied. Then came a reversal of fortune to complement the reversal of health. Louis's father sent a terse telegram: "Count on 250 pounds annually." Two hundred and fifty pounds was far from a fortune, but it meant that the couple would never again go hungry. Louis' first act was to go to a dentist to repair his teeth, which had virtually rotted away during his eight-month stay in California.

Louis and Fanny married in the home of a Scots Presbyterian minister on May 19, 1880; he was twenty-nine, she was forty. They set off on an unusual honeymoon accompanied by Fanny's son Lloyd, then twelve, and Fanny's dog Chuchu. They stayed in a bunkhouse in an abandoned Silverado mine on the flank of Mount St. Helena in the Napa Valley, sixty miles north of San Francisco. Their cabin was well above the fog line, and despite their primitive living conditions, the dry valley heat brought Louis back to full health. After a two-month pastoral recuperation, Louis took Fanny to Scotland to be accepted as a legitimate member of the Stevenson family. In his trunk were notebooks that would soon become The *Amateur Emigrant,* the story of his travels across the American continent and in California; *The Silverado Squatters,* the diary of his honeymoon trip, with charming character sketches and depictions of the natural beauty of the area; and *A Child's Garden of Verses*. These three books would bring him world recognition in the next few years.

XVII

The New "Overland Monthly"

At the Christmas Jinks of 1881, the Bohemian Club entertained a guest of honor, Count Thun of Bohemia. The members
were pleased to have a genuine "capital B" Bohemian in their
midst, and his presence inspired Charley Stoddard to tell the story
of another Bohemian, John of Nepomuk. In preparation for his
conversion to Catholicism, Charley had studied the lives of the
saints, and had become fascinated by these inspirational stories.
John of Nepomuk, he related, was known as "the saint who
wouldn't tell." In the thirteenth century, the King of Bohemia had
reason to suspect his wife of infidelity. The simplest way to investigate the matter, he reasoned, was to interrogate the Queen's
confessor, the priest John of Nepomuk. When the cleric refused to
divulge any information revealed to him in confession, the King
took him to the Moldan Bridge and told him to disclose what he
knew or be cast into the rapids far below. The priest remained
silent and was thrown over the rail. At that point, five brilliant
stars appeared around his head, and he landed gently in the water
and floated away unharmed.

The convivial bohemians were so taken by "the saint who
wouldn't tell" that they decided to make him the patron saint of
their club. And Count Thun was so impressed by Charley's recital
of the story that he commissioned a statue of the saint by
Bohemia's foremost woodcarver and sent it to San Francisco,
where it became one of the club's most treasured possessions.

Around the tables at the Bohemian Club that year, there was
much discussion of its two "honorary founding members," Bret
Harte and Sam Clemens. Each had left California before the club
was formed, but since it had been formed by men who had been
their friends and since they both had achieved considerable liter-

ary status, the club treated them as its Romulus and Remus. Although his best works were still ahead of him, Sam had completed three books since *Roughing It: The Gilded Age,* a satire on the political corruption and financial skullduggery of the Reconstruction Era; *The Adventures of Tom Sawyer;* and *A Tramp Abroad,* a humorous travel book on Germany and Switzerland. His name was a household word in America now, and he would have been a wealthy man had it not been for his unfailing talent for making poor investments.

Bret Harte was not so easily bragged about at the Bohemian Club. He had managed to get himself appointed Consul in Glasgow, Scotland, but the rumor was that he was spending nearly all of his time in London, leaving his consular work to his staff. A story was even circulating that, on a rare occasion when he took the train from London back to his post, the train stopped at a station and Harte looked out the window and absently asked the conductor what station it was. "This is Glasgow, sir," the conductor replied, and Harte had to gather his belongings quickly and get off before the train left again. Living in Glasgow, he wrote to his wife, was like "living in a damp cellar with an occasional whiff from a drain, from a coal heap, from a mouldy potato bin, from dirty washtubs." Mrs. Harte was convinced to remain in New Jersey.

There was also much discussion about Harte's relationship with the Van de Velde family. Arthur Van de Velde was Chancellor of the Belgian Legation in London, and his wife Marguerite had literary pretensions. The Van de Veldes had a town house in St. John's Wood, but their principal residence was an estate at Bournemouth where one room was permanently assigned to Harte. Marguerite Van de Velde was translating Harte's stories into French, so the two of them spent a great deal of time together, and naturally there was gossip about the extent of their relationship. Harte was still writing, and English magazines published his work, but even his admirers had to concede that his current stories were no more than diluted imitations of his early mining camp allegories.

There had been rumors also at the Bohemian Club about starting up the *Overland Monthly* again. Warren Cheney, the

owner of the California Publishing Company, was willing to
undertake the revival, and John Carmany graciously made him a
gift of the magazine's name. Ina Coolbrith had heard the rumors
but dared not believe them. One day, however, when she returned
from the library, she found in the mail this invitation:

Mr. and Mrs. Irving Scott
desiring to celebrate the revival of the
Overland Monthly
request your presence at dinner
at their residence
507 Harrison Street
Friday, December Twenty-Second, 1882
at half-past five o'clock

Ina had never met the Scotts, but she knew that he was an
engineer who had made his fortune designing mining machinery
and that he and his wife were among the leading socialites of San
Francisco with a mansion not far from Charley's place—though
on the part of Rincon Hill that had not suffered from slides and
settlement problems. They were friends of Warren Cheney, and
were lending their home for a party to launch the new project.
Included with Ina's invitation was a note from John Carmany,
asking her to send a short poem on some topic related to the original *Overland* that could be read at the dinner.

When Ina arrived at the Scott's mansion, she was ushered by
a butler into an enormous high-ceilinged dining room where a
huge table was set for forty-three dinner guests. The center-piece
was a large version of the *Overland's* bear logo, fashioned in vio-
lets. Many of the contributors to the original *Overland* were there,
but most of the principal ones were not. Harte was in Glasgow (or
London, more likely); Sam Clemens and Prentice Mulford were
back East, and Charley was in Hawaii working on a new book—
semi-autobiographical, he said—called *For the Pleasure of His
Company.* Consequently, Ina found herself to be somewhat of a
guest of honor. Carmany was acting as master of ceremonies. He
introduced Warren Cheney, who made a short speech, and then
introduced Millicent Shinn, a recent graduate of the University of

California who was to be the new editor, the first woman in America to be chief editor of a major magazine. After the dinner, Miss Shinn came over to Ina to extract a promise that she would submit poems to the new venture. Ina agreed and mentioned that just about everyone who had contributed to the old *Overland* and was still in the area had come to the party—with the obvious exception of Ambrose Bierce.

Miss Shinn replied, "Well, he wasn't invited. Mr. Cheney finds him pretentious and offensive and doesn't want anything to do with him."

It turned out that Cheney's snub of Bierce was ill-advised. When the first issue of the new *Overland* came out in January of 1883, Bierce referred to it as the "Warmed-Overland Monthly" and said that Ina's contribution, "Our Poets," should have been a dirge since "all of our poets are dead—or ought to be." Of another of Ina's *Overland* poems, "Unattained," he wrote that the verses were

> ...marred by this dainty writer's tiresome lugubriousness. Having in mind the whole body of Miss Coolbrith's works for the last fifteen years, we are compelled to ask—when is she going to 'attain'? If never, is it not time for her to remove her pretty lace handkerchief from her pretty brown eyes and put it comfortably in her pocket?

As editor of the *Wasp,* a satirical weekly of social commentary and vituperative color cartoons, Bierce had found his niche. Most of the copy of each issue came from his own pen, and he delighted in skewering corrupt politicians and dishonest businessmen. It was as if he found some compensation in his bitter attacks for his unhappy marriage and for being obliged to return to California from England, and he set himself up as the arbiter of literary taste for San Francisco. With good reason, every writer and editor feared his vitriol. When Oscar Wilde passed through San Francisco on a publicity tour, Bierce pulled out all the stops and wrote:

That sovereign of insufferables, Oscar Wilde...has mounted his hind legs and blown crass vapidities through the bowel of his neck to the edification of circumjacent fools and foolesses...the ineffable dunce has nothing to say and says it—says it with a liberal embellishment of bad delivery, embroidering it with reasonless vulgarities of attitude, gesture, and attire. There never was such an impostor so hateful, a blockhead so stupid, a crank so variously and offensively daft...His lecture is mere verbal ditch-water, meaningless, trite, and without coherence...With a knowledge that would equip an idiot to dispute with a castiron dog, an eloquence to qualify him for the duties of caller on a hog-ranch, and an imagination adequate to the conception of a tomcat when fired by the contemplation of a fiddlestring; this consummate and star-like youth...wanders about, posing as a statue of himself...emitting meaningless murmurs in the blaze of women's eyes. He makes me tired.

Despite Bierce's jabs, the *Overland Monthly* prospered, and once again regularly featured poems by Charles Warren Stoddard and Ina Coolbrith. Charley had completed his book but had not shown it to anyone. He was concerned that it was too audacious in both style and content for the public, so he simply put the manuscript in a trunk and waited. As for Ina, her life in Oakland had taken on a routine dictated by her seventy-two-hour work week in the library. When her mother died in 1876, Ina had become both mother and father to her niece and nephew as well as to Callie Miller. She worked hard, scrimped and saved, and was able to buy her own house near the library. As "her children" grew up, they had chores to perform: Henry and Little Ina worked at the library, shelving books and cleaning the kerosene lamp chimneys, and Callie took on the household duties of cleaning and cooking. By 1884, Callie had married a young Wells Fargo agent, Little Ina had found employment in the new field of typist-stenographer, and Henry at twenty-four was Ina's assistant librarian.

It was at this time that Ina's troubles at the library began. Until then, the library board had always been appointed, and had thus consisted of Oakland's leading business and professional men. But new regulations required that the board members be elected, which brought three new members to the five-man board: a lumber salesman and two railroad clerks. One of these, Eugene Trefethen, became a great thorn in Ina's side. First, he claimed that the library contained works that were "unsuitable to respectable people" and insisted that Defoe's *Moll Flanders* and all of Zola's works be removed from the shelves. Despite the protests of Ina, the editor of the *Oakland Tribune,* and the two incumbent board members, the new trio on the board carried the motion, and Ina reluctantly removed the books. Next Trefethen set out on a cost-cutting campaign. Through his control of the majority, he cut the annual book acquisition budget, curtailed newspaper subscriptions, and obliged Ina to send letters to all major publishers, begging for free books.

Then Trefethen added a new member to the library staff—his own widowed sister. Ina found herself obliged to work with a new assistant who was openly hostile to her and who reported her every action to the board. After a year, a new election replaced two of the three new board members with men who wanted to restore the library to its previous standards. To Ina's great relief, Trefethen's sister resigned, and Defoe and Zola came back up from the basement and onto the shelves.

In 1886, two years after Ina's "bad year," she was seated at her desk, absorbed in her work, when she became aware of some-one standing at her desk and glanced up. She almost missed see-ing a boy about ten in worn knee-pants and a large sweater with a hand-me-down look. He was standing back from her desk, a stack of newspapers under his arm, looking at her hesitantly.

"May I help you, young man?" she asked.

The boy looked around the library furtively and then back at her. "I was just wondering," he said, "how old you have to be to take out books."

"Well now," Ina replied, coming out from behind her desk, "officially, you have to be fourteen. Why, do you like to read?"

"Yes, ma'am. I really do," he said, looking up at her, apparently awe-struck that she had not sent him packing.

"What's your name?"

"Jack London, ma'am."

"And do you go to school here in Oakland?"

"Yes. Cole Elementary. Fifth grade."

"What's your father's name?"

"John London."

"Well, you take this card home. Have your father sign it, and then you bring it back to me. I'll give you a card in your father's name. You can use it to borrow books if you promise to take good care of them, keep them clean, and bring them back on time. All right?"

The boy took the card in a newsprint-smeared hand. "Really?" he said. Then he smiled at her, revealing a mouthful of rotting teeth. He returned the following day with the card filled out. Ina prepared a library card for him in John London's name and handed it to him. He looked at it and then up at her. "I can take out any book I want?"

"Yes..."

She was going to offer to help him, but he was off on his own, discovering the system, standing on a chair to read the titles on the higher shelves. A half hour later he returned with a history of Pizarro's conquest of Peru.

"A very good choice," Ina said. "I think you'll like it."

She had no idea of the impression her words made on him. No one had ever before encouraged him to read or complimented his choice of a book. This goddess had not only admitted him to the treasury but had praised him as well. He returned every few days to check out two more books. Before long he carried two additional library cards, one in his mother's name and one in his sister's, so he could check out six books at a time, mostly history and adventure.

One day Ina showed him a copy of *The Adventures of Tom Sawyer*. "Have you ever read anything by Mark Twain?" she asked.

"No, Miss Coolbrith. Is he any good?"

"Yes, he is. He used to live here, you know. He was a friend of mine."

The boy took the book and said with astonishment, "Here in Oakland?"

"No, in San Francisco. I lived there back then. But that was a long time ago."

Ina knew little of his background except that he was obviously poor and helped his family by selling evening newspapers.

He was the illegitimate son of Flora Wellman, a woman who was severely mentally unbalanced, and John Chaney, an itinerant astrologer. When Chaney discovered his mistress was about to present him with a second child, he wandered off. Flora, destitute, tried to kill herself. Fate had other plans, however, and the suicide attempt was unsuccessful. Flora found a kindly man, John London, who agreed to marry her and raise the child as his own. He was gentle and good-hearted but improvident. He failed in one business after another, lost one job after another, and was steady only in his fondness for the bottle. Eventually he became resigned to earning a meager wage as a night watchman.

Over the next three years, the scruffy boy turned into a scruffy young man, short but squarely-built and tough looking—an unlikely library patron perhaps, but one of its most faithful. At fourteen he was voted class historian, which meant that he would have delivered the graduation speech. But he had no suit, so he could not attend the ceremony. Yet this was a minor disappointment compared to the other one he was facing. His stepfather had lost his job due to a train accident injury, and Jack's plans to attend high school had to be abandoned. To support the family, he took a job at Hickmott's cannery, working ten hours a day, six days a week—a schedule that made it impossible to visit the library. His Sundays were spent sailing and drinking with waterfront companions. His sudden disappearance made Ina wonder what had happened to the boy who had been such an avid reader.

XVIII

The Hights

The 1880s were productive years for Mark Twain, who had by then completely abandoned his given name, Samuel Clemens. He published *The Prince and the Pauper* and *Life on the Mississippi.* As popular as they were, dishonest publishers cheated him out of his full royalties, and he was obliged to continue lecturing—"robbing the public from the platform," he called it—to support his family. Banquet speeches were another source of income for him, and he was in considerable demand. Most of these were all-male affairs, and he could let his humor loose with such antics as thumping on the table and shouting, "I assure you, gentlemen, I care *nothing* for ostentation—why I'd rather get into bed with Lillian Russell stark naked than with General Grant in full military regalia!" When he finished the manuscript for *Huckleberry Finn,* he set up his own publishing company and cleared fifty-five thousand dollars in the first year. That novel was soon followed by the enormously popular *A Connecticut Yankee in King Arthur's Court.*

Things had not gone so well for Bret Harte. The Democratic victory in 1884 had cost him his post in Glasgow. Unemployed, he moved in with the Van de Veldes and lived from their charity, churning out hack-work for British magazines so he could send a little money to his wife and children from time to time.

Robert Louis and Fanny Stevenson returned from Europe to New York. In the eight years since their Silverado honeymoon, the couple had traveled extensively, trying to find a climate that would accommodate Louis' delicate respiratory system. They had tried Scotland, but the dampness was too much for him. Switzerland worked for a while, but the winters were too severe.

They took a place on the Mediterranean in the town of Hyères, between Nice and Marseille, where he did well until an epidemic of cholera frightened Fanny into leaving. Despite the constant moving and bouts with ill health, his pen had not been idle. He had published *Treasure Island* and *Kidnapped,* two novels which would have by themselves assured him a place in the pantheon of writers in English; the classic novella that fixed in the public's mind forever the duality of human nature, *The Strange Case of Dr. Jekyll and Mr. Hyde;* and two of the best short stories ever written in any language, "Markheim" and "Thrawn Janet." The man who had nearly starved to death in San Francisco was returning to the States as one of the world's most famous and wealthy authors. The Stevensons, along with Louis' widowed mother, Fanny's son Lloyd, and their cook Valentine, went to Saranac, near Lake Placid, where a sanitarium for tuberculosis patients had been established. After a winter near the Canadian border, Louis felt invigorated and ready to realize the dream that had been born in Charley Stoddard's tilted mansion on Rincon Hill—to visit the South Seas.

When Stevenson and his family arrived in San Francisco and took up residence at the Occidental Hotel, he was disappointed to learn that Charley was not there, having taken a position as professor of literature and composition at the Catholic University of America in Washington, D.C. Fanny and Louis were astonished to see the remarkable changes that had occurred in the city during their nine-year absence. The summit of Nob Hill was now studded with unbelievably ornate and luxurious mansions owned by the Crocker, Stanford, Hopkins, Huntington, Fair, and Hearst families. Cable car lines now formed an extensive network all over the city and as far out as Cow Hollow by the Presidio. A new invention was being installed in all the major hotels and businesses, a device that made it possible to converse with someone on the other side of the city—the telephone.

The Stevensons' business in San Francisco was to persuade Dr. Samuel Merritt, the former mayor of Oakland, to lease them his ninety-five foot yacht *Casco,* one of the finest on the Pacific coast, for their trip through the South Seas. Merritt was skeptical about entrusting his treasure to "one of those cranks who write books," but was finally convinced when some of the Bohemian Club members vouched for Louis' sanity and financial soundness. Aboard the *Casco,* Louis and his family sailed to the Marquesas Islands, Tahiti, Hawaii, and then Samoa. Louis found that Charley had not exaggerated—everything he saw in the islands fascinated him. Even more important, his health had never been better. All of the specialists of the day recommended high altitudes for people suffering from tuberculosis, but Louis found the hot, damp climate of the tropics the most congenial he had ever known. He and Fanny bought 315 acres of land in the hills behind Apia, where they built their tropical paradise Vailima, and where Louis was christened by the Samoans *"Tusitala,"* the teller of tales.

Joaquin Miller's new wife was doing her best to discourage her husband from wearing his "Buffalo Bill" garb and acting the fool in New York, but her efforts brought few results. "Joaquin" was never cut out to be ordinary.

To no one's surprise, the marriage floundered, and he and Abby began living apart. To his credit, he did try to make amends with Minnie Myrtle. She had come to New York in utter desperation. She was fatally ill and completely without funds. Miller put her in a hospital and tried to send for their three children. He could not locate the two boys, but their daughter Maud came immediately, arriving shortly after her mother's death. Fed up with New York, Miller moved to Washington, D.C., bought a plot of wooded land in Arlington Heights, and—to the consternation of the whole city—proceeded to cut down trees and build a log cabin with his own two hands. The incongruous cabin became a local curiosity, and when visitors came, Miller would invite them to come in, serve them a glass of his special moonshine, and then endeavor to sell them the original bearskin he had worn over his shoulders when presented to her majesty, Queen Victoria. He sold several dozen of these "original bearskins" to gullible visitors.

In 1884, there was an International Exposition in New Orleans, and Miller, on the grounds that the fair might need a little extra *panache,* graced it with his presence. His old friend Miriam Leslie was there also, now a widow, and sole owner and editor-in-chief of all the Leslie magazines. The two of them— he forty-seven but posing as forty-two, and she forty-eight posing as thirty-three—were a familiar sight at the fair and the city's best restaurants.

When the Exposition was over, Miller hurried back to Washington to participate in Grover Cleveland's election campaign. A lifelong Democrat, Miller realized that, due to a split in the Republican party, this was the first time since the

Helen Hunt Jackson

Civil War that a Democratic candidate stood a chance of winning the presidency, and he wanted to be sure to take advantage of it. Cleveland won a narrow victory, and Miller, for reasons known only to him, presented himself as a candidate for the post of ambassador to Japan. As out of practice as the Democrats may have been, they did not entrust the frontier poet to represent the United States in Japan or anywhere else. Still, he had used his notoriety to good purpose in the campaign, and they did need to throw him a bone of some sort—something that no one cared about anyway. So they offered him the position of Superintendent of Indian Affairs. Insulted by the offer, Miller left Washington and returned to California.

What an ironic turn of events that was! A new government, in an effort to pay off a campaign worker, actually offered the job of supervising the administration's relations with the Indians to someone who knew something about Indians. Of course Miller was not qualified to run a government bureau, but the following years would prove that he could hardly have done any worse than those who did. Moreover, if Miller *had* accepted the post, at the very least he would have made sure that his office was regularly on the front pages of America's newspapers. But the real irony is that as Superintendent of Indian Affairs, Miller would have unquestionably come under the influence of the most devoted spokesperson for Indian rights at that time, Helen Hunt Jackson. Jackson had already published a scathing review of the treatment of American aborigines, a book titled *A Century of Dishonor.* At her own expense, she sent a copy to every member of congress with a quotation from Benjamin Franklin printed in red on the cover, "Look upon your hands! They are stained with the blood of your relations." At the time that Miller refused the post, Jackson was completing her principal work, *Ramona,* a novel designed to bring the plight of the Indians to the attention of the American public.

Just before the Stevensons left San Francisco, Miller returned home in time to make their acquaintance and show them around a little. He had lived in many different places in the forty-seven eventful years of his life, and now he was ready to settle down. He wanted to be near San Francisco but not confined to cramped city quarters, so he purchased eighty acres of barren hilltop land in Oakland whose only asset was a magnificent view of San Francisco and the Bay. No roads led to the property; it was accessible only by steep hillside trails, so he was able to acquire his estate at a very reasonable price. He called the place "The Hights," insisting on using his own idiosyncratic spelling, and set about building two structures, small rough-plank cabins with high peaked roofs and peaked windows to match. The first of these was his living quarters and studio, its floor covered in bearskins and its walls decorated with bows and arrows, tomahawks, and other frontier artifacts. The second structure, which he called "the abby," served as a place to entertain visitors as well as a guest bedroom.

While he was living in Washington, D.C., Miller had read about a special holiday that had been established in Nebraska on which school children were given a day off to participate in tree-planting in some public place; it was called Arbor Day. Miller had seen the devastation of the forests around San Francisco caused by the lumber-hungry growing population, and thought that the Nebraska holiday might well flourish in California as well. He wanted a particularly visible site to inaugurate his project, and managed to get permission to use Yerba Buena Island in the Bay, halfway between San Francisco and Oakland. The island had been denuded by early goat farmers. With his Bohemian Club connections, he obtained transportation from the U.S. Navy, eucalyptus seedlings from real estate magnate Adolph Sutro, financial assistance from wealthy city fathers, and cooperation from the school boards of local school districts.

Thus on November 26, 1886, three thousand school children and their teachers invaded the island, climbing the goat trails to the summit two hundred feet above the Bay, to witness the opening ceremony. Miller had arranged for General Mariano Guadelupe Vallejo, now seventy-eight, to serve as guest of honor. Vallejo, who had been sent north by the Mexican government in 1830 to investigate the activities of the Russians at Fort Ross, had remained there, becoming Northern California's first rancher and the first vintner in Sonoma and Napa Counties. Because of this, and because he had supported statehood for California, Vallejo had almost mythical status among Californians. He rarely went out any more, and his imposing presence, arriving on a white horse to open the proceedings, assured wide publicity for the event. After brief speeches, Adolph Sutro planted the first tree. Doña Conchita Ramirez, whose father had kept goats on the island before the Gold Rush, planted the second. Miller planted the third, and Calle-Shasta, his daughter, planted the fourth. (She was living with her father now, her husband having left her when he could not prevent her from self-destruction with alcohol.) Ina Coolbrith planted the fifth tree, followed by the old general. Then the school children went to work, and by mid-afternoon, thousands of saplings protruded from the island's rocky soil, awaiting the December rains. The following year, Miller repeated his Arbor Day project, this time reforesting San Francisco's Presidio, but his primary project was his own land. With only the help of visitors who came to see him or interview him, he planted over 75,000 trees on his property—Monterey pine, cypress, olive, and eucalyptus. Then, with his own hands, he constructed three great stone monuments: a pyramid in honor of Moses, a pillar in honor of John C. Frémont, and a tower in honor of Robert Browning. When these were finished and properly dedicated, Miller began work on a ten-foot-high stone platform which was to be his own funeral pyre.

XIX

The New Pagans

On the cusp of the last decade of the nineteenth century, a young journalist on his way back to England from India stopped off for his first look at America, beginning with San Francisco, which was by then a city of 300,000 people and a port whose trade was second only to that of New York. Rudyard Kipling was fascinated with what he found:

> San Francisco is a mad city—inhabited for the most part by perfectly insane people whose women are of a remarkable beauty.

He wrote back enthusiastically to the *Civil and Military Gazette* in Lahore of the peculiar people who went about "talking something that was not very different from English," of the bizarre eating and drinking habits he found, of the stuffy and long-winded members of the Bohemian Club who entertained him, of con men, of girls whose looks and frank independence stunned him, and—most incredible of all—the cable cars which

> ...take no account of rise or fall, but slide equably on their appointed courses from one end to the other of a six-mile street. They turn corners almost at right angles; cross other lines, and, for aught I know, may run up the sides of houses. There is no visible agency of their flight. I gave up asking questions. If it pleases Providence to make a car run up and down a slit in the ground for many miles, and if for two pence halfpenny I can ride in that car, why shall I seek the reason of that miracle?

Kipling discovered a people who seemed free from the various constraints that restricted the inhabitants of other places. On Kearny Street he "watched Young California and saw that it was expensively dressed, cheerful in manner, and self-asserting in conversation." This was a society that had never adopted the Victorian puritanism of Yankee New England, nor the pseudo-aristocracy and "quality folks" gentility of the South. It was a new and distinct region of the United States, whose style as well as its climate was distinctly Mediterranean. As California shook off its Gold Rush and frontier images, it took on one that was reminiscent of southern France, Italy, Spain, and Greece. The missions, vineyards, fruit orchards, huge flocks of sheep, and the influence of colonies of French, Italians, Portuguese, and other southern Europeans all conspired to create the concept of California as the world of classic antiquity reborn.

Certainly the good life had taken hold. Seafood was abundant, fresh fruits and vegetables were available year-round, and local wines were beginning to compete with imported ones. In San Francisco in particular and in other places as well, free lunch saloons were giving way to restaurants where the quality of cuisine greatly exceeded prices—French, German, Italian, Mexican, Greek, and, of course, Chinese. The Poodle Dog restaurant, renamed "The Old Poodle Dog," was now an establishment of five floors: the first one for family groups, the second for banquets, and the top three for gentlemen and their lady friends, who could carry out assignations while consuming twelve-course meals in private dining rooms with couches and locked doors. Here, as in the Mediterranean region, Nature seemed a smiling, kindly friend rather than the stern disciplinarian that she seemed to be in the East, and Californians were able to assemble and enjoy each other's company out-of-doors. The fandangos of the old Californios were recalled in outdoor dance pavilions where men in broadcloth suits and women in long skirts and leg-of-mutton sleeves waltzed and foxtrotted under the stars.

As the nineteenth century drew to a close, pageants celebrating everything—harvests, history, seasons, and debutantes—sprang up from one end of the state to the other. Pasadena's first

Tournament of Roses took place on New Year's Day, 1890, and the annual Fiesta de Los Angeles began in 1894. Two hundred acres of Golden Gate Park were devoted to the Midwinter Fair, which opened on January 1, 1894. The fair, purposely scheduled to show the world that San Francisco's climate was such that a fair could be held in winter, was the brainchild of M. H. de Young, publisher of the *Chronicle,* the man who had just built the city's first steel-frame structure, the ten-story Chronicle Building at Kearny and Market. Entrepreneurs such as de Young were now the mainstay of the Bohemian Club, whose patrician members amused themselves each summer at the Bohemian Grove with High Jinks and Low Jinks, which gradually evolved into the "Cremation of Care." This began as a ritual in which the members, gathered around a bonfire under the towering redwoods, watched club officials in mystic costumes cast Care into the flames to initiate a month of pagan abandon for men who were otherwise confined by stiff collars and competition. In the 1890s, the simple "pagan" ceremony became an outdoor theatrical production with a full orchestra, original music, and elaborate lighting effects.

The high priestesses of California as the reincarnation of Hellenistic culture were two women whose influence began just before the turn of the century and continues to this day—Isadora Duncan and Mary Austin. The first of these came to Ina Coolbrith's attention as a tall, pretty girl of ten who could be found regularly in the Oakland library after school. Although her clothes clearly indicated that she was poor, the girl was always lighthearted and carefree. She was most serious about her reading, however. She absorbed everything the library had on ancient Greece and Rome, and when she had exhausted the library's resources on antiquity, she turned to the poetry of Walt Whitman. Ina did not know much about her except that her mother was a music teacher and that the family moved to a different house every few months, presumably from getting too far behind in the rent. Wherever she lived, Isadora made her way to the library and devoured the books that Ina found for her, discussing them with her with such an intensity that Ina often had to remind her to lower her voice.

Isadora Duncan

One morning as Ina walked by the oak reading tables, she heard a familiar voice say, "Good morning, Miss Coolbrith." She looked back and saw Isadora, whom she had not recognized. In a long dress, with her hair pinned up, the ten-year-old looked sixteen.

"Dora! What are you doing here? Why aren't you in school?"

"Because I've quit," Isadora replied with a pleasant smile.

Despite Ina's efforts to convince the girl of the importance of staying in school, Isadora remained firm. She was wasting her time in school; she had too many important things to learn to bother with fractions and memorizing state capitals. Besides, she had her own business to run now. It was true. She was giving dancing lessons in her back yard, and on weekends she and her sister took the ferry to San Francisco to give private lessons in some of the finest homes. Frequently in the evenings they put on performances for private parties, dressed in light tunics and giving their impression of rustic Dionysian dances.

"I'm already earning more money than my mother does," the girl pointed out proudly. Ina's attempts to convince her of the need for a formal education were in vain. Isadora had determined to devote herself to Art; she was a dancer, not a schoolgirl.

As it turned out, Ina had to concede that Isadora took her own education very seriously. She came to the library to borrow every new book on mythology, ancient history, or the arts. When she discovered Ina's *A Perfect Day* and learned that the librarian was also a poet, her respect turned to adoration, and sometimes Ina would turn and find the girl's gaze focused on her in apparent worship. Two years after quitting school, she came in one day, breathless and once more childlike. She could hardly contain herself. Her father, whom she had not seen for years, had come up from Southern California for a visit. He had made his fortune and was going to make up for all the hardships that his former wife and their four children had endured. He was buying them a large house with a barn, a windmill, even a tennis court.

A week later, Isadora returned to the library with her fairy-tale father. When they reached the top of the staircase and Ina saw them, she gasped. "Joseph Duncan! *You're* Dora's father?" She had not seen him for twenty-seven years. His hair was gray now, and he had put on weight, but his charm and enthusiasm had not lessened in the least.

"Can you imagine how surprised I was when this wildflower daughter of mine told me that her mentor was Ina Coolbrith? I had no idea what happened to you after you left the *Overland*. What an amazing coincidence!"

Ina looked at Isadora, who was staring at her starry-eyed. "Your father was the first person up here to print my poems. It was through him that I made my first friends in San Francisco." Hearing them reminisce, Isadora conceived the fanciful notion that her friend and her father had been lovers long before she had been born, and determined that her intense attraction for Ina was an act of destiny.

Isadora's new barn quickly became a dance studio and shortly thereafter a theater as well. The Duncan children sold tickets to theatrical performances produced by Isadora's brother, Raymond, and dance recitals with Isadora as choreographer and lead dancer.

After a few years, Joseph Duncan's fortunes had reversed again, and he was unable to keep up the payments on the Oakland property. Deprived of her barn theater, Isadora, now seventeen, went to Chicago and convinced impresario Augustin Daly, whose company was touring there, that she would set Chicago on its ear with her new form of dancing; new, yet rooted in the classical dances of ancient Greece. When she auditioned for him, barefoot and dressed in a diaphanous gauze tunic, he signed her immediately and made her a regular member of his troupe. "I have discovered the art which has been lost for two thousand years," she pro-

Mary Austin

claimed to the world, "by the Pacific Ocean, by the waving pine forests of the Sierra Nevada." Her nature-inspired interpretive dancing, the antithesis of formal ballet, took Europe by storm, and her success—as well as her liaisons with several wealthy men—permitted her to construct a Temple of the Dance in Athens, Greece, where she and her company put on free public performances.

A much less flamboyant but equally unconventional classicist was Mary Hunter Austin. She grew up in Illinois where, as a lonely child, she had her first experiences with mysticism inspired by nature. She attended college but would take only courses in science. She had no interest in the scientific method; she simply wanted to accumulate facts and interpret them with her own intuitive, emotional approach. In 1888, when she was twenty, the lure of free land brought her family to homestead in the lower San Joaquin Valley. It was the first year of a three-year drought, and the newcomers had a difficult time adjusting to the hot, arid conditions of their new home.

She married Stafford Austin, the manager of an Owens Valley irrigation project, but it was not a satisfying relationship for either partner; Austin wanted a hard-working ranch wife, and Mary wanted time to be alone to study the desert and learn the secrets of survival from its plants and animals. Their marriage was further complicated by their only child, a daughter who was severely retarded. In the 1890s, Mary began writing essays on the desert and particularly on the Indians who lived there. She talked of the Spirit of the Arroyos, an indefinable mystic presence found only in the dry, remote areas—a presence older than, perhaps even the source of, civilization. Her works began to appear in the *Overland Monthly* and *The Land of Sunshine,* and gradually she left the desert, first for Los Angeles and then as one of the founders of the artists' colony at Carmel. There she completed her first and probably her best book, *The Land of Little Rain,* fourteen sketches with moving and thought-provoking depictions of the interrelationships between the desert and the people, animals, and plants that live there:

> Mind you, it is mostly men who go into the desert, who love it past all reasonableness, slack their ambitions, cast off old usages, neglect their families because of the pulse and beat of a life laid bare to its thews and sinews. Their women hate with implicitness the life like the land stretching interminably whitey-brown, dim and shadowy blue hills that hem it, glimmering pale waters of mirage that creep and crawl about its edges. There was a woman once at Agua Hedionda— but you wouldn't believe that either. If the desert were a woman, I know well what she would be like: deep-breasted, broad in the hips, tawny, with tawny hair, great masses of it lying smooth along her perfect curves, full-lipped like a sphinx, but not heavy-lidded like one, eyes sane and steady as the polished jewel of the skies, such a countenance as should make men serve without desiring her, such a largeness to her mind as should make their sins of no account, passionate, but not necessitous.

Mary Austin had discovered a form of spirituality which was different, even antithetical to the Calvinistic Protestantism with which she had been raised. She would spend the rest of her life delving ever more deeply into that spirituality and trying to convey its essence to her readers.

XX

Exits And Entrances

Jack London had quickly tired of being a wage slave in the cannery. His waterfront companions had shown him how to get more money in one night than he would ordinarily earn in a week, by raiding oyster beds on the shore of the Bay. His courage and aptitude for sailing made him sought after by the "oyster pirates"—a euphemism for *thieves*—and he yearned to have his own boat and go into business for himself. When the sloop *Razzle Dazzle* was put up for sale, he hurried to "Mammy Jennie," a black woman who had been his wet-nurse and who had cared for him during childhood when his mother was sick. He talked her into borrowing money on her house and lending it to him to buy the boat. Along with the *Razzle Dazzle* he acquired a consort, a woman twice his age named Mamie but called "Queen" by all the regulars at the wharfside Heinold's First and Last Chance Saloon, where Jack now spent most of his time. His reputation grew and soon the opposition courted him. He took the job of deputy of the California Fish Patrol at Benicia, at the north end of San Francisco Bay, preventing oyster bed theft. But after a few months he signed aboard the *Sophie Sutherland*, a three-masted sealing schooner headed for Japan.

When he came to the library for the last time before sailing, he told Ina Coolbrith he would be gone for seven months. She insisted he take some of her personal books along. "You'll die of boredom without something to read," she told him, "and you mustn't stop growing. Keep reading and, by all means, keep a journal of your experiences." When he returned from his voyage, he had discovered Socialism and began lecturing to working men in parks and on street corners. In 1893, he joined Coxey's March on Washington, a group of unemployed men marching from Ohio to Washington, D.C. to demand that the government provide more road-building and slum-clearing projects to put them back to work. Somewhere along the road to Washington, however, he became disillusioned with the movement and dropped out.

Education, he decided, was the key to self-fulfillment as a working-class leader. He "rode the rods" back to Oakland and enrolled, at nineteen, as a freshman in Oakland High School. During the one year he spent there, always on the edge of being expelled for his fiery Socialist speeches, he entered a writing

Jack London

contest sponsored by the *Sunday Call* and won first prize with his description of a hurricane at sea. He could not endure the idea of three more years of snail's pace learning in high school, and determined that he would enter the University of California by examination. Through his Socialist friends he met a young woman named Bessie Maddern who tutored him, and in 1896, having passed the examinations, he was enrolled in classes on the Berkeley campus. He lasted less than a year as a college student, and his major accomplishment there was founding the Intercollegiate Socialist Society. Bored, frustrated by the pettiness of the university system, he quit as soon as news arrived that gold had been discovered in Alaska, and with money borrowed from his sister, headed for the Yukon.

A year later, he returned with no gold, but with a wealth of experiences. Now his mind was made up—he was going to be an author. No more wasting time in classrooms; he just had to work at it until, by force of will, he succeeded. Living on the wages from menial jobs, he obliged himself to write 3,000 words a day, often copying Kipling's stories word for word to discover the secret of Kipling's style, which he was eager to emulate.

The first of the original San Francisco writers of the 1860's to receive an obituary in the *Overland* was Prentice Mulford. He had continued to live in his rustic cabin out in the woods of New Jersey, supporting himself from the sale of his White Cross Library pamphlets, which had become a blend of spiritualism, mental healing, common sense, and occasional reminiscences of his youthful days in California. His body was discovered in a small boat tied up off Long Island where he was born. There was nothing in the boat but his pipe, his banjo, and a writing tablet which contained his last words—completely unintelligible. There was no apparent cause of death and no one to care enough to request an autopsy. He had always felt that when a person slept, his spirit traveled and had experiences beyond the comprehension of the conscious mind. When he had lived on his boat on San Francisco Bay, he was convinced that he was in psychic contact with the spirits of the Bay whom the Indians knew well, but who eluded the notice of the preoccupied white man. Perhaps on that evening in 1891, he had been in communication with the spirits of Sheepshead Bay and just decided not to come back. He had lived so much apart from his fellow man in the East that his death was scarcely noticed, but those on the West Coast who had known him, remembered him and mourned for the strange little man who was, at the same time, a humorist and a serious spiritualist.

Just as Mulford was leaving this life, another Sag Harbor native arrived in San Francisco. His name was George Sterling, and he was destined to make an even greater impression on the city than his predecessor. Sterling was born in 1869, one of the nine children of a successful physician. The Sterlings were Catholic converts and determined that George should enter the priesthood. The young man made a three-year effort, but simply did not have the calling. So at twenty-one he was sent to work for his uncle, Frank C. Havens, a San Francisco insurance broker who was extending his fortunes by acquiring property in the East Bay and subdividing it into residential and commercial lots.

Sterling worked in his uncle's real estate company in San Francisco but chose to live in the small hillside community of Piedmont, next to Oakland. Probably one reason for this choice was that it permitted him two half-hour rides on the ferry each day, and he devoted that time to his secret passion, writing verse.

One Sunday, as the remarkably handsome young Sterling was returning from Mass, he noticed a strange sight. A small Asian - man dressed in a cowboy outfit was trudging up the hill carrying two bags of groceries. Out of curiosity, Sterling followed him up the street, then up the dirt paths, finally arriving at the "Hights" where he encountered the houseboy's master, Joaquin Miller. Miller invited him in and the two men became acquainted. Over numerous glasses of Miller's homemade "popskull" whiskey, Miller told Sterling all about his affairs with Miriam Leslie.

"When I last saw her," he said, "I swore to her that if she ever married anyone but me, I'd leave the country."

Miriam Leslie *had* remarried, her fourth marriage, this time to William Wilde, brother of Oscar Wilde, a drunken sponger who wrote pornography and was young enough to be her son. A man of his word, Miller wrote Miriam a sad letter and sent it to a friend in San Diego, asking him to mail it to her from Mexico. At the time of Sterling's visit, Miller was living with Alice Oliver, a sixteen-year-old girl whom he had met at Luna's restaurant in San Francisco, a favorite bohemian hangout. Alice had the advantages of several heritages—she was part black, part Mexican, and part Anglo-Saxon. Sterling was rather shocked to learn that the girl was carrying Miller's child.

When Sterling confessed that he too wrote poetry and showed some of his work to Miller, the old poet invited the young one to one of his "bandit barbecues." These parties began in the evening as a group of Miller's friends gathered around a large campfire where Miller had venison stew bubbling in a huge iron pot. Each guest had a large tin cup with a generous dose of Miller's "star juice" for *apéritif.* At the right moment, Miller would holler, "Bottoms up!" and then fill the same cups with stew.

At his first of these ceremonies, Sterling became acquainted with another Piedmont resident, Carleton Bierce, who invited him to a weekend picnic at Lake Temescal, a huge reservoir built to supply water to the growing cities of Oakland and Berkeley. Sterling accepted readily when he learned that Carleton's brother Ambrose would be there. By the time the picnic took place, Sterling had submitted one of his poems and Bierce had printed it in his *Prattle* column, giving George the opportunity to make conversation with Bierce by thanking him.

The Ambrose Bierce that Sterling met at Lake Temescal was no longer a mere columnist of wit and mockery; he had established himself as California's leading critic not just of literature, but of all the arts, as well as fashion, politics, and life in general. His skill in satire was so great that people read his column regularly just to get some wicked laughs, and through this, Bierce's influence had become absolute. Whatever he praised was successful, what he condemned was not, and what he ignored was unknown. And he was no longer writing for the small-potatoes publication *Wasp*. The scion of the Hearst family, William Randolph, had dropped out of Harvard in 1887 and returned home to San Francisco, where his father bought him the *Examiner* newspaper. Young Hearst began a new kind of journalism that would build a chain of newspapers around the nation and fulfill his dream: to be the most powerful man in America. Hearst knew the power of the pen better than anyone, particularly the vitriolic pen. He hired Bierce and moved his *Prattle* column to the *Examiner.*

Hearst's first targets were the Big Four: Charles Crocker, Mark Hopkins, Collis P. Huntington, and Leland Stanford, the developers of the transcontinental railroad, later named the Southern Pacific. These four men were the richest and most influential men in the West. They owned vast areas of land throughout California and controlled the legislature. Hearst wanted their power, and Ambrose Bierce was one of his principal weapons. While Hearst exposed the Big Four's Machiavellian activities on the front page, Bierce needled them in his column regularly:

> Stanford and Huntington, so long at outs,
> Kissed and made up. If you have any doubts
> Dismiss them, for I saw them do it, man;
> And then—why then I clutched my purse and ran!

George Sterling

When Sterling was finally introduced to Ambrose Bierce, he was even more intimidated. At fifty, Bierce was an imposing figure. Even though he was at an overnight picnic, he was dressed as if for a wedding. His curly hair had turned silver and he wore it long, like a gleaming crown. His meticulously trimmed mustache, turned up at the ends, gave him the look of a British military officer. Sterling could not manage to look directly into Bierce's startling blue eyes, and hung his head like a schoolboy. Nevertheless, Bierce had been impressed by the poem that he had accepted, and agreed to read more. He invited Sterling to lunch at Marchand's the following Sunday.

On that Sunday, the two men enjoyed a pleasant, leisurely lunch during which the critic interrogated his guest thoroughly. When they finished, Bierce ordered another bottle of wine and said, "Now read me some of the poems you've brought." He then sat back, glass in hand, eyes closed and listened attentively to Sterling's high Yankee-nasal voice reading his verses nervously. After each poem, Bierce held up his palm. When he had digested the work, he lowered his hand, indicating that he was ready for another. They spent the afternoon in that manner, and when Sterling had read his last poem, Bierce ordered cocktails. He then began asking questions of the young poet to determine the depth of his commitment to his art. The questions evolved into a lecture on a life devoted to the service of culture, of the sacrifices necessary in such a life, and the meaninglessness of any other. At seven o'clock they had dinner at the same table where they had lunched, and Bierce explained to his guest that the problem with America was that democracy had crept from politics into artistic endeavor where it had no business; the result was that American art rarely rose above the level of vulgarity and sentimentality.

At ten o'clock, they left the restaurant and walked down Sutter Street. Bierce led Sterling into a small café. He ordered two cups of *café filtre* and grimaced when Sterling said that he did not drink coffee. The young man felt embarrassed and wished he had not refused. A waiter came and performed his ceremony. He set a glass cup with a silver drip device on it in front of Bierce. Then, while the coffee filtered into the cup, he poured Kümmel over a lump of sugar in a small silver tray set over a candle and ignited the mixture. Bierce removed the filter from his cup and poured the burning mixture into his coffee. Sterling was fascinated with the process. "This is the only way to drink coffee, " Bierce said. "You should try it." He picked up the cup with the blue flame still dancing at the rim and sipped from it, somehow managing not to set his mustache on fire.

"Have you read Blake?" he demanded suddenly.

"One or two things. I find him rather obscure, difficult to understand..."

"Of course he is difficult to understand!" Bierce bellowed. "He is not writing homilies to be embroidered on satin pillow covers! He is grasping for eternal essences! Did you know that he used drugs?"

"He did?" Sterling asked incredulously.

Bierce signaled the waiter and ordered two more flaming coffees. "Yes. Not like so many in this mongrel city who take narcotics for thrills or to escape their demons. No, he uses them to disconnect his rational mind and thus reach into the farthest corner of his soul for truths that are otherwise unavailable." He was shaking his finger in Sterling's face now. "He did not use drugs for amusement; he was willing to risk his sanity in quest of a reality that is more real than the banal reality we perceive grossly through our senses. *That* is an artist. Are you willing to take risks, George?"

Sterling, having just managed to down the strong coffee and liqueur, said, "Ambrose, this has been a delightful and very instructive afternoon and evening. I can't tell you how grateful I am..." He pulled out his watch. "But I really must be getting home. My uncle doesn't like for me to be late..."

Bierce looked at him disgustedly. "You are talking like a timid little clerk. I think I have been wasting my time. Go on home, Georgie boy—curl up in your cozy little bed so you'll be bright-eyed tomorrow and ready for another day of boot-licking among the stock market courtiers. Run along now."

This was Sterling's first lesson. Many more followed. Bierce lectured his young admirer at length on various subjects during their forays in the city. He obliged him to visit the city morgue, where he bribed an attendant to display bodies for them to "strengthen the spirit." When Sterling had to rush from the place and vomit in the gutter after viewing the corpse of a drowned man, Bierce said, "Don't be embarrassed, George. When I was eighteen, I had to go out and bury soldiers and horses who had been lying in the sun for a week. I had my hard lessons in life too."

With Blake as a model and Bierce as a guide, Sterling began writing more seriously and striving for deeper meaning. Before long these poems appeared regularly in *Prattle,* and George Sterling was well on his way to becoming San Francisco's favorite poet.

In the last days of 1894, Robert Louis Stevenson's life ended, not from the tuberculosis that had plagued him for so long, but from a cerebral hemorrhage. The year he had spent in California was a time when he was poor in health and pocketbook, but by the time he died in Samoa fourteen years later, he was the most widely-read author in the world. He was buried on top of Mount Vaea near his estate at Vailima, and a plaque was placed on his grave with his own lines:

> Here he lies where he longed to be,
> Home is the sailor, home from the sea,
> And the hunter home from the hill.

Fanny Osbourne Stevenson was now a woman of extraordi-nary wealth, and when she returned to San Francisco, she commissioned Willis Polk, a rising young architect of the time, to design a mansion for her at the corner of Hyde and Lombard overlooking the serpentine block of Lombard called "the crookedest street in the world."

XXI

A New Job

Ina Coolbrith, now approaching fifty, came in for a difficult period, which all began with a ridiculous incident in her home just a few blocks from the library. When she had first moved into that house, Judge Boalt and his wife had presented her with a beautiful white angora cat which she named Calla. In the course of time, Calla presented her mistress with five angora kittens, all of which Ina found too adorable to part with. The kittens grew up and began doing what cats do best, so that eventually there were fourteen long-haired white cats in residence at 1267 Webster Street. They had the run of the house, and since Ina's nephew, Henry, now nearly thirty, was a bit of a dandy and wore a dark blue serge suit, he kept the door of his bedroom closed and forbade entry to all cats. When he returned home from his work as Assistant Librarian, it was necessary for him to change clothes before sitting down anywhere, since every chair and sofa was adorned with white cat hair.

A young Assistant Cataloguer had caught Henry's eye, and he was seriously courting her. On a warm Sunday, as he was about to leave the house to take the young lady to Idora Park for a pleasant afternoon at the rides and game booths, he came downstairs carrying his suit jacket in his hand and, realizing that his shoes were dusty, decided to go and brush them. He set his jacket down on the dining room table and went to the back porch. When he returned, his shoes now clean and shining, he discovered one of Calla's great-grandchildren curled up comfortably on his blue jacket. Uncharacteristically, Henry lost his temper.

"God damn you, get off there!" he shouted, jerking his jacket out from under the startled cat. Ina came in from the kitchen to see what the shouting was about. An argument ensued, resulting in Henry's moving into a boarding house and sending a letter of resignation to the library board. Within a few days, Ina managed to smooth his ruffled feathers and talk him into returning to work. Shortly thereafter, he married his cataloguer and took up residence in a small cottage. Relations between Henry and Ina were restored to normal and the incident would have been forgotten had it not been for a reporter from the *Oakland Tribune,* who heard of it from Ina's neighbors and wrote a humorous article called "Henry and the Fourteen Cats" which was reprinted in the San Francisco papers.

Some time later, Joaquin Miller decided to write an article about Ina Coolbrith. Without her knowledge, he proposed that she be given a post at the University of California as a "poet in residence." He deplored the fact that she was stuck at a dull job where, as he said with his penchant for dangling modifiers, she would be "dealing out books to children over a counter till she goes to her grave in the Oakland Library." The article was titled "California's Fair Poet. A Tribute to the Work and Worth of Ina D. Coolbrith," and appeared in the San Francisco *Call.* Miller's intentions were good, but this picture of Ina as a genius wasting her life as a librarian did not sit well with the library board. Facing financial constraints, they decided that they could best serve the public by requesting her resignation, promoting Henry to Head Librarian, and eliminating the Assistant Librarian position. There was an immediate hue and cry against this move in all the local papers, but the board remained adamant, saying that "due to strained relations between Miss Coolbrith and her nephew, this was in the best interest of the library."

Stunned, Ina cleaned out the desk where she had served for eighteen years. She moved back to San Francisco and set about collecting poems for a second volume of her verse, *Songs from the Golden Gate,* which appeared in 1895. Her friends at the Bohemian Club came to her rescue and offered her a job as the club's librarian. Over the years, as the club's membership had evolved toward members of wealth and influence, an extensive and valuable library had been built up. It was a self-serve and self-reshelve library, but it needed someone to catalogue its contents and to handle its records and correspondence. Ina was the ideal person. She accepted the part-time job at fifty dollars a month, and resolved to devote herself to a project which had long been in the back of her mind—a history of California literature. With her scrapbooks, her diaries, her photo albums, and her complete *Overland* collection, she had most of the resources she would need for such a book. She could produce something that would bring her economic security.

XXII

California Romance

Although Jack London is often given credit for being the first native-born California writer of note, the honor actually belongs to another novelist, one equally colorful, Gertrude Atherton, whose life was virtually the opposite of London's. She was born on Rincon Hill in 1857, well before its mansions began to crumble. Her parents were tumultuously mismatched: her mother, a descendant of Benjamin Franklin, had been raised in luxury on a Louisiana plantation, and her father was a stern Yankee businessman. Her mother managed to escape that marriage by divorce, then entered an equally disastrous one. When Gertrude returned to San Francisco from finishing school in Kentucky, she found her mother divorced again and contemplating a third marriage with a young man named George Atherton, the son of a wealthy New England merchant and a Spanish aristocrat from Chile. Atherton decided the daughter was more attractive than the mother, and George and Gertrude eloped.

He took his bride to live in Valparaiso Park, the family's estate on the peninsula south of San Francisco. The estate was ruled by George's mother, and Gertrude found life there exceedingly dull and artificial. Her husband, she later said, was a man who talked a great deal but never said anything. She was released from the restrictions of marriage, however, at the tender age of eighteen, when her husband died at sea while on a business trip to Chile. His body was preserved in a barrel of rum so it could be brought home for burial, and an apocryphal story grew out of the incident that the barrel had been delivered to the home and that Gertrude, thinking that her husband had sent home a cask of rum, ordered it opened—only to find her husband's pickled body inside.

Gertrude Atherton

Liberated from the stifling life at Valparaiso Park, Gertrude moved back to San Francisco and made two vows. The first was never again to be constrained by marriage, and the second was to devote herself to writing and spend her life with other writers in New York, Paris, London, and wherever else famous writers lived. She submitted a few stories to the *Overland* and the San Francisco weekly *Argonaut* and had them accepted; She then decided to try her first novel. Coming up with a plot and characters was not a difficulty for her; she would use the gossip about her neighbors, the Gordon family, a story more dramatic than any fiction she could concoct.

The story that was circulated began in England in 1849. George Gordon, the son of a well-to-do Yorkshire family, awoke one morning in a tavern to discover that, after an extended drinking party, he had married a local barmaid. He had been too drunk to know what he was doing, but a gentleman had to honor his commitments.

To avoid embarrassing his family, he took his bride across the ocean to San Francisco, where he started a sugar company. His wife had envisioned her married life on an English country estate, not in a rowdy mining camp, and pleaded to return to England. When her husband refused, Mrs. Gordon calmly informed him that she was an incurable alcoholic and, while she had kept her drinking a secret up until then, she saw no reason to continue doing so, since she was condemned to live in a distant outpost of civilization.

George Gordon left his wife to her indulgences, and threw himself into business and civic affairs with considerable success. He built an extensive estate as a summer home near Palo Alto and called it Mayfield Grange. Then he developed South Park at the foot of Rincon Hill. In a flat, undeveloped area near the shore of the Bay, he constructed an oval park five hundred feet long and seventy-five feet wide, modeled on the elegant districts of London. He planted elm trees and rose bushes there, and even imported English sparrows to complete the imitation of Berkeley Square. Around the perimeter he created a broad avenue which ran from Second to Third Street with sixty-four townhouse lots around it. The entire development was surrounded by a locked iron fence to which only residents had keys.

South Park soon became the most fashionable area of San Francisco in the 1860s. Meanwhile his wife had given birth to a daughter named Nellie, George Gordon's pride and joy. Mrs. Gordon, in an insane plot of jealousy and revenge, secretly began putting small amounts of whiskey in each of the baby's meals, so that by the time little Nellie was a toddler, she would not eat or drink anything that was not flavored with whiskey. The girl was in her teens before her father discovered that she was hopelessly addicted to alcohol. He sent her away immediately to a boarding school, but her mother simply smuggled bottles of whiskey to her in her laundry. When Gordon discovered what she had been doing, he ordered his wife out of the house. She countered by asking him how he would like reading in the morning papers every day that Mrs. George Gordon had spent the night in the drunk tank.

By then one of the wealthiest men in the city, Gordon tried everything possible to help his daughter overcome her addiction. Nellie was a willing volunteer in these efforts, for she had grown to hate herself for her weakness, but nothing seemed to work. During this time, she met and fell in love with a young Englishman who proposed to her. She told him she would marry him in one year and sent him back East. In that year she was determined to conquer her demon, and removed herself to a mountain lodge in Lake County. She bore her fiancé's child there, a girl who died ten days after her birth. Because of the Civil War, the letters the couple wrote to each other never arrived, and Nellie, assuming her young man had returned to England and deserted her, married an alcoholic who died a few years later—as did her father, broken-hearted over his daughter's fate. Nellie herself died before she was thirty, so that the huge Gordon fortune fell into the hands of her vicious mother. Mrs. Gordon sent for her brother to keep her company on the Mayfield Grange estate and the two of them quickly drank themselves to death. Mrs. Gordon's brother, however, had married a cook employed by the estate. When she died several years later, her peasant relatives on a farm in West Ireland were astonished to learn that they had inherited a magnificent estate and an enormous fortune. Later, Leland Stanford bought Mayfield Grange; eventually it became the site of Stanford University.

This was the story that Gertrude Atherton turned into *The Randolphs of the Redwoods*. Actually, George Gordon, whose real name was George Cummings, was a prominent San Francisco businessman whose life was much less lurid than Atherton's story. His wife, although an alcoholic, had never been a barmaid and did not feed her daughter whiskey. Atherton took her manuscript to the *Argonaut,* and the editor decided to run it as a serial. He paid her a hundred and fifty dollars for it, which she promptly spent on clothes and books. Later, the novel was reissued as *A Daughter of the Vine.* Now a published author, Gertrude left for New York, but she was disappointed to find that society and the literary crowd were unimpressed by her. Feeling snubbed, she departed for London, where she gained acceptance in artistic and social circles without having to resort to any of the foolishness that Joaquin Miller had used. Feeling quite superior to unsophisticated Californians and oversophisticated New Yorkers, Gertrude was shocked into an epiphanic realization when she read these words in a London weekly column:

> Why do California writers neglect the old Spanish life of that state? Never has there been anything as picturesque and romantic in the history of America, and it is a mine of wealth waiting for some bright genius to pan out.

"I read no more," Atherton later recounted, "Forked lightening was crackling in my skull. It illuminated a dazzling vista."

She realized that she was fated to be that "bright genius" and that, because of her husband's family, she had access to people who had known the Californio period. She hurried back to San Francisco and prevailed on her mother-in-law to give her letters of introduction to the old families of pre-Gold Rush California. She set up headquarters in Monterey and began researching her subject. The result of her efforts was *Before the Gringo Came,* published in 1894, a collection of romantic stories filled with fiestas, pious mission life, and moonlight serenades under the balconies of beautiful señoritas. The public was ready for such fairy tales of their heritage, and Gertrude Atherton knew that her home and her subject were in California.

XXIII

La Belle Époque

Of the new writers of San Francisco in the 1890s, the most outstanding was, without any doubt, Benjamin Franklin Norris, better known as Frank Norris. He came to San Francisco from Chicago in 1885 at the age of fifteen. His father, a wholesale jeweler, had had enough of Chicago winters and decided to try real estate speculation in the West. At Boys' High school, young Norris demonstrated considerable talent for drawing, and his mother, a former actress, encouraged his talent by convincing his father to let their son drop out of high school and study painting at the San Francisco Art Association. His instructors there affirmed his potential and recommended that he go straight to Paris for his training. So, at seventeen, the boy found himself enrolled at the Académie Julian, studying painting and learning French as rapidly as possible. After three years, he returned home an accomplished illustrator and sophisticated *boulevardier.*

While attending the University of California, Norris wrote a sort of medieval science fiction story called "Lauth," the tale of a scholar-turned-soldier who is killed in battle and then restored to life by a friend, a metaphysician. Alive but bereft of a soul, Lauth devolves progressively through lower forms of life and finally dies as a shapeless mass of protoplasm. Norris submitted this story along with several finely-wrought illustrations. Like many others before him, he saw his first work appear in the *Overland Monthly.* "Lauth" appeared in March, 1893. When the Boer War broke out, Norris, looking for adventure and experiences, obtained an assignment as a correspondent and sailed for Johannesburg. He had not been there long, however, before he contracted a fever and was sent home by the Boers. Back in San Francisco, he went to work for the *Wave,* a weekly magazine that had been under-

Frank Norris

written by the Southern Pacific Railroad to promote California tourism and to counter the attacks of Ambrose Bierce on the railroad.

By the time Norris joined the staff, the *Wave,* subtitled "A Weekly Journal for Those in the Swim," had become a general magazine of local politics, cultural affairs, original fiction and poetry, book reviews, and society news. The staff was small; Norris, along with Will Irwin, Gelett Burgess, and editor John O'Hara Cosgrave, wrote the whole thing. To give the impression of a larger staff, each wrote in a variety of styles with several pseudonyms. It was excellent training, and by the turn of the century, Norris had published three novels, all largely influenced by the naturalism of Emile Zola: *Moran of the Lady Letty*, an adventure in which a sea captain's daughter takes command of her father's ship when he is killed at sea; *Blix,* a tale of young love between a reporter and a San Francisco society girl; and *McTeague,* the story of a simple unlicensed Polk Street dentist who, deprived of livelihood, murders his wife for her savings. Norris' years on the *Wave* developed in him a keen eye for detail and a manner of description that permitted him to "sketch" representative individuals in prose much as an artist would have done with charcoal and paper. His sketch of "The Fast Girl" from the May, 1896 issue is a good example:

> She dresses in a black, close-fitting bolero jacket of imitation astrachan with enormous leg-of-mutton sleeves of black velvet, a striped silk shirt, and a very broad hat, tilted to one side. Her hair is very blond, though somehow coarse and dry, and a little flat curl

of it lies low over her forehead. She is marvelously
pretty. She belongs to a certain class of young girl that
is very common in the city. She is what men, amongst
each other, call "Gay," though that is the worst that
can be said of her. She is virtuous, but the very fact
that it is necessary to say so is enough to cause the
statement to be doubted. She loves to have a gay
time...which, for her, means to drink California champagne, to smoke cigarettes, and to kick at the chande-
lier.

Obliged to write articles on everything from fashion to football games, Norris immersed himself in the city, became intimate
with every level of its society, and in the process fell in love with
it as he had done with Paris:

Things can happen in San Francisco. Kearny
Street, Montgomery Street, Nob Hill, Telegraph Hill,
of course Chinatown, Lone Mountain, the Poodle Dog,
the Palace Hotel, and the What Cheer House, the
Barbary Coast, the Crow's Nest, the Mission, the Bay,
the Bohemian Club, the Presidio, Spanish town,
Fisherman's Wharf. There is an indefinable air about
all these places that is suggestive of many stories at
once.

Norris' work on the *Wave* attracted the attention of S. S.
McClure, who convinced him to move to New York and work for
the publishing firm of Doubleday and McClure. Norris had barely
begun work when the Spanish-American War broke out, and he
went off to Cuba as a war correspondent once again. But as in
Africa, he came down with a fever and had to return.

Although his novels were successful, Norris did not adjust to
living in New York. He wrote to his fiancée, society girl Jeannette
Black:

New York is not California nor New York City
San Francisco and I am afraid that because of the difference I shall never be reconciled to the East...I have
almost forgotten how a mountain looks and I can
never quite persuade myself that the Atlantic is an
ocean in the same sense as the Pacific...Indeed I have
come to look forward to the time when I shall come
back to San Francisco to live for good.

He did return in 1900, married Jeannette Black, and set to
work on *The Octopus,* the first novel of what he planned as a trilogy called *The Epic of Wheat.*

Although he knew all of them and worked on the *Wave* with
some of them, Norris was never a part of the group that became
known as *Les Jeunes* (the youngsters). Norris was much too serious, and seriousness was the last thing on the minds of the talented young people who rejected the stuffiness of the Bohemian
Club—although some of them were members—and formed their
own bohemian gathering. Its principal members were Gelett
Burgess, Bruce Porter, and Willis Polk.

Burgess had come to San Francisco from Boston after graduation from the Massachusetts Institute of Technology to work as a
draftsman for the Southern Pacific Railroad. Eventually he
obtained a position as instructor in topographical drawing at the
University of California, but he lost that position after being
apprehended in an act of vandalism. It had to do with a fountain
at the corner of Market and California Streets erected by Dr.
Henry D. Cogswell, a forty-niner and retired dentist. Cogswell
was an ardent crusader for abstinence from alcohol. Wherever he
found a cooperative city council, he would install a fountain in a
public place where passersby could slake their thirst (if they were
willing to risk drinking from a public tin cup) without going into
a saloon. On top of the pedestal that held the fountain, Cogswell
would place a life-sized cast-iron statue of himself holding out a
water glass. The glass, by means of a pipe running through the
statue's arm, was kept perpetually full. Gelett Burgess and some
of his mischievous friends were offended by the statue. Not only

Gelett Burgess

was it pretentious and ugly from an aesthetic point of view, its pious condemnation of spirits was antithetical to the philosophy espoused by Burgess and his companions.

One night, after considerable celebration, they climbed the statue, tied a rope around Cogswell's neck, and pulled him down off his pedestal, water glass and all. Discovered to have participated in the affair and thus deprived of his university position, Burgess moved to Russian Hill in San Francisco and went to work for a local furniture manufacturer as a designer. He soon made friends with Porter Garnett, a calligrapher, wood carver, and fine printer, and Willis Polk, an up-and-coming architect, best known at that time for his boisterous parties. The three of them conceived of a new magazine that would be unusual, irreverent, and creative. With one hundred dollars of their own capital and the support of William Doxey, who owned Doxey's bookstore (located on the Market Street side of the Palace Hotel), they launched the *Lark*.

Everything about the publication was whimsical and light-hearted. In Chinatown they located a cheap paper made from bamboo fiber with red and green characters stenciled on the edges. They dampened and pressed the paper so that it took on large yellow splotches with smears of red and green dye in the margins, and they printed on one side of it only and used unjustified lines of hand-set type. On May 1, 1895, the first issue of the monthly went on sale at Doxey's bookstore, at "five cents an issue or one dollar a year." The contents of each copy were as nonsensical as the format. As editor, Burgess contributed largely to it, particularly with his immortal poem:

I never saw a purple cow
I never hope to see one
But I can tell you anyhow,
I'd rather see than be one.

Moreover, Burgess contributed cartoons. His characters, called "Goops," were line drawings of noodle-limbed people who came in two types: the "sulphites" who were original thinkers, and the "bromides" who spoke only in platitudes. Eventually "bromide" entered the language as a synonym for a hackneyed expression. *Les Jeunes* were great admirers of Robert Louis Stevenson and wanted to use some of his lines for one of the *Lark's* covers, but they needed permission. It was not hard to come by. Isobel Osbourne Strong was working in Doxey's bookstore and convinced her mother, Stevenson's widow, to cooperate. The resulting cover shows a clerk at work in an editorial room. On the floor around him are strewn rejected manuscripts, partially covering a human skeleton. Under the illustration are Stevenson's lines:

The rose on roses feeds; the lark on larks.
The sedentary clerk all morning with a diligent pen,
Murders the babes of other men.

In the course of getting permission to use this quote, Gelett Burgess befriended Fanny Stevenson and proposed a gravestone for her late husband. Fanny liked the idea and had two tablets cast in bronze. For her own marker, she had these lines from the Book of Ruth: "Wither thou goest, I will go, and where thou lodgest, I will lodge." For Stevenson's grave, she chose his own line, "Gladly did I live and gladly die." As his relationship with Fanny deepened, Burgess designed the Stevenson monument for Portsmouth Square, and with the help of *Les Jeunes* raised $1,500 to build the monument. Although Fanny was sixty-two and Burgess only thirty-seven, the two became lovers. Their affair did not endure, however, and Fanny soon took an even younger lover. His name was Ned Field; he was a playwright and only twenty-three when he cast his lot with the strong-willed Fanny. In addition to her San

Francisco mansion, Fanny owned a ranch in the Santa Cruz mountains, a hacienda in Mexico, and a large house in Santa Barbara, and the couple moved at a leisurely pace among these various residences whenever they felt the urge to travel.

Yone Noguchi

The *Lark* attracted numerous talented young artists and writers to contribute to its mockery of conventions: the painter-, book illustrator, and author Ernest Peixotto and the muralist Bruce Porter were first published there, as were the liberated women of the day Florence Lundborg, Juliet Wilbor Tomkins, and Carolyn Wells. But the most unusual of the contributors was a young Japanese poet named Yone Noguchi, who had come to San Francisco to seek his artistic fortune. He began as a dishwasher, but eventually made a pilgrimage to the "Hights" to meet fellow poet Joaquin Miller. Miller took him on as a houseboy, and he worked in exchange for room, board, and English lessons. It was he whom George Sterling had seen dressed in a cowboy outfit, lugging groceries up the path to Miller's home. Noguchi had stayed with Miller for four years but was disillusioned by the fact that Miller never read anything but his own writing and spent much of his energy trying to impress friends and visitors. One of Noguchi's jobs had been to slip behind Miller's cabin and turn on a concealed sprinkler when Miller was demonstrating an Indian rain chant for his guests. Through Miller, Noguchi met Charley Stoddard and found him a much greater help. Charley was still teaching at the Catholic University of America in Washington, D.C., but he returned to San Francisco every summer. Noguchi stayed with Charley both in San Francisco and Washington, continuing his efforts at writing verse in English. His command of the language was still sufficiently imperfect to lend an exotic air to his verses.

Through the *Lark,* Noguchi developed a following, and his first collection, *Seen and Unseen,* "nocturnes set to the music of an unfamiliar tongue," was published in 1896. The *Lark* lasted only two years and was ended by its founders—although its circulation had reached 3,000—so that it would never be said that the magazine had lost its spontaneity. Gelett Burgess went off to New York; Bruce Porter and Porter Garnett remained in San Francisco but settled down to more serious and remunerative work. Willis Polk went on to become, along with Bernard Maybeck and Julia Morgan, one of the founders of the San Francisco Bay region style of architecture. It was a good time for a talented and ambitious young architect to be in San Francisco. The *Chronicle's* ten-story building had proven that tall buildings were possible in earthquake country. It was followed by the even taller Spreckels building across Market from the *Chronicle.* As Market Street grew elegant, a new ferry building at the foot of Market was erected, with a central clock tower modeled on the Giralda Tower in Seville. The graceful new Ferry Building quickly became the unofficial symbol of the city. Willis Polk, former *Jeune,* was one of its principal architects. Horseless carriages were beginning to appear on San Francisco's streets, coughing and backfiring and causing horses to rear and bolt, and motion pictures, a new fad, were exhibited in the city for the first time. Obviously, a new age was just around the corner.

The Lark tickled San Francisco's imagination for two years, but before they broke up, *Les Jeunes* created another institution with a longer life—Coppa's. Giuseppe Coppa had been a cook in some of the city's finest restaurants before opening his own place in North Beach, a simple Italian home-style restaurant that met with immediate success. By 1900, he had moved into the Montgomery Block building in the corner opposite the Bank Exchange Saloon, where in earlier years Bret Harte and Sam Clemens had profited from the free lunch. Coppa's became a favorite hangout for the artists of the day for two reasons. First, the food was very good, and twenty-five cents would buy a plate of fresh pasta, a pint of hearty red wine, and half a loaf of thick-crusted Italian bread. Second, "Papa" Coppa had a fondness for artists and would extend credit to them.

Then one day in 1903, Coppa decided his restaurant was looking a little dingy and had the walls repapered. His artist clients found the new red paper objectionable and offered to redecorate the place free of charge. Coppa agreed, and the next Sunday, three men went to work using colored chalk. Porter Garnett drew a mural on one wall of a five-foot lobster standing on an island marked "Bohemia." Robert Aitken, who later sculpted the Dewey monument in Union Square, created two large nudes on another wall, and Perry Newberry did a third wall in a similarly irreverent manner. The following Sunday, more *Jeunes* joined the project. A decorative frieze ran all around the dining room containing the names of great artists and thinkers from Aristotle to Zola, intermingled with the names of *Les Jeunes* and those of their friends. Above the frieze, Mexican artist Xavier "Marty" Martinez drew a border of black cats. The work continued for several months. It included artists' caricatures of one another; quotations in English, Latin, Hebrew, and medieval French; devils, satyrs, nymphs; Father Time supporting the wall clock with his feet while holding a bottle of wine; and wherever there was a bit of space left, some of Gelett Burgess's contorted Goops. "Papa" Coppa was sure that with all this artistic graffiti adorning his walls, respectable people would never frequent his place again. But he found, on the contrary, that once word of the murals got around, *everybody* wanted to come and see them and, as they dined on chicken Portola, try to link the caricatures on the walls with the artists eating at nearby tables. Coppa's had become the most celebrated restaurant in town.

XXIV

A New Century

As the nineteenth century came to an end, Jack London had a drawer stuffed full of rejection slips. Confident that he had talent and that it would eventually be recognized, he continued writing and submitting his Kiplingesque stories. Finally, his first published story, "To the Man on the Trail," appeared in the January, 1899 issue of the *Overland Monthly*. He received only five dollars for it, but to him the recognition that he had not been wasting his time was a sweet victory. The following month the *Overland* carried the first of his "Malamute Kid" stories. They were enormously popular, and his next story was accepted by the *Atlantic Monthly*. By 1900, his first collection of stories, *The Son of the Wolf,* was a best-seller, and the *Overland* was paying him fifteen cents a word. He had married Bessie Maddern, his former tutor, and now had two daughters. At last, he could support his family. London's meteoric rise in popularity was all the more stunning because it had occurred without the aid of Ambrose Bierce. It was a source of considerable annoyance to Bierce when this upstart London, who wrote, Bierce said, "as if his digestion, like his politics and rhetoric, was out of order," began to be spoken of as the founder of a new school of realism.

London and his family lived in the Oakland hills, not very far from George Sterling and his socialite bride Carolyn Rand Sterling, known as "Carrie," the younger sister of Sterling's uncle's wife. Also not far away was the painter and former *Jeune* Marty Martinez, who had moved with his wife to Oakland to get away from the constant partying in San Francisco and get some work done. And not far from Martinez was Joaquin Miller in his "Hights." The teenaged girl with whom Miller had been living when he met Sterling, Alice Oliver, had delivered a baby boy, but the child died shortly thereafter and was buried near Miller's funeral pyre. When Alice became pregnant again, Miller sent her off to Arizona, where she had a girl. She returned only to get pregnant again. This time, Miller sent her to Hawaii where she bore his eighth child, and she never returned. So, at the time that London, Sterling, Martinez, and Miller became acquainted with each other, they formed a new artistic group in the Oakland hills. Introduced to Sterling's family, Miller fell in love with Sterling's fourteen-year-old sister and had the nerve to ask her parents for her hand in marriage. He was politely shown the door.

The grizzled old poet was something of a role model for Jack London. Miller also had gone to Alaska during the Gold Rush, not to look for gold but to write articles for Hearst's *Examiner*. Hearst, ever the promoter of American imperialism, instructed Miller to paint a rosy picture of the frozen north, minimizing the dangers and hardships and exaggerating the opportunities for instant wealth. Miller complied, and there were many who went off overconfident and underprepared to seek their fortunes who came to curse Miller for his false reports. When the Boxer Rebellion broke out in China, Hearst sent Miller there to cover the story, instructing him before he left on what to write. This time, Miller wrote what he saw rather than what he was told to write—and hardly any of his reports were used. But his neighbors heard of these adventures from Miller himself, and, as usual, the old man told heroic stories with himself as the central character.

Marty Martinez might just as well have saved himself the trouble of moving from San Francisco. He was now caught up in a different but equally distracting bohemian whirl. Wednesday nights were open house at the Londons' where various artists mingled with Jack's Socialist and waterfront associates. And on Sundays when the weather was fair, everyone trudged uphill to the "Hights" for one of Joaquin's "bandit barbecues." When the weather was not so fair, the Sunday gatherings took place at Martinez's studio-home for chili con carne and red wine. They were an odd assortment, this "Oakland gang": Miller, with his long white beard and frontier outfits; London, in his flannel shirts, looking like a workman on holiday; Sterling, strikingly handsome and always elegantly dressed; and Martinez, dark-skinned, with a mop of jet-black hair and mustache to match, wearing corduroy suits and flowing silk bow ties. They were often joined by the muralist Maynard Dixon, in cowboy boots and floppy-brimmed hat and the huge Norwegian sailor-turned-sculptor, Finn Frolich. This group had replaced *Les Jeunes* and were now the center of attention at Coppa's.

While Sterling was fascinated by Jack London's rough background and his aggressive intellectualism, he could not overcome the feeling that London could learn to appreciate the finer things in life if he could just experience them and overcome his prejudice against "snobs." Accordingly, at one of their gatherings he invited London to lunch with him the following Saturday at Marchand's. London accepted the invitation to be introduced to San Francisco's most fashionable restaurant—but on the condition that Sterling, in return, devote the evening to letting London show him a side of the city that would, no doubt, be a new experience also.

At Marchand's that Saturday, Sterling ordered breast of quail *à la Marengo* and recommended it to his guest, but Jack chose a tenderloin steak and french fries. He was, Sterling was pleased to note, impressed with the food and the decor of the place, but he ridiculed the patrons—the men in high starched collars and close-fitting jackets, the women in enormous feathered hats and gowns with huge puffed sleeves and tightly corseted waists.

"The food's good," he said, "but these dandies don't appear to be having a very good time. They all seem more concerned with looking proper and not speaking above a whisper than with enjoying themselves." He was the only man in the restaurant in a flannel shirt, but he had put on a necktie for the occasion. When they had finished their lunch, Sterling ordered a glass of Lachrymae Christi to end the meal. London preferred Hennessy Three-Star cognac, neat. He was on his fourth glass while Sterling continued to sip his wine.

"Why don't you drink that stuff and be done with it?" London said impatiently. "Let's get out of here and find someplace livelier."

He led Sterling down to the Barbary Coast to a disreputable-looking, gaudy saloon on Pacific Street. Inside, in an atmosphere so thick with cigar smoke that Sterling could hardly see, a bar ran the length of one wall. The rest of the place was crowded with tables except for a small dance space next to an elevated stage, alongside which a six-piece band hammered out polkas. Men in rough clothes were dancing clumsily with obviously bored young women in cheap, bright-colored dresses. London tipped the hostess, obtained a table near the stage, and ordered two schooners of beer.

"You've shown me a slice of your world," he said, shouting so Sterling could hear him above the music, "and I appreciate it, really. Now I want to show you a slice of mine. Take care that you don't lose your watch or your pocketbook."

The band played a fanfare, and an unhealthy-looking master of ceremonies came out in a suit whose flashy pattern could not hide the generations of stains on it. He told a series of vulgar jokes that brought guffaws from the male audience, then introduced a group of hootchy-kootchy dancers—corpulent, perspiring, middle-aged women with bleached hair who cavorted awkwardly, more or less in time with the band.

Sterling looked around at the leering men swilling beer and spitting tobacco juice on the sawdust-covered floor. "Let's go, Jack," he said. "I really don't like this place."

"In a few minutes. The headliner's coming up."

The star of the show was a belly dancer called, like a legion of others, "Little Egypt." Younger and darker than the other dancers, this one performed her lascivious motions to the band's rendition of a vaguely Mediterranean melody. When she had finished, Jack tipped a waitress and "Little Egypt" appeared, still in costume, and sat down at their table, ordering a bottle of champagne and three glasses. London led her on, eliciting her life story which was, predictably, that of a talented young daughter of a prosperous and respectable Pennsylvania family, who was seeking to develop her art but had fallen on hard times, necessitating her appearance in such a low dive as this. London called her "Little Pittsburgh" and began to pinch and tickle her until she stood up and said huffily that if he could not behave like a gentleman, he could do without her company.

"Come on, George; we've other places to see,' London said, and Sterling, with considerable relief, followed him out to the street. The sky was just turning dark. It was still light in the west, but thousands of garish electric lights had come on along Pacific Street, giving the neighborhood a carnival aspect, enhanced by the line of barkers outside the dance halls enticing passers-by with lurid descriptions of the pleasures they would find "just behind these doors."

They walked up Grant Avenue and Sterling told London about the evening that Bierce had dragged him around the city, ending up at the morgue.

"That figures," London snorted. "Bierce is fascinated with death because he detests life. He's afraid of it, I think. He doesn't want to live in the real world. Anyway, I'm not taking you to any damned morgues tonight—nothing so tame as that." They were in the heart of Chinatown, working their way along the crowded sidewalk among the Chinese residents and the tourists gawking at the exotic goods in the shop windows. London turned suddenly down a narrow alley and knocked at an unmarked door. An impassive Chinese man in a black smock and skull-cap admitted them and led them down a dim hallway to a precarious wooden stairway that descended below the street level and ended at another corridor, this one so dark that their guide had to light a candle to proceed. The corridor floor was of loose wood planks that sank into the muddy soil as they stepped on them, and Sterling began to gag on the fetid air, a hideous combination of incense, damp earth, and sewage.

"Where are we going, Jack?" he asked. "We seem to be descending into Hell."

"On the contrary, we're at the gates of Paradise," London replied.

They stopped at a door. Their guide tapped on it softly, opened it, and hastened them into a room fifteen feet square whose floor was also of loose planks, these with water seeping between them. The ceiling was barely six feet high and from it was suspended a single kerosene lantern for illumination. In its feeble light, Sterling could see that the walls were lined with rough wooden bunks three tiers high, each one large enough to hold two people. The bunks were nearly filled with men lying prostrate, insensible to their surroundings, their eyes open but vacant. Two men, still conscious, were lying on one of the bunks with an oil lamp burning between them; next to it stood a jar of opium. From time to time, each would dip a piece of wire into the jar and then hold it over the flame of the lamp until the beads of black tar melted and bubbled. Then they would scrape the burning mixture into the bowls of their long pipes, suck white smoke from it and then, with slow, dreamy movements, start the process over again, oblivious to their observers.

London indicated the unconscious patrons. "Would you like to see what they're seeing? Want to try it?"

"And end up like them? God help me, no thanks. Why do they do it?"

"I guess it's because they're like your friend Bierce. They find reality unbearable, so they come here and transport themselves somewhere else, in an existence of absolute pleasure, where trouble, pain, and sickness cease to exist. Say what you will, George, you and I will never know the ecstasy that these clods are experiencing at this very moment."

"I'll forgo the pleasure. Let's just get out of here. The stink is awful."

To Sterling's dismay, the guide, instead of leading them back-up to the street, took them down another rank staircase to a door guarded by a large Chinese of sinister appearance. A lengthy discussion ensued in Chinese, and then they were admitted to a small dark room. The guard stood inside the room now, scowling at them.

"That's a hatchet man if ever I saw one," Sterling whispered. "What's going on here?"

"Whatever you do," London whispered back, "don't let on that you're afraid."

The guide lit a lamp, and they could see that a bamboo cage was hanging from the ceiling. In it was a Chinese girl of fourteen or so, dressed in a flowered kimono, kneeling disconsolately with a frightened expression on her face. There was a knock at the door, and the guard admitted four Chinese men, their heads shaved except for the spot from which a long shining queue dangled. One of them spoke to the guard who barked an order, and the girl sadly removed her kimono, her only garment. Sterling watched, indignant but fascinated, as the man who had spoken to the guard approached the cage and examined the girl, reaching through the bars to touch her skin while she sat trembling. A brief conversation followed. Then another of the men pulled out a large purse, counted out a handful of bills, and handed them to the guard, who untied a rope and lowered the cage to the floor. London's guide motioned him out, and Sterling was glad to see that they were returning up the staircases.

Once back on Grant Avenue, he remarked, "It is absolutely incredible that these things are taking place right under our feet as we walk about this quarter thinking how quaint and colorful it is."

"You can't know what's in the depths unless you descend into them, but you have to make sure at all times that you can get back out," London said, amused that his friend did not realize that what they had seen in the second room had been a performance designed to let locals impress out-of-town visitors.

"When you get down to it," Sterling said, "the Oriental is a callous beast who treats women and children like cattle."

"Oh yes," London replied. "Ever been in there?" He pointed to the brick church at the corner of California Street, Saint Mary's. Sterling, a Catholic, assured him that he had attended Mass there more than once. Then London asked if he had ever been in Quincy Alley, right next to the church. When Sterling said he had not, London led him into the narrow cobblestone passage between two rows of wooden buildings with overhanging balconies and staircases. It was less than a block long and ended in a cul-de-sac. On the front of the church, a large cross outlined with electric light bulbs was affixed, perpendicular to the church facade. The light from it illuminated the entrance to the alley. A policeman stood there, leaning against the church wall, indifferently eyeing those who entered. As they proceeded, Sterling saw that both sides of the alley were lined with cubicles barely two feet wide and three feet deep, fronted with iron bars. In each cubicle sat a grotesquely painted prostitute in a dressing gown, cajoling and enticing the men strolling by. There were faded blondes, red-haired girls with thick Irish brogues, and the daughters of Hawaii, Mexico, and Africa, all rolling their eyes and making kissing sounds to the young men strutting by the cribs.

"God, it's like a zoo!" Sterling said.

"So much for the callousness of the Oriental," London laughed. "I can assure you that the proprietors of these establishments are every bit as white and as Christian as you and I."

They left the alley with London mocking his companion for having prayed in Saint Mary's without even realizing that on the other side of the brick wall was a temple of Aphrodite that, like the church, received sinners twenty-four hours a day. London took Sterling to a saloon and ordered two beers and two "cannibal sandwiches." When the sandwiches arrived, each a large portion of a loaf of French bread filled with raw hamburger and chopped onions, London ordered two glasses of Hennessey's.

"The cognac's an important part of the meal," he said. "This is good for you. Gives you strength." Sterling tried the sandwich but left nearly all of it on the plate when they departed for what London said would be their last stop. They walked up the hill out of Chinatown to Powell Street, and rang the bell at a fashionable Victorian residence with large bay windows and elaborate carved decorations adorning its front. A maid admitted them and took them into a parlor, where a heavily corseted woman with dark red hair greeted London enthusiastically by name. A black man was playing ragtime softly on a piano, and several attractive young women in deeply décolleté evening gowns were gathered around the piano. One of them approached as London and Sterling sat down on a red velvet couch and asked them if they would care for a refreshment.

"Cognac for me," London told her. "And bring one for my friend too. He needs it." He introduced Sterling to the large woman on the love-seat facing them as his old friend Maggie Sanderson, whom he had met in Alaska where she had run an establishment much less elegant than this one. Then he signaled for one of the girls by the piano to come over. Her name was Flossie, and Sterling was surprised to see how demure she was. Had it not been for her revealing gown, he realized, she could have fit in comfortably at one of his uncle's dinner parties in

Piedmont. Before long another young woman, a dark-haired girl with clear blue eyes who told him her name was Nanette, had joined them, sitting next to him and engaging him in casual conversation. When she asked him if he would like another brandy, he replied that he did not care much for it—it was too strong. Somehow an open bottle of champagne and two glasses appeared, and Sterling found himself sipping it and telling Nanette all about his incredible evening in the depths of Chinatown with Jack.

Later, without knowing quite how he had gotten there, Sterling was in an upstairs bedroom, all lace and chintz and ruffles, as Nanette undressed and slipped between lavender-scented sheets. In the morning, when he awoke with a considerable headache, Nanette was gone, but the aroma of patchouli in her dark hair and the feel of her skin in his memory crowded out the pangs of guilt pleading for his attention.

Despite all the trouble his wife Carrie gave him for staying out all night, and despite the week of vindictive pouting he had to endure, Sterling could not resist further adventures with London, who delighted in dragging him through the worst parts of the city, showing him abject slums, illegal prize-fights, tawdry burlesque shows, and saloons with pornographic performances. These were always just preludes to a visit to one of the city's fancier brothels, and before long, Sterling's classic features were familiar to most of the parlorhouse madams.

Saturday nights in the fleshpots of San Francisco became a ritual for the two friends. Bessie London and Carrie Sterling did all they could to discourage their husbands' carousing, but to no avail. Sterling's mother and his uncle (who was also his employer) banded with Carrie in an effort to pull him away from London's influence. Carrie moved to another bedroom and refused to sleep with him. His mother wept. His uncle threatened to fire him, and even got Bierce to point out that Sterling's debauchery was causing him to write less than he should. Sterling could not deny any of the charges levied against him. He was always contrite and promised to "do better," but he could no more give up his escapades with London than the opium addicts in Chinatown could relinquish their next pipe.

The two spent Sundays nursing their hangovers, usually at the "Hights," where Joaquin Miller would be showing the "sleeping maiden" of Tamalpais to young female admirers who had come up to visit the poet. He would explain the Coastanoan legend that the Sun-God had come to earth one day and, seized by the beauty of an Indian chief's daughter, swept her up in his arms to carry her to the skies. His foot caught on Mount Diablo, and he fell with his captive into the huge lake that was separated from the ocean by the coastal hills. As he fell, his arm broke an opening in the range of hills, creating the Golden Gate. The chief's daughter was crushed to death in the fall, and the Sun-God laid her gently beside the coast where she remains to this day.

If constant partying caused a decline in Sterling's writing, it had no such effect on London. He wrote his thousand words a day without fail. The publication of *The Call of the Wild,* first as a serial in *The Saturday Evening Post* and then as a book published by Macmillan, catapulted him into the position of one of America's most promising young writers. Knowing the value of publicity and taking a cue from Miller's career, he made sure that his name was in the paper every week. He was indifferent to what the press said about him, so long as they kept printing his name.

And then suddenly both Bierce and London disappeared from San Francisco, both for the same reason—William Randolph Hearst. In addition to the *Examiner,* Hearst had acquired numerous other papers across the country, and he was ready to begin his campaign to become president of the United States. His first step was to establish residency in New York and get himself elected to the U.S. House of Representatives. He knew that a man with plenty of money and editorial control of influential newspapers could win elections. His father, after all, although virtually illiterate, had become a U.S. Senator. Hearst had sent Bierce to Washington, D.C. earlier when he had battled the Southern Pacific Railroad lobby; he sent him there now on a permanent basis. Nothing could destroy an opponent faster than Bierce's ridicule. As for Jack London, his assignment was South Africa. Hearst had no use for London's politics, but he wanted a reporter who could bring the Boer War to American readers as a cliffhanger, and London's terse, vigorous style was just what he needed.

London himself found working for Hearst distasteful, but the opportunity to add "war correspondent" to the list of occupations that appeared on his book jackets—oyster pirate, seaman, factory worker, Socialist orator—was too good to pass up.

Moreover, his marriage was in trouble and he needed some distance. Bessie was a good wife; he could not argue against that, and she had always been tolerant of his Wednesday evening open-house sessions with all sorts of people in the house until all hours. She even looked the other way when he came home in the early morning hours drunk and smelling of heavy perfume. But maternity had brought out in her a growing conservatism that he had not seen before they were married. She began to quarrel, demanding that he be more responsible, spend less time acting like a sailor on leave, think more of his wife and two daughters. His home began to seem like a prison to him. Hearst's assignment was an escape. By the time he reached England the Boer War had ended and there was no reason to continue on to South Africa. Rather than return home, however, he decided to adopt a new role: investigative reporter. At a pawnshop in London, he bought old worn-out clothes to disguise himself as one of the city's homeless unemployed. He walked the streets of the West End all night—people were forbidden to sleep in public places, and all parks were locked up. He learned to earn a few shillings by procuring cabs for people coming out of the theaters on rainy nights. He learned the heartlessness of the bobbies who chased off starving old men and women from sleeping in doorways so that people returning to their homes would not have to see them huddled in the cold.

On his way home, he put it all together in his first book of nonfiction, *The People of the Abyss.* It was a moving indictment of the capitalist system that rang with authority and whose theme was "Has civilization bettered the lot of the average man?" As the train rolled across the Nevada desert, he wrote a powerful conclusion, comparing the poor of England to the Innuit Indians of Alaska, who lived in one of the most inhospitable places in the world. While the Innuits had periods of starvation, chronic starvation was unknown to them, and they always had adequate shelter and clothing. The reason that poor people in England were worse off than the Alaskan Indians, London wrote, was that funds had been misappropriated by the government. "Civilization has increased man's producing power a hundred fold," he declared, "but through mismanagement, men of civilization live worse than beasts."

When London left Oakland, Sterling's family breathed a sigh of relief, certain that George, free from London's influence, would mend his ways. They were sorely disappointed. Sterling rented one of the studios in the Montgomery Block above Coppa's, where a variety of painters played Rudolph to a succession of Mimis. He spent his weekends there to facilitate his amorous rendezvous with young women eager to be immortalized by San Francisco's favorite poet.

XXV

Death And Homecoming

The citizens of San Francisco were shocked when the morning newspapers of May 5, 1902 announced that Francis Bret Harte, 66, had succumbed to cancer of the throat in Surrey at the house of his friend, Madame Van de Velde. The Bohemian Club was buzzing with the news all day that Harte, an honorary member for life, had died. Few of the present members had ever met him, so the club turned to Ina Coolbrith and Joaquin Miller to help them plan an appropriate ceremony for a man whom they were beginning to call "one of our founding members." They arranged a Memorial Jinks and transformed one room of the club into a replica of a mining camp. Members were selected to dress as well-known characters from Bret Harte stories: John Oakhurst, Kentuck, Stumpy, Tennessee's Partner, Colonel Starbottle, Yuba Bill, and others as recognizable as old friends to those who loved Harte's stories. Ina and Joaquin each wrote a poem of homage for the occasion. In Ina's poem, after recalling many of his characters, she wrote:

> I knew them all—but best of all I knew
> (Who in himself had something of all of these)
> The Man, within whose teeming fancy grew
>   These wondrous histories.
>
> I see him often, with the brown hair half
> Tossed from the leaning brow, the soft yet keen
> Gray eyes uplifted with a tear or laugh
>   From the pen-pictured scene.

Not long after Harte's memorial, the city and the Bohemian

Club lost another bright star, Frank Norris. He had been working on *The Wolf,* the third book in his trilogy, *The Epic of Wheat,* and was planning a trip around the world to complete the research he needed for the novel. In San Francisco, he and his wife Jeannette had become friends with Fanny Stevenson, who invited the young couple to her ranch *Vanumanutagi* (Vale of the Singing Birds) in the Santa Cruz mountains. The Norrises had become enchanted by the place and had arranged to buy a ten-acre portion of it that had an old log cabin at the edge of a redwood grove. They envisioned using the cabin for a writing retreat until, after their trip, they could enlarge it into a permanent home.

The voyage, however, had to be delayed. Jeannette needed an operation for appendicitis. A month later, Norris complained of severe indigestion, and when his wife suggested that he also might be suffering from appendicitis, he laughed off the idea, saying that one operation in the family was enough; he was anxious to begin their trip. But a few days later he was in the hospital, where doctors discovered a ruptured appendix with peritonitis and gangrene. He struggled for his life for three days, but tropical fevers had weakened his system, and he lost the battle. Harte's memorial had been a celebration for a legend who, for most Bohemians, had been as dead for many years. It was different with Norris. He had been one of them, a young man of thirty-two, cut down at the height of his career. There was grief, not nostalgia, at the club's ceremony for Norris.

When the *Lark* folded its wings and *Les Jeunes* disbanded to seek their respective fortunes, Yone Noguchi was at loose ends. He wandered down to Southern California, then to Chicago, and finally to New York. There he made the acquaintance of Leonie Gilmore, a young woman, half Irish and half American Indian, with an excellent education and considerable editing experience. She helped Noguchi polish his manuscript: *The American Diary of a Japanese Girl*, a fictional account based on his own experiences. Excerpts from it were printed in *Leslie's Monthly,* and two years later the complete book was published.

Noguchi, a highly romantic young man, became deeply involved with three lovers at the same time. He was intimate with

Leonie Gilmore while he was sharing Charles Warren Stoddard's bed on frequent visits to Washington, D.C. At Stoddard's, he met a Washington Post reporter, Ethel Ames, and fell in love with her at first sight. Partially to escape his amorous complications, the young poet went to London. In 1902, Stoddard wrote to him:

> Ethel has gone to her mother in the south. I think you are very fond of her. I am sorry, for one of your temperament should not marry. I think you would soon weary of the marriage tie. You are a Poet—a Dreamer—an Idealist. You should be solitary, free to go and come, without let or hindrance...A thousand thanks, my dearest Yone for this lovely and beloved picture. I shall keep it by me. How I wish I could see Yone in his native costume; I wish I could see him as God made him—naked and not ashamed....If anything happens to me in Washington...if I cannot stay to make my living, I want to go to the Hights and live with my Yone. You shall be my young eagle; I shall nestle you and watch your flight in the heavens. Once more a thousand embraces! I fold you in my heart with a number of kisses.

But the young poet did not marry Ethel nor become Stoddard's "young eagle." On his return to the U.S. after the successful British publication of his collection of poems, *From the Eastern Sea,* Noguchi discovered that Leonie Gilmore was pregnant with his child. She moved to Los Angeles and gave birth to a boy, Isamu Noguchi, whom she determined to raise by herself. Noguchi returned to Japan and in 1906, by then a respected professor of literature, he invited Leonie to bring the boy and live with him. By the time she arrived, however, Noguchi had already married his housekeeper.

When Jack London returned from England, he made a sincere effort to become a devoted husband and a good father to his daughters. He gave up his Wednesday night open houses, and quit, with occasional relapses, spending nights in saloons and brothels. It did not seem to help. Marriage and motherhood had turned Bessie into a devout homemaker and there seemed to be no end to her demands on him.

Once again he dealt with the problem by removing himself from it. War had broken out between Russia and Japan over the efforts of Czar Nicholas II to establish ports in Manchuria. Anxious to try again to become a war correspondent, London convinced the Hearst Syndicate to sponsor him. When he arrived in Japan, he found that the Japanese were refusing permission for any foreign correspondents to travel to Korea where the battles between Russian and Japanese forces were taking place. An international collection of correspondents had to content themselves with remaining in Japan and relaying official Japanese press releases to their respective newspapers.

Using his knowledge of boats and waterfront life, London bribed a fisherman to take him to the port of Inchon. From there, he hitched rides on military vehicles moving north from Seoul until he reached the front on the Yalu River, the border between Korea and Manchuria. London's reports and box-camera photographs were the only ones to reach the outside world that had not been censored by the Japanese War Office. The Hearst papers had exclusive stories and photos, and made the most of them. When the Russian fleet was destroyed off Pusan, it was clear the Czar had no further hope of victory and would have to make a humiliating peace with Japan. The fighting was over, and London returned home to a hero's welcome.

Nothing in his domestic life had changed, however, and he soon left his family and moved into an apartment in Oakland. Bessie finally agreed to a divorce, and the day after it was final, London married Charmian Kittredge, a young woman with whom he had been keeping company and on whom he based the character of Maude Brewster in the novel he was writing, *The Sea Wolf.*

In 1903, Charley Stoddard returned to San Francisco from Washington, D.C.—this time on a one-way ticket. He was sixty now and had been teaching for eighteen years. An offer from *Sunset* magazine to do a series of articles on the California missions had helped him decide to retire. In his leather grip on the train across the country was the completed manuscript of the novel he had begun twenty years earlier in Hawaii, *For the Pleasure of His Company.* He had put it aside then, fearing it was too revealing. Five years later, in Washington, he had met William Dean Howells through Mark Twain, and Howells had made complimentary remarks about Charley's earlier book, *South Sea Idyls.* Inspired by Howells' encouragement, Charley had rewritten his manuscript, but in deleting and disguising most of the parts likely to cause scandal, he produced a hodgepodge of scenes with no discernible structure. When Rudyard Kipling was in New York, Charley showed the manuscript to him. Kipling took it with him, promising to go through it and write suggestions on how to revise and improve it. It had taken him several years, but Kipling faithfully sent back one chapter after another, his suggestions sometimes taking more pages than the original.

Now, at last, it was ready for the public. It concerned the adventures of a Paul Clitheroe and his attempts to "find himself," vacillating between sensual aestheticism and a life of humility and service as a monk. Charley had purposely avoided any reference, no matter how oblique, to his most famous friends. Harte, Twain, Bierce, Mulford, and Miller were absent, but his characters were all based on people he had known. He had included Ina Coolbrith as Elaine, the poet-librarian, but there was no scandal in that character. The other people he had included would be recognizable only to those of his friends who lived on the fringe of respectability. Any direct reference to sexual relations between two people of the same sex would, of course, cause his book to be banned and himself to be ostracized. But he was confident that he had managed to deal with the subject in such a way that most people would not catch on, while for those with personal experience in such matters, the references and relationships would be quite clear. It was a risk, but it was one that he had been challenged to take for twenty years.

When *For the Pleasure of His Company,* subtitled *An Affair of the Misty City,* came out, Charley wrote a flowery inscription and delivered Ina's copy personally to her in the Bohemian Club library. The early reviews in the newspapers were generally good, and Charley was anxious to get Ina's opinion. When he visited her at her house on Russian Hill, he was astonished to find her furious. "You have portrayed me as an insipid, dreary, self-pitying drudge!" she told him. "How could you do such a thing?"

He protested that the character Elaine was only vaguely based on Ina's situation, but his attempts to mollify her had no effect. "Listen to this," she commanded, opening his book to a marked page.

> Her life had been one long bitter disappointment. Her poems had won the praises of the noblest poets in the land, but they had not sold as they should have sold; even to the literary portion of the world, her name was too little known. Losing one after another of all who were nearest and dearest to her, she was by force of destiny compelled to lead the life of a slave, in order to clothe and feed herself though modestly enough. From morning till late in the evening she was on duty in a public office. This was Elaine, the sweetest singer in all the tribe in that golden land of song—and saddest by right of silent, prolonged helpless and hopeless suffering.

"Now Charley," Ina said, "look me in the eye and tell me that the miserable, unappreciated wretch you've described there isn't me!" Charley was filled with chagrin. In attempting to arouse the reader's sympathy for the unfortunate fate of his old friend, he had revealed to Ina how she appeared to him and to others who knew her. It was not the image she had of herself, and she did not want Charley's "poor Ina" picture to take root in the mind of the public. She resolved to work harder, finish her history of the literary crowd of the early days, and erase the drab image of her that Charley had depicted.

XXVI.

Destruction

Unable to sleep because of the rheumatic pains in her joints, Ina lay in bed, too tired to sit up and read. She looked at the alarm clock on her night stand. It was just after five, still dark outside. She tried to think of nothing, hoping that sleep might return, but she could not keep her mind from focusing on the day ahead. She needed to be at the Bohemian Club library by nine. That meant she would have to arise by six-thirty. She was so slow and creaky in the mornings lately that it took her forever to get up and get out. At least now that it was April, the mornings were starting to get warmer. She had nearly finished her manuscript of memoirs and had made a collection of old photographs to go with it, and she was going through the whole thing one last time before talking to potential publishers. On the whole, she was quite pleased with how it had turned out, and was wondering which publisher to approach first.

Suddenly there was a tremendous noise, like an explosion. She found herself on the floor, which was pitching wildly like a small boat in rough seas. The clock and a vase were rolling back and forth across the carpet, and the bed was dancing up and down as if it wanted to jump on top of her. *Earthquake!* she thought. But it couldn't be, the noise and the shaking continued so violently. She got to her hands and knees, then was thrown crashing against the wall. She clutched the leg of the dresser and hung on desperately. Then it stopped.

She realized the floor was covered with broken glass from the window, and when she looked up at the walls she saw huge spaces of lath work where the plaster had broken away. The light suspended from the ceiling was swinging crazily overhead. *Out! I've got to get out!* The floors and the stairway were covered with glass, plaster, books, and the remains of furnishings that had been hanging from the wall; but she walked barefoot over them, realizing that her teeth were chattering uncontrollably not from cold but from sheer fright. *Let them rattle. Just so my knees don't fail me!*

Out on Taylor Street she was astounded to make out in the darkness all of her neighbors standing in the street in various stages of undress. Most of them were in nightgowns, as she was; some were in their underwear. A few had shoes on and several men had grabbed their hats as they fled their houses. They looked ludicrous standing there in little groups, but she rushed toward them. "Look out for the wires!" several of them shouted as she approached the sidewalk. She looked down and saw that the electric lines were down in the gutter, sparking like huge snakes. She stepped over them cautiously and joined the others. It was still dark, but the sky was illuminated by several fires in the central part of the city. The ground was still shaking, and everyone was talking at once—then suddenly there was a particularly violent jolt and they all fell to the pavement, several of the women screaming and children crying. Ina felt a deep nausea come on her from the jelly-like shaking of the street under her hands and knees. She fought it back and heard herself saying out loud, "Stop. Please stop!"

Chimneys and bricks came crashing to the ground and men began shouting: "We should go north, toward the Bay!" "No, it's better to stay put and wait till it's all over!" "No, no. We should go west, toward Van Ness!" But no one moved. They could not trust the ground they were sitting on. After a desperate half hour of watching more and more fires break out in the city below, the sky began to lighten with dawn. Like many others, Ina was shivering with the cold, but there was some comfort in seeing, through the dust-filled air, a pale sun climb in the sky over the Oakland hills, illuminating the devastated streets. One of her neighbors, she noticed, was holding an empty birdcage. Then the shaking stopped.

Someone was speaking to her. "Miss Coolbrith, I'm going back in." It was the student who rented her spare bedroom. He said, "I don't think it's safe for you to return yet, but I'll dash in and get a few things, some clothes at least."

"Oh yes," she said, "and Moona."

"Moona?"

"My cat."

"I'll try." He was off, leaping nimbly over the electric wires and running into the house. Then came another jolt. Ina could see actual waves moving along the street. She could hear more crashing chimneys and screams and wails. Down the block, the front of a two-story house pitched into the street, scattering refugees. It left the interior of the house exposed. The rooms were all visible, like those of a doll house, each one patterned in a different wallpaper. There was something vulgar about it, Ina thought—intimate parts exposed. She stared at her doorway. Was her tenant all right? Could he be injured, trapped in there? Then he appeared. He was dressed. In one hand he had a small briefcase along with Ina's coat and shoes. In his other hand he held a yowling Moona by the scruff of the neck.

"God bless you," she said. "Thank you so much." She put on her coat and shoes and took the squirming cat from him.

"I was coming down the stairs," he said, his voice a high-pitched squeak, "when it hit again. The staircase just crumpled out from under me, but somehow I managed not to let go of the cat." He was displaying the scratches Moona had inflicted on him. "What is it, Miss Coolbrith?" She must have looked shocked.

"My manuscript. It's in the cedar chest in the parlor."

"There's no way to get up there now. You'll have to retrieve it with a ladder after the fires are out. It's not safe to go in there yet. There may be more tremors."

"Oh God, I hope not. I hope it's over."

All day the neighbors remained in the street, waiting for someone to tell them what to do. They watched the terrible progression of the fires downtown. At first they could see and hear fire trucks racing to the fires and spraying water on them, but as the day progressed the fires in the commercial center spread and joined each other. The Russian Hill residents watched and identified landmarks as the flames advanced. "There goes the Palace Hotel." "The Stock Exchange is burning." "It's reached Chinatown now." Night fell, but the sky was aglow with the light of the flames reflected in the smoke, and they watched in horror as the fire climbed to Nob Hill, consuming the Fairmont Hotel and the mansions around it. To the southwest, it spread to Van Ness and destroyed City Hall and began devouring the beautiful Victorian residences there one by one. *Where is the Fire Department? What are they doing?* Then they saw a squad of soldiers climbing the hill, shouting orders.

A weary and impatient sergeant brushed off their questions and ordered them to go down the hill to Fort Mason, at the waterfront. He explained gruffly that the earthquake had broken all the water mains and that the fire department had no water to fight the fires. The army was dynamiting areas downwind of the fire to try to stop it. He assured them that unless the wind shifted, Russian Hill would be spared, but everyone must evacuate to open spaces.

He marched his men off, and the neighbors began slowly moving northward toward the Bay. Most of them had some things they had rescued from their houses in suitcases, laundry baskets, or small trunks which they dragged along behind them. Ina had nothing but her cat, which she dared not put down for fear the frightened animal would run back into the house. As they descended the steep hill, enveloped in the frightening odor of gas escaping from broken pipes under broken sidewalks, they were joined by hundreds of other refugees silently dragging their belongings, their way illuminated by the harsh glow of the growing fires behind them. It was a grotesque pageant, people in ridiculous assortments of clothing walking along in the night, all with the same dazed expression on their faces. The only sounds were the harsh scraping of all those trunks and baskets along the pavement, and the occasional explosions in the distance.

At the "Hights," Joaquin Miller was awakened by a strong bump at 5:12 am. He arose and went outside. Columns of smoke were rising in the downtown area across the Bay. His first thought was of his manuscripts at the Bohemian Club. He kept them there because he felt they were better protected from fire in a stone building than they would have been in his wooden house in the dry grasses of the Oakland hills. Now he could see the irony of that choice: San Francisco was burning down. As quickly as he could, he made his way to the ferry slip, hoping that the ferries would still be running. They were, but when he arrived at the San Francisco Ferry Building he found a chaos of people scrambling to get out of the city. Abandoned horses and buggies clogged the foot of Market Street. He helped himself to one and headed up Market. A line of soldiers turned him back. He tried a dozen different streets to find an access to the club, but the whole downtown area was blocked off. He could see that Russian Hill was still untouched and decided to go there to rescue Ina, but once again he ran into army blockades. Finally, he abandoned the horse and buggy and rejoined the frantic San Franciscans headed for Oakland.

When Ina and her neighbors arrived at the fort, which consisted of a few barracks and large open flat drill fields, soldiers directed them to the area they were to occupy. Thousands of people were there, just sitting or lying on the dirt field, watching the flames shoot up over the hills illuminating the thick black clouds of smoke that covered the night sky. Thoroughly exhausted, Ina stretched out on the ground. She had not slept on the earth, she realized, since the late spring nights over fifty years before when she was crossing the plains with her family. She tucked her cat inside her coat and, with her arm for a pillow, fell fast asleep.

She awoke early the next morning. The sun was up, but the sky was so covered with smoke that it seemed still to be night; the air was heavy with soot and the acrid smell of burnt wood. Moona was no longer in her coat, but she found the cat nearby. She picked her up and carried her over to the line in front of the women's latrine tent that the soldiers had hastily erected. Standing in line, she learned that the army was serving breakfast for the refugees over near the barracks. She realized that she had had nothing to eat or drink for over thirty-six hours. In the huge, slow-moving breakfast line, there was lots of talk:

The fires are still burning. The fire department is powerless to do anything but blow up more buildings to try to stop the fire's spread.

No doubt about it—the whole damned city's going up in flames.

No it won't, if the wind just dies down.

They're shooting looters, did you know that? Just shooting them and leaving them in the street.

Serves them right.

Around her, Ina saw children running and playing as if they were on a picnic, and young girls were gathered with some young boys, laughing and flirting. They don't realize what's happening, she thought. *This wonderful, irreplaceable city is burning up. It's gone and we are all homeless paupers!* After a breakfast of corned beef, biscuits, and coffee, she returned to the spot where she had spent the night. She had no belongings to mark it, but she could recognize her neighbors' things. Some one handed her a four-page newspaper. All three of the city's major newspapers had been destroyed, but they had combined their efforts and, using the *Oakland Tribune's* presses, run off a *"Call-Chronicle-Examiner Special"* which they brought to the city by ferry and distributed free to the people of San Francisco to give them some sense of the magnitude of the destruction. The first page had one huge black headline:

EARTHQUAKE AND FIRE
SAN FRANCISCO IN RUINS

The news on the four pages was all bad. All of the northeast quarter of the city, which contained the major commercial centers, was reduced to rubble and ashes. The fire was still spreading. The Mechanics Pavilion had been converted to a makeshift hospital; injured people and hospital patients had been transferred there in automobiles commandeered by the army. Inmates from the insane asylum had been taken there also, but most of them had run off.

Ina spent two more days and nights at the fort, most of the time standing in line holding Moona in her arms. Then, sitting on her patch of ground, she looked up through the morning fog and saw Judge Boalt, an old friend and Bohemian Club member, the man who had given her Calla, her first cat.

"Ina! Thank God I've found you. I came down here looking for friends, you especially. Come. Come home with me now."

"Home?"

"Yes. To our house. We're in the Western Addition over by

the Presidio. Come and stay with us."

"Is it safe? Are you sure?"

"Yes, yes. The fire is out. They stopped it at Van Ness. We're fine. Come, we have a bedroom for you."

Judge Boalt led her on the two-and-a-half mile walk to his house, much of it uphill. Ina's progress was slow and painful, but the thought of shelter and privacy gave her the courage to keep going. When they arrived, Mrs. Boalt offered her a bath. They were not permitted to use their stoves until their chimneys had been inspected, but every household had set up a makeshift camp stove in the street, and Mrs. Boalt put a kettle of water on to heat.

When Jack London felt the earthquake and saw the smoke rising across the Bay, like Joaquin Miller he too got on the first ferry to San Francisco. His object was not to rescue manuscripts or friends, however, but to report on what he saw. His account of the day of the earthquake appeared in the next issue of *Collier's* magazine. In it, he described the end of Union Square:

> At 8 o'clock on Wednesday evening I passed through Union Square. It was packed with refugees. Thousands of them had gone to bed on the grass. Government tents had been set up, supper was being cooked, and the refugees were lining up for free meals. At half past one in the morning three sides of Union Square were in flames. The fourth side, where stood the great hotel St. Francis was still holding out. An hour later, ignited from top and sides, the St. Francis was flaming heavenward. Union Square, heaped high with mountains of trunks, was deserted. Troops, refugees, and all had retreated.

Gertrude Atherton was staying at the Berkeley Inn working on her sixth novel, *Rezanov,* when the earthquake struck. Her daughter was living in Belvedere at the time, and her friends were in San Francisco. She took the ferry across the Bay with the idea of checking on her friends and then crossing to Marin County to see her daughter. When the boat arrived at the Ferry Building,

My eyes were met by a truly appalling sight. On the far side of the Embarcadero, a wide expanse into which the streets running from east to west debouched, was a curtain of smoke and flame. The city was blotted out. This part of San Francisco is on "made ground," for the waters of the bay once lapped Montgomery Street, many blocks west. The surface of the Embarcadero looked like a leaden sea, its waves arrested and immobile. Here and there were wide cracks. My fellow passengers were all running in the direction of Telegraph Hill a quarter of a mile north and beyond the present range of the fire. A solitary policeman was walking slowly up and down the middle of the Embarcadero. I went up to him and asked him how I could reach the Occidental Hotel. He stared at me as if he were looking at a lunatic. "There's no one left in the Occidental Hotel unless they're crazy," he said. And then he added in sepulchral tones: "City's doomed... Where did you come from anyhow?" I told him I had come from Berkeley, and he said with the voice of authority: "Well, you go straight back there while you can...this is no place for you." I spent that night watching San Francisco burn; columns of flames that looked to be miles high; rolling, twisting, gyrating masses of smoke shot with a billion sparks.

The fire had burned for three days and two nights. When it was over, San Franciscans came out of whatever shelter they had found, tens of thousands of them living in army tents, and began to asses the damage. One-fourth of the city, the oldest and most densely-populated part, had been burned to the ground. Throughout the rest of the city, thousands of structures were unsafe to use because of earthquake damage. Judge Boalt took Ina up on Russian Hill. Ever since she had left her house, she could see that a group of buildings at the very top of the hill had survived. As the judge's horse pulled the buggy slowly up the hill, Ina said to herself, *It's too much to hope that my house has been spared, but please God, let me recover my cedar chest.* As they went up Taylor Street, however, she could see that there was no chance. The house three doors from hers was at the edge of the surviving buildings, blackened by smoke but otherwise undamaged. Where her house had been the stark chimney stood alone like a tower over a pile of rubble covered with a powdery gray ash. The whole eastern part of the city looked just the same—chimneys, rubble, and ashes.

"There's nothing here, Ina," Judge Boalt said gently. "It's all gone."

"Yes, everything I owned—cremated. I don't even have a comb!"

He took her back to Van Ness Avenue. The mansions on the west side of the street had been spared and were turned over by the owners to businesses so that commerce could begin again and the city could start to rebuild. Raphael Weill had lost his White House department store, but his warehouse had survived. He was offering one free suit to ladies who had lost everything. Ina entered a huge ornate Victorian house, a bedlam of customers and salespeople. She selected a suit and, with money loaned to her by Mrs. Boalt, purchased some blouses, undergarments, and a bathrobe. As they returned home, they could see soldiers supervising the laying of temporary tracks throughout the burned sections of the city. The rubble, some of it still smoking, was being loaded into shuttle cars and dumped into the Bay in the area between the Presidio and the end of Van Ness. The ashes were not yet cool and the air was still heavy with a bitter, smoky odor, but San Francisco had already begun to rebuild.

That night, after she had gone to bed, acknowledging her good fortune at having a bed and friends with a house intact, Ina permitted herself to grieve for her manuscript, her scrapbooks, letters, photographs—everything that had been in her cedar chest and could never be replaced. She knew that many in the city were grieving for loved ones burned to death or buried in falling walls, and that she, so far as she knew, had not lost anyone close to her. But she could not help but feel that her cedar chest was a loss not only to her but to all those who had known and loved the city in the previous century. The idea of trying to write her book again, without her notes and documents, was too overwhelming even to consider.

XXVII

Creation

Ambrose Bierce, Charley Stoddard, and George Sterling were all absent from San Francisco when the earthquake occurred on April 18, 1906. Bierce was virtually a full-time resident in Washington, D.C. by then, even though his family was still in the Bay Area. Charley had moved to Monterey, eighty miles south of San Francisco, as a headquarters for his series of articles on the California missions, and George Sterling was living nearby in the small settlement of Carmel.

This was the same place where Robert Louis Stevenson, deathly ill and trying to escape the summer fogs of Monterey, had collapsed and would have died had he not been rescued by a goat farmer. But there had been no community there then, just the nearly-abandoned mission and ranches on the pine-covered land that slopes down to the sea from the high ridges behind Monterey. Carmel's only other literary connection before 1903 was as the setting for Gertrude Atherton's potboiler, *Patience Sparrowhawk and Her Time,* a novel filled with sex, scandal, and violence that begins in this remote place of rugged forest and sapphire-blue sea where the lonely heroine spends her childhood.

But in 1903 two developers, James Devendorf and Frank Powers, formed the Carmel Development Company, created Ocean Avenue, a road straight down from the ridge to the beach, and put in a grid of streets along either side of it. To prevent winter floods, they lined Ocean Avenue with wooden sidewalks and planted a row of trees down its center. Thus "Carmel-by-the-Sea" was born. The developers decided that the rustic setting would make an ideal artists' colony, and the first step in creating one was to encourage some established artists to take up residence there to attract other buyers. The timing was perfect for George Sterling, who had sunk deeper into debauchery and had been spending most of his time in his Montgomery Block studio. Desperate to get him away from these habits, his wife and uncle abandoned their hope of making a businessman of him and agreed to let him devote himself to poetry if he would just move away from the city and start over, away from his bohemian friends.

Sterling went down to Carmel in the summer of 1905 with two friends and started to build a simple cabin with a stone fireplace and a large living room. By October, Carrie Sterling was able to come down with Skeet, their terrier, and a pet mockingbird and move in. Sterling entered the project with great enthusiasm. He was leaving the fleshpots behind and devoting himself to chopping firewood; raising vegetables, rabbits, and chickens; gathering shellfish; and hunting game. There was little time left for poetry, but he managed to escape from his bucolic chores for an hour or two here and there and devote the time to his muse. The essential thing was that he and Carrie were experiencing a renewal of their marriage.

The colony began when two more artists moved to Carmel. The first was Mary Austin, who had just published *The Land of Little Rain,* left her unsympathetic husband, and placed her retarded daughter in an institution. She had a cabin constructed near the Sterlings and then erected her "wickiup," a precarious tree house modeled on Indian dwellings, to which she would climb to seek solitude, communion with nature, and inspiration for her writing. Her writing, at this point, concerned the simple life of Indians, Mexicans, and Basque sheepherders. She rejected the turn-of-the-century fashions of corsets and tight clothing; she wore soft, comfortable, flowing dresses and let her long hair hang loose. In San Francisco, she would probably have been arrested as a suspected lunatic for appearing like that in public, but in Carmel she could do as she pleased.

The second artist was Arnold Genthe, a German intellectual who had come to San Francisco to try his hand at painting. He despaired of ever making a living as a painter, but found that his new hobby, photography, held more promise. He had begun by taking pictures of the exotic scenes of Chinatown, but soon acquired a reputation for portrait photography. While other photographers strove for clarity in their portraits, Genthe was the first to discover the value of soft focus and printing through screens or even Irish linen. The results of these techniques permitted Genthe to produce photographs in which plain girls looked pretty, middle-aged women looked young, and the dullest of people looked interesting. He joined the Bohemian Club, increased his social contacts, and quickly became the most prominent portrait photographer in the city.

Like Sterling, Genthe came to Carmel to get away from the temptations and distractions of San Francisco, but his escapes were only temporary. Carmel remained a second home for him. His house was no less impressive for that fact. His living room was thirty by sixty feet with a high ceiling and two skylights; a huge deck overlooked the ocean through the pines; and his darkroom was located in the town's only concrete basement.

For a while, these three compatible characters shared an idyllic life in their Eden with occasional visits from friends like Charley Stoddard, Ina Coolbrith, and Joaquin Miller, but after the earthquake, more people moved into Carmel and visitors became more numerous and more frequent. The destruction of a large part of San Francisco seemed to bring out an urgent sense of carpe diem in the Carmel residents and their guests. Every weekend became a celebration, a festival of wine and song with large beach parties and huge abalone or mussel feasts around the open pit fireplace outside the Sterlings' house.

The princess of the revelers was a beautiful young woman with startling blue eyes and golden hair named Nora May French. She had grown up in Los Angeles and when still an adolescent had had her precocious lyric poems published in *Out West.* In that manner, she came to the attention of Harry Lafler, editor of the short story magazine *Blue Mule.* He arranged to place some of her poems in the *Argonaut,* and the two began a correspondence. When Lafler, who was separated from his wife, visited Nora May in Los Angeles, the two became lovers and she moved to San Francisco. She had achieved considerable status there by having one of her lines reproduced on the murals of Coppa's restaurant: "I fancy that all sensible people will ultimately be damned." "Sensible" was a description never applied to Nora May. Her

Nora May French

moods ranged from near-hysterical gaiety to inconsolable depression. She flitted from lover to lover, and the Sterlings never knew with whom she would show up from one weekend to the next, but they were always confident of her visits.

Each weekend, the Sterlings hosted an ever-increasing group of guests: "Marty" Martinez, the muckraker Lincoln Steffens, and Jimmy Hopper—football hero turned short story writer—became regulars. As the parties intensified, Sterling's devotion to chores and poetry began to falter. It became thoroughly lost with the return of Jack London. The press had not been kind to London when he left Bessie and married Charmian. One newspaper said that "a moral leper had married an ugly-faced girl from whom children ran in terror." London's friends did not much care for Charmian either, but they were less cruel than the press.

London's response to the disapproval was a plan to sail around the world with his bride on a yacht designed by himself, seeking adventure and continuing to produce his thousand words a day. The trip was a disaster from beginning to end. The building of the yacht, the *Snark,* took twice as long and twice as much money as originally estimated. His crew was somewhat less than competent. The captain was Roscoe Eames, Charmian's uncle, who had no ocean navigating experience and firmly believed that the earth was a hollow sphere in which we live on the inside surface. For cook, London chose a twenty-year-old, Martin Johnson, later to become a well-known explorer and adventurer, but who at the time had no experience either in seafaring or cooking. The able seaman was Herbert Stolz, whose only qualification was that he had just graduated from Stanford after four years of outstanding performance as an athlete. These three, plus the Londons and Jack's Japanese valet, made up the boat's company. They were gone for twenty-seven months but got no further than the Solomon Islands due to problems with the yacht, problems with the crew, and bouts of malaria and yaws, which kept London in a Sydney hospital for six months. Nonetheless, London had kept up his literary output; he had produced the novel *Martin Eden* and his best short story, "To Build a Fire," during the voyage.

The Londons arrived for a two-week visit at the Sterlings' cabin in Carmel. George and Carrie Sterling found that marriage and the cruise seemed to have changed London. His socialism had vanished somehow and had been replaced by a kind of idealistic capitalism. He was traveling with a different crowd now, and showing up at such San Francisco events as the sumptuous Christmas party given by the sugar magnate Adolph Spreckels and his wife, the former artists' model Alma de Bretteville, in their new Pacific Heights mansion. London had started buying land near Glen Ellen in Sonoma County, some fifty miles north of San Francisco, and he was full of ideas on building the most modern, most efficient ranch in the world. He had 240 acres in his "Valley of the Moon" ranch, but that was just a beginning. There would be more land, vast crops, scientifically bred livestock, forests of eucalyptus trees, and—of course—a mansion appropriate for a world-famous author and self-made land baron.

London, busy as he was with his writing and the development of his ranch, found occasion to slip away to San Francisco from time to time. Much of the old Barbary Coast had disappeared in the earthquake and fire, but in a short five-year period after the cataclysm, the city was rebuilt, and there was no shortage of saloons or brothels. Sterling would arrange to have "business" in the city to coincide with London's visits, and the two of them, to their respective wives' chagrin, fell easily back into their old habits.

The Sterlings, whatever their own troubles were, had grown deeply concerned about Nora May French. She had financial troubles, she had trouble with her lovers, but mostly she had trouble with being what the French call "comfortable in her own skin." She had begun to neglect herself and looked as bedraggled as she

Jimmy Hopper

obviously felt. The Sterlings invited her to come down to Carmel and stay with them. Nora knew that Sterling kept a supply of cyanide available so that, whenever he felt the time was right, he could accomplish his own death in a manner befitting a poet. She asked him to give her enough to do the same, but Sterling refused. He had no intention of giving poison to someone as prone to despondency as Nora.

One weekend, Jimmy Hopper was in town and Nora fixed her attention on the handsome athletic young man with blond curls that rivaled her own. Jimmy was fond of her, sympathetic to her, but that was as far as he would go. He was married and, though separated from his wife, he was a faithful man. Nora was not used to being rebuffed and took deep offense at Jimmy's indifference to her flirting. At a poker party at the Sterlings' when Carrie provided roast beef sandwiches for her guests, Nora served one to Jimmy, but nervously dropped it on the floor. Before she could retrieve it, Skeet, the Sterlings' terrier, ran off with it. Later that night, Sterling discovered Skeet lying dead in the garden. A mysterious death—what could have happened to him?

A few nights later, Carrie was alone in the house with Nora. George had gone to San Francisco "on business." The two women had passed a cheerful evening together and retired to the twin beds in Carrie's bedroom. Around midnight, Carrie heard Nora get up, get a drink of water, and then return to bed, making strange noises in her throat. Carrie turned on the light and saw Nora lying stiff in bed with foam on her lips. Thinking that the girl was in hysterics, Carrie went to her and found her cold. She climbed into the bed to warm her. She held the girl close and then tried to massage her, but finally realized that she was trying to comfort a corpse. Later a doctor discovered traces of cyanide in

Nora's water glass. She had purchased the poison at the local pharmacy, saying that she had some badly tarnished silverware to clean.

The San Francisco papers made much of the tragic death of the beautiful and talented young bohemian poet: MIDNIGHT LURE OF DEATH LEADS POETESS TO GRAVE was the *Examiner's* headline. But the Carmel colony was more burdened by guilt than grief. They all felt that they had neglected to take the warning signs seriously. Jimmy Hopper summed it up by saying, "We had the lifeboat out, but we were only hitting her on the head with our oars." Nora's body was cremated, and her friends gathered at Point Lobos to scatter her ashes. There was considerable drinking, and several of her former lovers quarreled over who should do the honors. When the quarreling turned to wrestling on the rocks, a neighbor quietly took the urn and cast Nora's ashes into the sea.

After Nora's death, a sobered community saw a new project begin in Carmel that was gathering people of talent to an enthusiastic joint effort under the auspices of Herbert Heron Peet. His mother, Jeanie Spring Peet, was a writer, sculptress, utopianist, and had been wife to several gifted and creative men. Herbert Peet had grown up in Los Angeles, where he earned his living as a stock actor, but when he first came to Carmel to meet his idols George Sterling and Charley Stoddard, he saw the opportunity he had been dreaming of—a community theater. The Little Theater movement was gaining momentum in the nation at the time, a part of the growing experimentation in the arts and reaction against the formulaic professional theater, and Peet envisioned a theater group in Carmel that would utilize the manifold talents of the residents and visitors. He talked the Carmel Development Company into donating a block of wooded land to the project, and the Forest Theater was on its way. The site formed a natural amphitheater, and the "stage" was a flat area of bare ground in the woods. Logs were laid out for the audience to sit on, and torches provided illumination. There was a great sense of mystery and atmosphere to the rustic theater. Audience members arrived bundled in warm clothes and carrying "bugs," or candles stuck in tomato cans to light their way through the woods. Before the play began, they sat listening to the surf and watching wisps of torch-lit fog float through the tops of the pines. The magic of the theater was already well-established before the first actor came out from behind the trees.

Peet had dreams that he hoped his new venture would help bring to realization. He had written a play called *Montezuma,* and he thought that a successful production in Carmel might capture the attention of someone connected with Broadway. That was Peet's plan, but he soon found that the Forest Theater project would become the center of controversy in Carmel for years to come. To begin with, Peet's plans to mount his play were thwarted by the aggressive involvement of Perry and Bertha Newberry in the theater society. Both of them had been active earlier in San Francisco with *Les Jeunes,* and Bertha had been immortalized on Coppa's walls as "Buttsky," a nickname she had earned from her habit of smoking other people's discarded cigarettes. Perry Newbury had written a pageant about Junipero Serra and convinced the society to inaugurate the Forest Theater with that rather than Peet's play.

The first season, 1911, was well received, and the theater was in the black. For the second season, Peet was dismayed to learn that he was in competition with the Newburys again. "Buttsky" had written an Egyptian melodrama called *The Toad* and insisted on its being produced next. Sterling and others objected to the play on the grounds that it was filled with plagiarisms. After much wrangling, a compromise was reached and both plays were mounted for that summer. From then on, the Forest Theater became a bone of contention among the artistic crowd in Carmel: Whose play would be chosen? Who would direct? Who would get the choice parts? George Sterling, with his experience in writing and producing pageants for the Bohemian Club's High Jinks, was the most logical choice for a leader of the group, but creative egos were deeply involved, and there was a surfeit of would-be leaders.

As the theater group was forming, an editor and novelist named Harry Leon Wilson retired to Carmel. He could afford to retire after the great success of a play he had written with Booth Tarkington, *The Man From Home,* in which a sharp Midwestern lawyer protects naive young Americans from scheming European aristocrats with titles but no money looking for a meal ticket. By the time Wilson came to build his magnificent "Ocean Home" on the site which would later become Carmel Highlands Inn, *The Man From Home* had earned its authors over $600,000, an incredible fortune in those days. Wilson was forty-five and chose for his wife the prettiest girl in Carmel, seventeen-year-old Helen Cooke, who had been living with her mother in Helicon Home Colony, a socialist cooperative commune founded by Upton Sinclair in Englewood, New Jersey. When Helicon burned down, Sinclair and several of his followers, including Mrs. Cooke and her daughter, moved to Carmel. Helen was the object of the affections of several men, including Sinclair Lewis and Arnold Genthe, but Wilson, the wealthiest of her suitors, won out. Wilson was a committed writer who spent eight hours a day at his desk, and during this period he created three comic novels serialized in the *Saturday Evening Post* that made him one of America's most popular writers: *Bunker Bean, Ruggles of Red Gap,* and *Merton of the Movies.* He generously allowed the Forest Theater to stage *The Man From Home,* a play which the amateur theater group could never have otherwise afforded, and he lent his young bride as well. Because of her beauty, Helen Cooke had a major role in every Forest Theater production.

The squabbling that had been going on in the theater society came to an end when Mary Austin returned to Carmel from Europe. She had gone there just before Nora May French's suicide, convinced that she was dying of breast cancer. In Italy she had found a miraculous cure with the Blue Nun order; gone on to do a serious study of the prayers of early Christian martyrs, finding them similar to American Indian religious practices; gathered enough material for two books, *Christ in Italy* and *The Man Jesus;* and traveled through Europe and England in the company of a young matinée idol, meeting every important writer who would receive her. Now she was back and determined to put order in the community theater. She wrote an Indian pageant-play in verse called *Fire,* starred in it, and directed it. It was a great success, and the following year she produced another of her Indian folk plays in verse, *The Arrow-Maker,* starring Helen Cooke Wilson. The play firmly established Mary Austin's authority as the creative leader of the Carmel artistic colony.

The theater group prospered, though not without bickering and some offstage melodrama. Young Mrs. Wilson remained the annual leading lady until the year when her leading man's efforts to accomplish convincing love scenes in rehearsals so aroused Harry Leon Wilson's jealousy that he challenged the younger actor to a duel with fists. Wilson was ignominiously defeated; Helen divorced him and left Carmel for good.

In the midst of these controversies, George Sterling was to see his best-known poem published, an event which initially brought him great pleasure but ultimately left him embarrassed and disillusioned. It was called "The Wine of Wizardry." He had been working on it for years and considered it the finest thing he had ever written, a long, rambling series of unrelated fantastic word pictures brought about by contemplating the reflection of a sunset in a glass of red wine, the contemplation done by "a brow caressed by poppybloom." He sent it to Ambrose Bierce back in Washington, D.C. who responded, "No English poem of equal length has so bewildering a wealth of imagination. Not Spenser himself has flung such a profusion of jewels into so small a casket. It takes the breath away." Despite his enthusiasm, it took Bierce three years to get it published, but when he did, he did it with style. The poem appeared in Hearst's *Cosmopolitan* magazine with flamboyant illustrations and an accompanying article by Bierce in which he praised the poem to the skies, comparing Sterling to Poe, Keats, Coleridge, and Rossetti, and declaring, "I steadfastly believe and hardily affirm that George Sterling is a very great poet— uncomparably the greatest...on this side of the Atlantic...Of this poem I hold that not in a lifetime has our literature had any new thing of equal length containing so much poetry and so little else."

Such extravagant praise invited reaction from all the other critics, most of whom had little use for Bierce's outdated literary tastes. The old curmudgeon had wielded absolute critical power in San Francisco, but in the East he had become little more than a propagandist for his employer. Outside the Hearst publications,

"The Wine of Wizardry" was panned as a lurid and pointless series of hyperbolic fantasies, and the lines most often quoted:

And blue-eyed vampire, sated at her feast,
Smiles bloodily against the leprous moon,

were used to illustrate its excessive imagery. Sterling had hoped that this poem would convince his wife and family that he was, after all, a great poet and that their efforts to get him to settle down in journalism or business would have resulted in a loss to American literature. "The Wine of Wizardry" had no such effect.

In 1909, the Carmel artistic colony lost a good friend and neighbor when Charley Stoddard died in his rooms over Mike Noon's Casa Verde restaurant in Monterey. He had enjoyed living there above the sounds of conviviality, and when he had felt lonely, he could always descend to the bar and find companionship. At the end, he lay in his bed in a silk dressing gown surrounded by his relics and souvenirs, admiring the portrait he had had painted of himself in monk's robes and going through all his old manuscripts and letters. As he reread each one, he placed it on a pile to be burned in the fireplace by his landlady. His funeral took place at the Mission San Carlos Borromeo in Carmel, and both the old priest who conducted the mass and the one who delivered the eulogy were former students of Charley's. Ina Coolbrith, though she needed a cane to get around now, came down on the train to say farewell to her oldest friend, barely able to accept the fact that the airy young poet to whom Joseph Duncan had introduced her had grown old and died.

Bierce wrote to Sterling:

I observe that Charley Stoddard is dead. You know I did not care for him, but I knew him for more than forty years, and, naturally, have a little feeling in the matter of his death. Can you acquaint me with the circumstances of his passing?

Sterling replied that he guessed "the old man was glad to die" after all:

> ...for he had hardly a sound organ in his body. What really killed him was alcohol—he couldn't leave it alone and give his heart a rest; and so his heart finally "lay down on the job." I'd not seen him for three months before his death, as he was a case of inversion of sex, and it gave me the "jims" being with him after I found that out. But two days before he died I called, with several others, and found he was asleep. No one thought he was seriously ill; but I wouldn't let them awaken him. I left him some books. A day or two after he "passed peacefully away."
>
> He was a lonely old man and the gentlest creature I ever knew—the woman's soul it may be...Ina Coolbrith came down to the funeral looking like a sibyl of stone.

And Bierce, with a similar lack of charity, replied:

> Thank you for letting me know about Stoddard. I did not care for him—my objection to him was the same as yours—he was not content with the way God had sexed him.

Charley's funeral was small, and only the local newspapers remarked on his passing. But the following year, when his old friend Mark Twain left this world as he had entered it, with Halley's Comet visible in the sky, he was mourned and honored throughout the world.

XXVIII

Dreamers And Builders

In 1904, Reuben Hale, owner of Hale's Department Store at Fifth and Market, had proposed to his fellow members of the San Francisco Merchants' Association that the city begin planning a world's fair to celebrate the completion of the Panama Canal, which would cut the shipping distance between San Francisco and New York by nearly 8,000 miles. Work on the canal had just begun; no one knew how long it would take to complete—or even if the Americans, like the French twenty years earlier, would have to give up the project, defeated by yellow fever and malaria. But the city's mercantile leaders thought the fair was a capital idea and began raising seed money. After the earthquake and fire, nearly everyone forgot about the project, but not Hale. By 1910 he had organized a week-long festival and managed to raise five million dollars. At that point, the Panama-Pacific International Exposition was under way, and San Franciscans were determined to show the world that a new city had arisen from the ashes of the earthquake and fire of 1906. San Francisco now had more than half of all the steel-and-concrete buildings that existed in the United States. It was a new city, and it was going to introduce the Age of Technology in typical California style—the best damned fair the world had ever seen.

Ina Coolbrith was ending her term as President of the Pacific Coast Women's Press Association, and at the final meeting for that year—a meeting devoted to Gertrude Atherton, who was by then California's leading woman novelist—a suggestion was made that the Association sponsor an International Author's Congress at the Exposition. Women had just gained the right to vote in California, and activism was in the air. The idea was enthusiastically accepted by the membership. Ina, as the member whose name was best known and most respected throughout the world, was chosen to head the committee whose awesome task it would be to decide who the world's most deserving two thousand authors were, and then send them invitations to come and attend the Congress.

Unfortunately, Ina's friend Joaquin Miller, the undisputed master of public relations and general ballyhoo, was not able to participate in the preparations for the Congress. Miller was beginning to slow down. Around the turn of the century he had gone on the vaudeville stage, appearing in a Yukon costume, parka, fur pants, and sealskin boots, and pulling a sled. His act was called "My Impressions of the Klondike," and was peppered with occasional lines of poetry in Chinook—an Eskimo language which, Miller assured his audiences, had defied linguists for decades but which he had managed to learn during his first month in Alaska. While on tour, he visited his wife Abby in New York and discovered to his surprise and delight that his daughter Juanita, now eighteen, had grown up to become an attractive young woman who was about to launch her career as a professional singer. He retired from the vaudeville circuit and returned to the "Hights" to write poetry and take advantage of the constant stream of feminine admirers who came to pay their respects to the great bard-adventurer. He continued his flamboyant life until 1911, when he suffered a stroke and was paralyzed. Abby and Juanita came out from New York to look after him, his daughter giving up her singing career (which had amounted to nothing more than one appearance at the Empire Theater).

Miller recovered somewhat from his paralysis but was no longer the same vibrant man. When he appeared at a 1912 Democratic rally for Woodrow Wilson in Oakland with Gertrude Atherton, people barely recognized him. The following year, Lily Langtree was appearing on the stage in Oakland and, despite her sixty years, climbed up to the "Hights" to visit the old man who had strewn rose petals on a staircase for her to walk on some forty years earlier in London. A few days later, at seventy-five, Joaquin Miller died in his bed, his wife and daughter at his side.

He had left strict orders that his body be taken immediately to the funeral pyre he had built and there burned in the company of his family and friends. In his life, Miller had always managed to get around the rules and have his own way, but once he was gone, that control was lost. First, the undertakers' association prevented the cremation of an unembalmed body. Then the City of Oakland prohibited an outdoor cremation. Despite his wishes, Abby decided to have a preacher come and provide a standard church eulogy. Moreover, she permitted Joaquin's body to be on display at the "Hights" so that all his friends could come to say farewell. His friends came, but so did thousands of curiosity-seekers who overran the place, taking souvenirs. Everything that was movable disappeared in the stampede, including some of the clothing from the body. The police had to come to rescue the coffin and take it to a mortuary. Three months later, a private ceremony was held at the "Hights," and a wooden urn containing Miller's ashes was burned on the funeral pyre. As the urn disintegrated, the earthly remains of Cinncinatus Hiner Miller were carried off by the winds.

Later, George Sterling received a quill pen from Juanita Miller, with a letter assuring him that it was the one her father always used to write his poems. Sterling prized it highly until he discovered that Juanita had sent a similar feather to all of Miller's friends.

Initially, the response to Ina Coolbrith's invitations to the Authors' Congress was excellent, and she felt a growing sense of excitement over the prospect of the world's greatest authors all coming together for the first time in history in San Francisco, with her as their hostess. But after November, 1914, when the Age of Technology in Europe became caught at the level of tanks, machine guns, and long-range artillery, Ina began receiving one letter of regret after another from every European country, from England to Russia: due to the war, the authors could not participate after all. There was some talk of delaying the Exposition, but money had been raised, commitments had been made, and the project had a momentum of its own. Besides, it was clear that this war in Europe was not going to finish quickly. A site for the Exposition had been chosen: the north shore of the city between the Presidio and Fort Mason, where all the rubble from the earthquake had been dumped into the Bay, creating a large, flat landfill of over six hundred acres with panoramic marine views. Already, wagons were carrying loads of topsoil to the area to cover up the surface of the debris.

Mary Austin had accepted an offer to be a member of the Exposition Planning Commission, and had moved up from Carmel to devote all her time to this work. The commission decided from the beginning that this was to be the most impressive exposition the world had ever seen. They hired George Kelham, designer of the Palace Hotel and the Bohemian Club, as chief architect, and he devised a general plan for the area that would provide architectural harmony for all its parts: a Tower of Jewels as a centerpiece, eight main exhibition palaces, a huge Festival Hall, a thousand-foot-long Palace of Machinery on the east with an amusement park behind it, Bernard Maybeck's Palace of Fine Arts on the west end, along with exhibit halls from various countries and states—and all of this linked by expansive thematic landscaped courtyards with huge fountains of dancing waters and large reflecting pools. At the water's edge, a marina was created, forming the St. Francis Yacht Club. Bordering the exposition grounds on Chestnut Street, a thirty-foot-high "vertical lawn" was built, a wood fence whose sides were covered with growing ice plant. Henry Ford even constructed an operating assembly plant for the Palace of Transportation that turned out a Model T every ten minutes for three hours each afternoon, a particularly appropriate exhibit since the Exposition celebrated not only the Panama Canal but also the nearly-completed Lincoln Highway, the transcontinental road that made it possible to drive an automobile on paved roads all the way from New York to San Francisco. In the arches over the Fillmore Street entrance, planners decided to add a touch of culture by engraving the names of great writers and thinkers of the ages: Homer, Sophocles, Aristotle, Chaucer, Shakespeare, Cervantes, Milton, Descartes, and...among these giants, their own favorite local writer, George Sterling. Sterling knew nothing of this until it was done and was as embarrassed as he was pleased. He took a great deal of teasing over it, particularly from Jack London, who felt that if any contemporary writer's name should have been there, it was his own.

On February 20, 1915, at 6:00 am, every bell was rung, every fire engine siren was sounded, and automobile horns throughout the city ougahed to announce the opening of the exposition. A fife and drum corps marched through the residential streets to bestir the populace. Governor Hiram Johnson and Mayor "Sunny Jim" Rolph led fifteen thousand people down Van Ness Avenue to the main entry, where a prayer was given. In Washington, D.C., President Wilson pressed a gold key that sent a radio signal across the continent for the first time. When the signal was received by an antenna atop the Tower of Jewels, the gates were swung open, the fountains began to flow, and the Panama-Pacific International Exhibition was under way. Before it ended ten months later, nineteen million people would pass through the entry gates.

Ina's Authors' Congress did not begin until June, so she had plenty of time to enjoy the exhibits, the architecture, the gardens, and the special events before her actual duties began. As an Exposition official, however, she was included in many ceremonies and was thrilled to meet some of the famous people who came out to see the fair: Thomas Edison, Henry Ford, Maria Montessori, Buffalo Bill, Helen Keller, Charlie Chaplin, and a man she had already known as a Bohemian Club member, Luther Burbank. He came often to distribute thousands of seed packets to fair-goers, and at one ceremony, he made an elaborate show of naming a new hybridized poppy, calling it *crimson eschscholtzia Ina Coolbrith*. Everybody who was anybody came to the fair. Theodore Roosevelt, Rough Rider hero of San Juan Hill in the Spanish-American War, had later become president and had encouraged the revolution that made Panama a nation, thereby facilitating the canal project. "Teddy" Roosevelt came and spoke to a crowd of two hundred and fifty thousand at the Exhibition's Court of Nations.

On June 29, Ina opened the International Congress of Authors. After her brief introductory remarks there followed a series of talks, all in English, but delivered by authors from around the world. There were papers on Norse Literature, Irish folk songs, Shakespeare, Medieval Jewish poets, and the influence of literature on Chinese politics, among many others. The following day, the morning was devoted to lectures on the literature and history of California. In the afternoon, the auditorium was filled to capacity, and there were many there who were dear to Ina's heart: Mary Austin; Gertrude Atherton; Bret Harte's former secretary, Josephine McCrackin; the "Man With the Hoe," poet Edwin Markham; and Ina's niece, "Little Ina" Cook with her daughter, also named Ina Cook. Governor Johnson's message of greetings and congratulations was read, Edwin Markham gave a short address on "The Saving of Poetry," and then Senator James Phelan recalled the early days when Harte, Twain, Stoddard, and Coolbrith established California's literary beginnings. Finally, the president of the University of California, Benjamin Ide Wheeler, presented a wreath of bay laurel to Ina and proclaimed her California's first Poet Laureate. As she received it, she noticed how similar it looked to the one she had fashioned for Joaquin Miller to place on Byron's grave forty-five years earlier. *My God,* she thought, *Forty-five years!*

She spoke briefly, acknowledging the honor and saying that she felt it was given to her, not on her merit alone, but in memory of the group that Senator Phelan had just mentioned, of which she was the sole survivor. "For those who are passed away and for my sister women—I accept this laurel with deep gratitude and deeper humility."

XXIX

Wolf House

Jack London was not much involved with the preparations for the Exposition or the Authors' Congress; he was too busy with his own project. He threw himself into "scientific ranching" with a near-frantic enthusiasm. His original holdings had now grown to fourteen hundred acres. His "Beauty Ranch" was going to be the model of the latest techniques in farming, vineyards, livestock, and orchards. As San Francisco developed its Exposition, Jack London was preparing an equally grandiose one-man exposition that would last forever. To a friend he wrote:

> I am rebuilding wornout hillside lands that were worked out and destroyed by our wasteful California pioneer families. I believe that the soil is our one indestructible asset, and by green manures, nitrogen-gathering crops, animal manures, proper tillage and drainage, I am getting results which the Chinese have demonstrated for forty centuries.

Drawing on every resource he could find, particularly his neighbor, Luther Burbank, London installed the latest ideas in agriculture: a silo made of concrete blocks; a stone piggery;   a modern winery; and imported European purebred goats, cattle, and horses to improve his stock. Not every idea worked. For example, he invested heavily in the cultivation of eucalyptus trees, only to discover that their lumber turned out to be unsalable. While the ranch was being developed, Jack and Charmian lived in a small farm house on the original piece of land he had purchased. It served as his headquarters, but a farm house was not appropriate to what was to be the world's finest ranch. London dreamed

of a house that would befit his project, a completely unique residence that would someday welcome scientists, artists, and
philosophers from every nation. With his architect, he planned,
on the top of a rise that overlooked his property, Wolf House, a
vast mansion made of ten thousand-year-old redwood logs with
their bark left on, chocolate-colored concrete, volcanic rocks, and
blue slate. The living room was to be fifty feet long and adjoined
by a huge patio with swimming pool.

The ranch and the house required large sums of money, but
at this time London was earning over $70,000 a year, more than
any other author in the world. Still, he increased his output. A
thousand words a day was no longer sufficient. Everything he
wrote was mailed to George Sterling for editing, and in one period of three months, Sterling received a quarter of a million words.
London had no time to go down to Carmel and cavort on the
beach with his old friends. He wrote to Sterling:

> The only chance I get to go away is when I rush
> off to buy a Jersey cow, or look at a silo, or to buy a
> stallion or an angora goat herd or a shorthorn bull or
> such truck.

What he was writing was, to a large extent, what he was living—a novel called *Valley of the Moon*. In it, a young Oakland couple, fed up with industrial life, sets off on a journey around
California seeking a new life, one worthy of the children of "the
pioneers who settled this country." They discover the artists'
colony at Carmel (where all the characters were based on the
actual residents) but find it too arty and sense a superficiality in
the bohemianism that pervades the life there. Eventually, they
arrive at the Valley of the Moon in Sonoma County and begin a
new life as ranchers, determined to put into practice the truths
they have absorbed on their journey. Nearly every character in
the book can be readily identified as someone London knew, and
two of them are based on London himself. One, a waterfront boy
in Oakland, tells the heroine that "Oakland's just a place to start
from." The other alter ego of London himself is Jack Hastings, a
rancher and war correspondent who lives on a yacht on the

Sacramento River. A pair of characters based on Charmian's aunt and uncle, the Hales, establish what the two main characters have to look forward to at the end of the novel. The Hales live in the country, in a redwood bungalow lined with books. They spend their days working the soil and their evenings reading and enjoying the fruits of their labor. They are the epitome of well-deserved contentment and a life in perfect balance.

Since London would not leave his ranch, Sterling took to visiting Jack and Charmian, but found that the idyllic life portrayed in *Valley of the Moon* did not much correspond to reality. Early each morning, London would prop himself up in bed and begin writing, sustained by coffee, whiskey, and Russian cigarettes. Over his bed a clothesline was rigged up, on which he fastened notes and pages torn from books and magazines. When he wanted one, he simply reeled it within reach. As he finished each page, he dropped it to the floor, where his Korean manservant retrieved it and took it into the next room, where Charmian was typing the morning's production. The afternoons were devoted to frantic efforts to practice scientific ranching. London had abandoned the flannel shirts and wool caps of his socialist days and now sported a riding outfit, a bandanna, and a Baden-Powell hat. If his efforts at being the world's most modern rancher frequently ended in fiasco, at least he managed to look the part.

On August 22, 1913, Jack and Charmian London retired in their small house for what they thought would be the last time. In the morning they would begin moving into Wolf House, which was finally completed. In the night they were awakened to cries of alarm and the smell of smoke. They ran out in their nightclothes only to see the mansion on the knoll above them engulfed in flames, torched by a disgruntled former employee. London had not bothered to take out any fire insurance. He had felt that the design of the house had made it impervious to fire, but he had not foreseen arson—a fire set inside the building. When the flames were finally out, the house a total loss, he took to his bed in a deep funk and lay there for four days, weeping.

The loss of his dream house seemed to be a blow from which London could not recover. He lost his enthusiasm for his ranch and turned over its management to his sister Eliza. His drinking increased and, worst of all, his writing suffered considerably. All the things he had failed to accomplish in reality, he tried to put into his new novel, *The Little Lady of the Big House.* It was pure wish-fulfillment. When he asked Sterling for an evaluation of it and received a negative report, he became enraged. As much as he sought to compensate for his own failures through the fantasy of his novel, he could not find a life-affirming end for it as he had done in *Valley of the Moon. The Little Lady of the Big House* ends in suicide.

Not long after its publication, London was dead at forty-one. He had been suffering terribly from renal colic, and his doctor had given him morphine tablets to ease the pain. One night, suffering a severe attack, he took an overdose, and his houseboy found him dead on the floor in the morning. The papers were filled with gossip for weeks. Some journalists claimed it was a suicide by a man grieving for his lost estate, his failing ranch, and the declining quality of his writing. Others scoffed at that, saying that London would never have removed himself from life until he had seen the outcome of the war in Europe. Still other friends agreed, saying they knew that he had just begun a love affair with an English girl and that his death had to have been accidental. While the speculation continued, everyone agreed that he had been one of the highest-paid and best-known authors in the world, and unquestionably one of the most prolific. In the last seventeen years of his life, he had produced eighteen novels, twenty volumes of short stories, seven books of non-fiction, and hundreds of articles and essays. While the quality of his writing had suffered greatly at the very end of his life, the rest of it would remain valid and popular for generations to come. At the time of his death, his work had been translated into eighty languages.

XXX

The Satyr's Dirge

George Sterling had not only lost his closest friend, he lost his mentor as well. In a letter from New Orleans in December of 1913, Ambrose Bierce had informed Sterling that he was on his way to Mexico, ostensibly to observe the progress of Pancho Villa's revolution. After several months with no news, Sterling checked with Bierce's family. They had not heard from him since Sterling had, and his last letter had contained the disquieting sentence, "To be a Gringo in Mexico—ah, that is euthanasia!" Sterling had discounted that merely as the old man's frustration at getting his publisher to publish his collected works as he wanted them done. Still, Bierce was seventy-one now and really not in shape to be chasing Mexican revolutionaries across the desert.

Rumors began to circulate. There were reports that Bierce had been executed personally by Pancho Villa in Chihuahua; that he had been killed in the battle of Ojinaga; that he was incarcerated at the insane asylum at Napa, looked after by a female admirer. Sterling wrote to the War Department, urging them to send a search party into Mexico to look for him. The War Department declined. They had plans for involvement in Mexico that were incompatible with search parties around the border, and they did not want any complications. In addition, Bierce had insulted just about everyone in Washington, and the general feeling was that it was just as well that he was missing.

Eventually, Sterling had to accept that Bierce was gone—that he was unquestionably dead, but that no one knew for sure where or how he had died. Perhaps, Sterling had to admit, that is what the old man had wanted. All his adult life, Bierce had mocked death; wherever he traveled he kept a human skull on his desk "for inspiration." He had ridiculed eulogies and pious grieving for decades. How, then, could he simply grow old, stiff in the joints, and die like any other man? No doubt he had chosen to exit in this dramatic fashion. Sterling gave up any further search.

Not only Sterling's two closest friends, but his wife, as well, had gone. Although he and Carrie had quarreled and separated numerous times, she had always come back, always hoped that this time George's promises would be kept. But shortly before the Panama-Pacific Exposition, she gave up. Sterling's uncle, Frank Havens, had given the couple $40,000 to invest so they would always have an income. When Carrie discovered that George had spent the money rather than investing it, she moved into the Claremont Hotel and filed for divorce on the grounds that her husband was failing to support her.

America entered the war in Europe, and Sterling threw himself into jingoistic poems of maudlin patriotism. The Carmel colony was breaking up: Jimmy Hopper went to France as a war correspondent; Mary Austin moved to find a more spiritually inspiring environment in New Mexico; and Upton Sinclair, far from the best of the Carmel writers but unquestionably the most influential, left for Southern California in 1916 to begin his sprawling novel on the rapid growth of the area, *Oil!*

Sterling left also and moved to San Francisco, where Barbour Lathrop, a wealthy fellow club member, paid for his room at the Bohemian Club. Sterling seemed to be trying to cram as much dissipation into his life as possible. Already the city's favorite poet, he became its favorite *bon vivant* as well. From the wealthiest neighborhoods to North Beach, no party was complete without him. He was especially fond of costume parties, where in leopard skins or a brief Roman toga he could show off his physique and be the center of attention. His name was the one most frequently seen in the gossip columns—one day for staging a boxing match with a professional prize fighter, the next for carrying the head of the dragon in the Chinese New Year's parade, and the next for rolling milk cans down Telegraph Hill at three in the morning after a boisterous party. Although he had never held an office, he was clearly the spiritual head of the Bohemian Club. As that organization moved further away from its artistic roots, it needed a connection with its origins, at least one genuine bohemian, and

Sterling provided that link. His antics permitted the members to associate themselves vicariously with disreputable behavior without taking any personal risks. And they rewarded him by giving him top billing in their summer High Jinks at the Bohemian Grove. Although a few serious poems appeared from time to time in the *Overland Monthly,* most of his output consisted now of humorous rhymes that appeared in newspapers and general interest magazines.

About the time that Sterling left Carmel, a new poet arrived—a tall, broad-shouldered young man with intense blue eyes, seeking sanctuary from a society which had already condemned him and his wife. His name was Robinson Jeffers. He was the first son of William Jeffers of Pennsylvania, a Presbyterian minister and professor of Latin, Greek, Hebrew, and Ecclesiastical History. Most of Robinson's early education had been in Europe while his father taught at various universities. In 1903 the elder Jeffers retired to Los Angeles, and Robinson entered Occidental College, already fluent in Latin, Greek, French, and German. As a graduate student, he studied medicine at the University of Southern California, and in an advanced German class he made the fateful acquaintance of a young woman, Una Call Kuster. She was two years older than he, beautiful, extremely intelligent, passionately involved in the life of the mind and the spirit—a perfect match for the young medical student, except that she was already married. Several years earlier, as an undergraduate at the University of California at Berkeley, Una had met and fallen in love with a fellow student, Teddie Kuster. Now Kuster was a prominent lawyer in Los Angeles and Una was a young socialite, her life centered around the country club and the Junior League. It was a busy life but not a satisfying one, and her soul-thirst for something more meaningful than parties and fashionable clothes had led her to return to university courses. As Una and Jeffers became friends and shared long conversations sitting on the steps of USC buildings, they became aware that their attraction for each other was too intense to remain platonic. Jeffers withdrew. He transferred to the forestry department at the University of Washington, but the exile did not work. A year later he was back in California and Una was asking her husband for a divorce. Kuster, in an attempt to salvage his marriage, asked his wife to spend a year in Europe before making a final decision. She agreed. During that year, from the summer of 1911 to 1912, Jeffers lived in "drunken idleness" at the beach, but his sabbatical was not entirely idle. It resulted in his first book of poems, *Flagons and Apples.* When Una returned, her mind unchanged, she filed for divorce.

Robinson Jeffers

The Kusters were a prominent enough family for the Los Angeles *Times* to do a feature article on the affair titled "Two Points of the Eternal Triangle" with pictures of Una and Jeffers and a copy of "On the Cliff" from *Flagons and Apples,* a love poem clearly written for Una.

When the young lovers were finally able to marry, they decided to move to some remote village in Ireland and devote themselves to poetry and music, but the outbreak of World War I prevented them from going to Europe. They had heard of the artists' colony at Carmel-by-the-Sea, and thinking that they might find refuge from gossip and social obligations there, decided to go and have a look. Later, Jeffers wrote:

> When the stagecoach topped the hill from Monterey and we looked down through the pines and sea fogs on Carmel Bay, it was evident that we had come, without knowing it, to our inevitable place.

Jeffers and the rugged coast that runs from Carmel to Big Sur, where mountains plunge spectacularly into the ocean, seemed made for one another. From the sparsely populated land, the poet drew inspiration for a new style that centered around the beauty and indestructible forces of nature and the passions of the people who lived in the countryside there, seeking to tame the land but often finding instead that they were made wild by it. Robinson and Una Jeffers bought a five-acre plot of land among the wind-blown cypress trees about a mile from the village and just a few yards from the rocky ocean shore. They hired a mason and Jeffers worked as his apprentice to build a small cottage on their property from the granite stones of the beach. When the house was completed, Jeffers, having fallen in love with masonry, constructed by himself a three-story stone tower next to the house. The couple lived a rustic life: Jeffers wrote in the mornings and laid stones in the afternoons. Una tended the garden, prepared their simple meals, made most of their clothes, and cared for the fruit of their marriage, twin sons. The remote and obscure life they had hoped to find in Ireland they created for themselves in Carmel, but it was not meant to last.

Without Sterling and Austin to stir things up, Carmel had settled down again to a peaceful community of artists, but San Francisco had taken on a frantic gaiety. World War I had brought about a national wave of reform. Dance halls and houses of legalized prostitution were closed, and the Eighteenth Amendment shut down all saloons, bars, and liquor stores. The effect on the city was to move vice from the lower classes to the middle and upper classes. Anyone with money could find a drink in the hundreds of speakeasies throughout the city, and brothels for white-collar clients still functioned demurely in residential neighborhoods, illegally but without interference from a tolerant police department. As the city moved into the roaring twenties, George Sterling became the quintessential playboy. Nearly every evening he could be found presiding over a table at his favorite restaurant, Begin's Bologna in North Beach, where good wine was still available and where his check was discreetly picked up by the management since his presence attracted paying customers; and the girls of the Jazz Age knew that they could not be considered "popular" in San Francisco until they had twirled around Begin's dance floor at least once in the arms of the tall, graying poet with a face like a Greek god. And nearly every night, after he had dined and titillated the flappers, he would wrap himself in his overcoat and stroll along Montgomery and Market Streets to Coffee Dan's at Powell and O'Farrell, a basement speakeasy that customers could enter by a staircase or, if they preferred, slide in by way of a chute.

In his room at the Bohemian Club, Sterling covered the walls and even the ceiling over his bed with photographs, some showing Bierce and London and his Carmel friends, but mostly of himself in various costumes at a party or at some outdoor pageant. He was virtually living inside his own scrapbook. He went to New York where the works of Carl Sandburg, Robert Frost, T. S. Eliot, and Ezra Pound had created a renaissance of poetry, but Sterling felt like a country bumpkin at literary discussions there, which were too obscure for him. He went to Los Angeles to write titles for silent movies, most notably Douglas Fairbanks' *The Thief of Baghdad*, but he always returned to the only city where he was considered seriously as a poet.

Carrie Sterling, his former wife, viewed his antics with several kinds of regret. She was no longer living at the Claremont Hotel. Frank Havens, her brother-in-law as well as Sterling's uncle, like many men who had a talent for amassing huge fortunes, had a talent for losing them as well. Havens was broke, and Carrie had been obliged to go to work. She was reduced to living in a small pagoda behind the Havens' house in Piedmont. She felt that a reconciliation might be beneficial both for Sterling and for herself. She arranged a dinner party at the Berkeley home of Ambrose Bierce's brother, and did her best to vamp her errant mate, but it was no use. Sterling still loved her, but he was more in love with his own image, the urban troubadour. Reconciliation was impossible. Shortly before the Armistice was signed, Carrie wound up her Victrola, put on a record of Chopin's funeral march, lay down on the bed, and drank a lethal dose of cyanide.

Carrie's death shocked Sterling at least partially out of his jester role. He began to attend to his writing more seriously, and eventually the Book Club of California asked him to edit a collection of California poetry. This event coincided with Sterling's discovery of Robinson Jeffers' work, and he titled the book

Continent's End after its lead poem by Jeffers. After the success of
the book, Sterling was given a column in the *Overland Monthly*
called "Rhymes and Reactions," in which he published and criticized the work of new poets. One of his first reviews was of the
long narrative poem *Tamar* which Jeffers had written in 1916 and
printed at his own expense. Some publishers were sticking their
necks out with controversial themes that stirred up censorship
among the sanctimonious, particularly the current works of
Gertrude Atherton, dubbed by journalists as a member of the
"Erotic School." Her novel, *Black Oxen,* the most widely-read
book in America in 1923, tells the adventures of a fifty-eight-year-
old woman who regains her youth through a glandular operation
and is courted by men half her age. But no publisher was willing
to risk taking on *Tamar* because its themes were too bleak and
violent and its content too explicitly sexual. On the literal level, it
is the story of a young woman living on an isolated farm near
Carmel who becomes pregnant after an incestuous relationship
with her brother and who eventually destroys herself, her family,
and her lover in an all-consuming conflagration. On a deeper
level, it is the recapitulation of the story of the earth goddess who
creates the seasons of the year and who symbolizes the cosmic
rhythms. It is a stark and powerful poem, devoid of any charm or
elegance but written in a slow rhythm as relentless as the pound-
ing surf:

> Passion and despair and grief had stripped away
> Whatever is rounded and approachable
> In the body of a woman, hers looked hard; long lines
> Narrowing down from the shoulder-bones, no appeal,
> A weapon and no sheath, fire without fuel.

It was the kind of poetry that Sterling had dreamed of creating himself but had never been able to rise to. He praised it thoroughly, calling it "the strongest and most dreadful poem that I
have ever read or heard of." At the same time, James Rorty, a San
Francisco editor, published a review of *Tamar* in the New York
Herald Tribune, and Mark Van Doren in *The Nation* wrote, "the
necessity of its being printed at the author's expense is a disgrace

to American publishing." Shortly thereafter, Boni & Liveright brought out *Tamar and Other Poems,* and Robinson Jeffers was no longer obscure. His idyllic life was now cluttered with interviewers, budding poets, and a succession of famous people who made pilgrimages to his stone outpost: Carl Sandburg, Edna St. Vincent Millay, Langston Hughes, Dorothy Parker, Sinclair Lewis, George Gershwin, Charlie Chaplin, Martha Graham, Charles Lindburgh, Krishnamurti, and Ansel Adams. Finally, Jeffers hung a sign on his front door which read "Not at Home before 4 p.m." on one side and "Not at Home" on the other.

For the next few years, George Sterling continued to promote Jeffers in his column. He praised the poet's works with the same unbridled enthusiasm that Bierce had once lavished on him. His own life, however, had degenerated badly. Years of overindulgence were taking their toll. In 1926, he received a letter from his old friend and editor of the *American Mercury,* H. L. Mencken, saying that he was coming to San Francisco for a visit. Mencken had published two of Sterling's articles in the *Mercury,* one on Joaquin Miller and another on Ambrose Bierce, and that represented the extent of Sterling's success in the Eastern press since Bierce's disappearance. For that, Sterling was grateful and was determined to make Mencken's visit a memorable one. Mencken had been to San Francisco before to cover the 1920 Democratic convention. He fell in love with the place and could not praise it enough: its sunny but cool weather, its friendly people, its new luxurious civic auditorium, and—most of all—the quality of the food and the generous amounts of bourbon whiskey that Mayor Rolph had made available to all the delegates. "Whenever I meet an old timer who took part in it," he wrote in later years, "we fall into maudlin reminiscences of it, and tears drop off the ends of our noses." Sterling was planning major celebrations. First there would be a Bohemian Club banquet in Mencken's honor. The following night would bring a huge spaghetti feed in the Montgomery Block, with the main dish served on an authentic Roman shield. Then a "Buddhist meal" was planned with lavish decoration, exotic music, and dancing girls in flimsy costumes. To prepare for what was to be a week-long binge, Sterling began to collect, from the many sources available to him, wines and liquors to accompany the celebrations. Through his bootleggers and providers of questionable prescriptions, his small room became filled with cases of illegal beverages.

Twice, before he reached California, Mencken was delayed and sent telegrams to Sterling, apologizing and rescheduling his arrival date. In Los Angeles, he was detained again several times, each time postponing his arrival with pleas to forgive the inconvenience. But Sterling had not been able to stave off temptation that long. The constant anticipation, followed by the letdown of delay, had driven him to begin sampling the stash in his room, and by the time Mencken arrived, Sterling was too hungover to attend the Bohemian Club banquet. Waiters came up to his quarters to take cases of wine down to the banquet room, and later, Sterling could hear the laughter coming up the stairwell from the celebration, where Frank Norris' brother Charles was filling in for Sterling as master of ceremonies. It was a final irony: Sterling detested Charles Norris. Late that night when the dining and drinking and storytelling were over, Mencken came up to Sterling's room to say good night and see how he was feeling, but could not rouse him. In the morning, the club manager, unable to get a response, used his passkey to enter the room and found Sterling's body on the floor. He had taken the vial of cyanide that he always carried with him. All around him on the floor were ashes. He had burned all his manuscripts.

A large and elaborate funeral, provided by the Bohemian Club, attracted hundreds of San Franciscans to say goodbye to the colorful man who had given them their favorite home-town poem, "The Cool Grey City of Love." At Begin's Bologna that night, patrons lowered their heads in silence as the orchestra played a tribute to the poet, Debussy's *Prélude à l'Après-midi d'un Faune.*

XXXI

When The Grass Shall Cover Me

For Ina Coolbrith, Sterling's death seemed to be the loss of her last link to the world of writers. When she mourned Sterling, she was grieving as well for Harte, Clemens, Mulford, Stoddard, Stevenson, Miller, London, and certainly for her own youth. The *Overland* asked her for a memorial poem for Sterling and she complied, but was greatly dissatisfied with the results. She begged for more time, but there were deadlines and the editor did not want to delay the memorial issue, so her "George Sterling," much to her chagrin, appeared in its unsatisfactory form.

Later that same year, Ina put together a collection of what she considered her own best poems written since *Songs From the Golden Gate* had first been published in 1895. There were 116 poems in all, and she chose *Wings of Sunset* for a title. Charles Phillips, with whom she had edited the posthumous collection of Stoddard's poems, wrote a biographical introduction to her book based on the information Ina supplied to him. It contained no reference to her mother's marriage into the Smith family or even to Ina's being born in a Mormon settlement. Even though her stepfather had abandoned the family and obliged Ina to devote herself to their support, she remained faithful to her promise to him never to reveal her true origin. Also, there was no mention of Ina's own early marriage and divorce, although she did include a very personal poem that had never before been published and that contained obvious references to Robert Carsley:

Within that nameless realm where Dead meet Dead
I met that one through whom my life was banned,
   Who gave for love fierce hate.
So wan the eyes, reflecting eyes as wan,

I reached my hand to clasp the outstretched hand
    And touched—but icy air!
'Alas!' I said: 'Alas! Alas! poor shade!'
And he: 'Alas! Alas! poor shade!' he said.

By 1928, Ina was in her eighty-seventh year and was for the most part confined to the small back bedroom of her niece's house in Berkeley, but she managed to get out of bed each day and sit in the armchair close to the window that overlooked the garden. The arrival of a bird among the flowers was an event for her, and she was resignedly conscious of the constrictions of interest that old age had brought. She sat observing the birds in the garden, reminiscing, half-dozing, then quietly she stopped breathing, and the last of those writers who had known the Gold Rush passed into history.

She was buried in an unmarked grave next to her mother in Mountain View Cemetery in Oakland. A memorial service was held at St. Mark's Episcopal Church in Berkeley, where her friends once more heard the poem she had written sixty years earlier:

When the grass shall cover me,
Head to foot where I am lying—
    When not any wind that blows,
    Summer-bloom nor winter-snows,
Shall awake me to your sighing:
    Close above me as you pass,
    You will say, 'How kind she was,'
    You will say, 'How true she was,'
When the grass grows over me.

When the grass shall cover me,
Holden close the earth's warm bosom—
    While I laugh or weep or sing,
    Nevermore, for anything,
You will find in blade and blossom
    Sweet small voices, odorous,
    Tender pleaders in my cause

That shall speak of me as I was—
When the grass grows over me.

When the grass shall cover me!
 Ah, beloved, in my sorrow
 Very patient, I can wait,
 Knowing that soon or late
There will dawn a clearer morrow;
 When your heart will moan: 'Alas!
 Now I know how true she was;
 Now I know how dear she was—
When the grass grows over me!

Through the efforts of Fanny Stevenson's sister, Nellie Van de Grift Sanchez, and two of Ina's closest friends, Derrick and Eunice Lehmer, Summit Peak in the Sierras, which overlooks Beckwourth Pass where Ina first entered California riding on the saddle of Jim Beckwourth, was renamed Mount Ina Coolbrith.

Later, in 1947, a steep terraced park that runs down the eastern slope of Russian Hill was dedicated to the poet. Ina Coolbrith Park—just a few blocks from her last San Francisco residence at 1067 Broadway—looks out on the downtown area of the city, the Bay beyond, the campanile of the University, and the tree-covered hills of Oakland.

XXXII

Hard Times

The legend which Robert Louis Stevenson created around himself during his brief stay in California lived on through his family. When Fanny Stevenson died in Santa Barbara at the age of seventy-seven, it was her lover of ten years, Ned Field, then thirty-three, who closed her eyes. During those years, Field had assisted Fanny in editing the collected works of her late husband. After Fanny's death in 1914, Field married her daughter, Isobel Osbourne Strong, who was fifty-six at the time. Understandably, many people saw him as a fortune-hunter, but those people were very wrong. Field was a member of a wealthy publishing family and was financially independent. Isobel had inherited a sizable fortune from her mother, but Field had no need of her money. He was genuinely in love with her, just as he had been with her mother. The couple settled in Los Angeles, where Field wrote scripts for Hollywood. In 1921, they became millionaires when oil was discovered on property that Field had encouraged Fanny to buy years before. For the next fifteen years, the Fields were leaders among the "new royalty" that motion pictures had created in Hollywood. Field died in 1936, but Isobel, the young girl who had discouraged her mother from running around with that "disreputable Scotsman," enjoyed good health and great wealth until the age of ninety-three.

The Wall Street crash of 1929 had little effect on people as wealthy as Ned and Isobel Field, but for the majority of Americans, it was the collapse of what President Herbert Hoover had optimistically called "the permanent plateau of prosperity." Suddenly there were no jobs, and in San Francisco, as in every other American city, the residents adopted a tenacious and sullen resolve to survive "until this thing is over." San Francisco had been a strong union town since the Gold Rush days, when skilled workers were at a premium and organized to protect their rights and gain good wages. In 1916, however, someone threw a bomb into a patriotic rally, killing ten people. Labor radicals Tom Mooney and Warren Billings were convicted of the crime, mostly on the basis of perjury and tainted evidence, and the strength of independent unions gave way to company-sponsored unions. The Great Depression brought about a renewal of independent unions when workers saw that the company unions were not going to help them survive the hard times. The most important of the new organizations was the Longshoremen's Union, which called for a strike that shut down the port of San Francisco. That strike spread to other West Coast ports from Seattle to San Diego and led to a confrontation—striking longshoremen versus the police and California National Guard—that left two people dead and hundreds injured. At that point, members of all the San Francisco trade unions walked off their jobs, creating a general strike and a clear expression of solidarity. Federal arbitrators settled the strike, and from that point on, even though unemployment was high, San Francisco was a union town again.

In San Francisco, as well as in the United States in general, library lending went up forty percent in the four years after the crash; the libraries, as often as not, were filled with people who had nothing to do or who were just looking for a warm place to rest. But bookstores were folding in rapid succession. Book-buying had decreased to the extent that book production went from two hundred million in 1923 to half that in 1933. Magazines were not faring much better. As advertising revenues dried up, the *Overland Monthly,* California's undisputed leading literary magazine since 1868, was struggling to stay alive. Its final issue came out in 1935. Literary life in San Francisco, it seemed, was a thing of the past.

It wasn't that people were not reading, but what they were reading was not thought of as literature. Pulp fiction and pulp magazines not only survived but prospered during the depression. They were cheap to produce and offered escapist fare for a population with too little money and too much time on its hands.

From the thick pages of pulp magazines emerged a new San Francisco writer named Dashiell Hammett. Born on a small tobacco farm in Maryland in 1894, Hammett had to leave high school and go to work as a messenger boy to supplement the family income. He was an indifferent worker and longed for a more sophisticated way of life, which led him to answer an advertisement in a Baltimore newspaper for agents (or "operatives" as they were called) for the Pinkerton National Detective Agency. He envisioned himself as a protector of law and order, but when he was sent to Montana to help keep striking miners in line, he realized he was little more than a goon for the mine owners. His sympathies were with the miners, but it was the owners who were paying his wages.

When America entered World War I, Hammett decided to carry a gun for Uncle Sam instead of Pinkerton and enlisted in the Army. But before he could get to France, he contracted influenza which quickly worsened to tuberculosis. Discharged, he returned to the detective agency and was sent to Tacoma, Washington. His health failed again and he entered a Veteran's Administration hospital there and met a young nurse named Josephine Dolan. Shortly after Hammett was transferred to a hospital in San Diego, he received a letter from Josephine notifying him that she was carrying his child. He arranged to be released from the hospital and agreed to meet her to start a new life at a place somewhere between Tacoma and San Diego. That place turned out to be San Francisco, where Hammett went back to work for Pinkerton's at six dollars a day. As a gumshoe, he became familiar with every aspect of the city, from the waterfront dives to the luxury hotels on Nob Hill. During his time with Pinkerton he worked on the *Sonoma* liner case, where $125,000 in gold sovereigns had been stolen, and on the Fatty Arbuckle rape/murder case. He and other Pinkerton agents found witnesses whose testimony convinced the jury that the portly silent film comedian had been framed. Although Arbuckle was acquitted, the scandal ruined his career.

Hammett's tuberculosis had never left him, and the long nights of standing in the fog waiting for someone he was following to make a move were taking a toll on his health. He had always had an itch to write and managed to land a job as an advertising copy writer for Samuel's Jewelry a few doors down Market Street from the Pinkerton office. Hammett had always been amused by the detective stories he read. The genre, created by Edgar Allan Poe with "The Murders in the Rue Morgue" in 1841, had degenerated into stories in which a clever private eye aided a bumbling police department to apprehend an evildoer. Hammett knew from experience that these formulaic whodunits were far removed from the real world of detective work, and he felt sure he could do better.

H. L. Mencken and George Jean Nathan had started a pulp magazine of detective stories in 1920 called *The Black Mask.* Hammett submitted a story to them with a very different kind of hero. "The Continental Op" (an operative for the Continental Detective Agency) was short, fat, and so unromantic that his name was never even mentioned. In his world, the noncriminal characters were as sinister and unprincipled as the crooks, and he performed his job not out of heroism or altruism but rather out of pride in doing well what he had to do. The story was well-received and was followed by several others, and by 1929, the Continental Op appeared as the protagonist of a novel, *Red Harvest,* set in the miners' strikes of Montana, where Hammett could give free rein to his cynicism and sense of ambiguity. By then he was considered the nation's expert on detective stories and was writing reviews of them for the *Saturday Review of Literature.*

Of all the cities he had known, Hammett preferred San Francisco as a setting for his works. The place seemed to him to have been created for mystery and sinful indulgence. In 1930 he developed the quintessential San Francisco novel, *The Maltese Falcon,* and a character, Sam Spade, who is as much a part of San Francisco as Sherlock Holmes is a part of London. The detective story takes place during a five-day period and in a twenty-five-square-block area of downtown San Francisco centered around the Geary Theater.

After the success of *The Maltese Falcon,* the former six-dollar-a-day detective was rolling in money at a time when people all over the country were standing in bread lines and "riding the

rods" in a futile search for employment. Most of what Hammett
earned was donated to left-wing
causes; the rest was spent on gambling, women, and bootleg liquor.
His principal source of income during the thirties was the series he
developed called *The Thin Man,*
popular as stories, radio shows, and
films.

Down in Carmel, the writers'
colony had disappeared, its members having either died or moved
away. Two remained, however, and
had become good friends: Jimmy
Hopper, who continued sending stories to the *Saturday Evening Post,*
and Robinson Jeffers, who had
another critical success with *The
Roan Stallion.* One day while wandering around the countryside,

Dashiell Hammett

Jeffers and his wife came upon an abandoned cabin with no trace
of a road to it. When they asked about it they were told that it had
been abandoned ever since the owner was killed by his stallion.
The image of the desolate cabin began to germinate in Jeffer's
mind as a story. *The Roan Stallion* concerns a woman named
California, half Mexican-Indian and half Scottish, who lives in a
remote cabin with her white husband, who devotes himself to
drinking and gambling. One day he returns from town with a
magnificent roan stallion he has won in a card game. To
California, the horse is more than just an animal; it is a divine
creature worthy of worship. At night, when her husband is sleeping, she rides the horse through the hills and experiences a mystic ecstasy. One night, when her drunken husband tries to force
her to make love, California escapes to the corral. When her husband follows, the stallion attacks him and kills him with his
hooves and teeth. Torn with conflict, California finally shoots the
stallion.

The major critics were enthusiastic, and Mark Van Doren in *The Nation* went so far as to call *The Roan Stallion* a masterpiece. Jeffers was naturally pleased with the recognition and the book sales, but the main effect of his success was more visitors and distractions; once more he and Una had to protect themselves and their twin boys from a world that pressed in on them. Two years later, with the publication of *The Women of Point Sur,* the world began very much to leave him alone. Another long narrative poem, it told of a minister who experiences a crisis of faith from which he emerges with a firm conviction that Christianity is a hoax and that God is indifferent to questions of right and wrong. He wanders down the coast of California, preaching his doctrine to anyone who will listen to him, until he reaches Point Sur, where he takes a room at an isolated farm. His influence on the residents there encourages a maelstrom of infidelity, incest, bisexuality, suicide, murder, and madness. The critical press was unanimous in condemning the poem as obscure, pretentious, unnecessarily complex, sordid, and ridiculous. Jeffers was indifferent to their comments. He stood by his work and defended it. If it caused him to be less of a celebrity and if people were less motivated to beat a path to the doorstep of his stone fortress in Carmel, so much the better.

XXXIII

Dubious Battle

Twenty-five miles northeast of Carmel is the town of Salinas, Spanish for "salt marshes." It is the administrative and shipping hub for the "salad bowl of America," the Salinas Valley, and from this agricultural center emerged in the twenties a writer who encompassed the virtues of many of his predecessors. John Steinbeck would equal the storytelling skill of Bret Harte, the wry humor of Mark Twain, the biting wit of Ambrose Bierce, the virile realism of Jack London, and the poetic symbolism of Robinson Jeffers.

He was born in 1902 into an upper middle-class family; his father would become Treasurer of Monterey County, and his mother was a teacher who introduced her son to the classics and, when he showed signs of talent, encouraged his writing. The young Steinbeck grew up in two places, Salinas and Monterey. Salinas, at that time, was a virtually feudal agricultural area where farms were large and frequently owned by corporations rather than farmers. There were two classes in the town, the conservative, land-owning upper class and the exploited farm workers. His second environment, Monterey, where his parents had a summer home, was a multi-cultural fishing and canning port, filled with honky-tonks for the benefit of fishermen and the soldiers from nearby Fort Ord. Steinbeck attended Stanford University, but was not a well-focused student and dropped out after five years of attendance with no degree. He wandered to San Francisco where, as he later wrote:

> I spent my attic days there, while others were being a lost generation in Paris. I fledged in San Francisco, climbed its hills, slept in its parks, worked

on its docks, marched and shouted in its revolts. In a way I felt I owned the city as much as it owned me.

John Steinbeck

Then he moved to New York City to work as a reporter, but gave it up because every time he was given an assignment he got lost. He returned to California by working as a deck hand on a freighter, and, as Richard Henry Dana had done nearly a hundred years earlier, he conceived a book while aboard ship. This one, its style due largely to Steinbeck's lifelong hero, Robert Louis Stevenson, was the story of the buccaneer Henry Morgan. The novel, called *Cup of Gold*, was not very good, but its timing was even worse. It was published two months before the stock market crash of 1929, and its sales were dismal. The following year, Steinbeck met Ed Ricketts, the marine biologist who would become his closest friend and mentor, and he married Carol Henning, a woman of taste and intellect who encouraged her husband's efforts to write, even though it meant living on the twenty-five-dollar-a-month allowance that his parents provided. The couple lived in the Steinbeck summer home, actually located in Pacific Grove, a quiet and conservative town next to Monterey that had been a Methodist campground when Stevenson had stumbled on to it fifty years earlier and which remained "dry" long after Prohibition was repealed.

Steinbeck wrote short stories in this period, some of which were published in the waning *Overland Monthly,* and in 1932 appeared his first collection. Entitled *Pastures of Heaven,* it described refugees from urban life who had come to seek the good life in Corral de Tierra, the bleak land west of Salinas, but who fail to find it due to their own illusions and self-deception. The book was not a commercial success—it earned the author four hundred dollars—but it brought him critical recognition.

His reputation was established and his life style drastically changed in 1935 with the publication of *Tortilla Flat.* The novel concerns a group of ne'er-do-well Monterey *paisanos,* people of Mexican, Indian, and Spanish blood, who live irresponsible, carefree lives and cluster around their friend Danny, who returns from World War I to find that he has inherited a small house. The humorous adventures of these simple folk involved in complex situations are told in the style of Mallory's *Morte d'Arthur,* with Danny in the role of King Arthur and his friends as the Knights of the Round Table. After being rejected by nine publishers, the house of Covici, Friede published it—and all of Steinbeck's books thereafter until 1964. Suddenly Steinbeck was rich and famous. *Tortilla Flat* won the Commonwealth Club's Gold Medal for the best work by a native Californian, and the Steinbecks moved to the town of Los Gatos, in the foothills of the Santa Cruz mountains at the southern end of San Francisco Bay.

The following year, a vicious struggle between growers and lettuce packers took place during an extended strike in Salinas. Steinbeck returned home to observe the events and the result was a realistic novel, *In Dubious Battle,* concerning two Communists who organize a hopeless strike for the purpose of converting workers into revolutionaries. The work was praised for its objectivity and its indication that the causes of the turmoil were more psychological than economic, but the author was castigated in his home town by both sides, each of which felt that it had been unfairly portrayed. This was Steinbeck's first novel about "man's eternal, bitter warfare with himself."

In 1937 appeared *Of Mice and Men,* a novella about two itinerant ranch hands who travel from job to job, dreaming of the couple of acres they will buy someday so they can "live off the fatta the land." The story was poignant and rich in symbolism, and its selection by the Book-of-the-Month Club brought Steinbeck a national reputation. The couple toured Europe in grand style and then moved into the home of George F. Kaufman to work on a stage adaptation of the novella.

When they returned to California, they found the Central Valley in turmoil over the immigration of more than 350,000 "Okies," refugees from Oklahoma, Arkansas, and Texas, where the combined effects of the Depression and years of drought had created the Dust Bowl, forcing small farmers off their land. These unfortunate farmers then migrated west in wheezing cars and trucks to seek jobs as pickers. The influx of these agricultural workers from the Midwest created "Hoovervilles" throughout the Central Valley—collections of shacks made of cardboard and scrap metal where hordes of impoverished families lived in squalid and unsanitary conditions. It was a situation ideal for the exploitation of farm labor, and it brought about an explosive escalation of tensions between the haves and the have-nots—the residents who feared unionization and "contamination" pitted against the newcomers who feared starvation.

Steinbeck accepted an assignment to cover this situation in a series of articles for the San Francisco *News* called "The Harvest Gypsies." From his research for the series came his best work, *The Grapes of Wrath*. It is a multi-layered novel of the experience of farm people from the Dust Bowl and their subsequent adversities in California, recounted through the tribulations of the Joad family. On a literal level, *The Grapes of Wrath* illustrates the social history of the "invasion" of California by desperate people from the Midwest. On that level alone, it had a greater impact on American public opinion than any novel since *Uncle Tom's Cabin*. As critics, who were lukewarm toward it at first, began to investigate it more thoroughly, they found other levels of meaning in the novel. The biological level revealed an objective picture of the transplanted Joads and their fellow sufferers simply as creatures whose normal environment had been destroyed and who had to use their adaptive abilities to survive in unfamiliar situations. On the anthropological level, the Joads are a symbol for the family, the fundamental unit through which human beings, in all times and places, orient themselves. In the course of the novel, the family evolves; conventional roles change as the members cling desperately to their rituals in an attempt to retain their identity. At another, deeper level, *The Grapes of Wrath* is a Biblical allegory, in which the catastrophes in Oklahoma parallel the oppression and bondage of the

Jews in Egypt. Their migration parallels the exodus; the arrival and trials in California parallel the Jews' flight, their wandering in the wilderness, and their entrance into the land of Canaan, where the chosen people encounter the hostility of the Canaanites. On a fifth level, the novel is an epic in which the Joad family fills the role of a single character—the hero who expresses the ideals of a people. Gradually, its members come to realize that the family, which has always been their basic unit of survival since frontier days, must give way to a larger sense of community, a bonding together and common action by an oppressed people to achieve security for the group by unified opposition rather than flight.

The Grapes of Wrath was the best-selling book in America in 1939 and earned its author a Pulitzer Prize, an invitation to dine with the Roosevelts at the White House, and royalties beyond his fondest dreams. More important to him was the fact that his book had raised social consciousness. Both state and federal funds were made available to help the Dust Bowl refugees obtain food, medical care, and better living conditions.

XXXIV

The New Bohemians

Among the thousands who thronged the Panama-Pacific International Exposition in 1915 was one who surely must have stood out: a beautiful woman, still young, with jet-black hair piled up on her head and large intense eyes that were equally black. She had in tow her four children: two daughters, Zabel and Cosette, and two sons, Henry and William, all of them with the same black hair and eyes as their mother. Her name was Takoohi Saroyan, and she was delirious with joy because she had just saved enough money from her job as a maid to take her children out of the orphanage and return to Fresno with them. Takoohi had immigrated to New York from Armenia with her husband, a poet-minister, and her three eldest children, then moved west to the Armenian community in Fresno in the San Joaquin Valley. Her husband's parish assignment did not work out, and he took to chicken farming to try to support his family. Three years after the birth of his son William, he died of appendicitis, and Takoohi was obliged to put her four children in the Fred Finch Orphanage in Oakland, where she could visit them only on her Sundays off. They remained there for five years. Their visit to the Exposition was to celebrate their liberation, and later, William Saroyan would recall that he, as an eight-year-old, perceived it as "a place that couldn't possibly be real."

When Takoohi took her brood back to Fresno, they all went to work, even little William, who sold the *Fresno Evening Herald* on a street corner after school. From an early age, William Saroyan knew that he would be a writer. As soon as he had learned to type, he dropped out of junior high school, much to the relief of the Fresno Unified School District, and focused his attention on saving enough money to buy a typewriter. He worked for

William Saroyan

the Postal Telegraph Company, flying through the flat streets of Fresno on his bicycle delivering telegrams; before his classmates had graduated from high school, he had become manager of the Fresno telegraph office. Takoohi realized that career opportunities were limited in Fresno, where most Armenians spent their lives as farmworkers, so she moved her family to San Francisco. Again, everyone went to work—everyone except eighteen-year-old William, who was determined to become a writer and spent his days reading and writing in the San Francisco Public Library. Other members of the family objected to his failure to contribute to the household expenses, but Takoohi—uncharacteristically, because she was a hard, stern woman—told them to leave him alone.

For two years, Saroyan collected rejection slips...until August, 1928, when the *Overland Monthly* accepted a story titled "Preface to a Book Not Yet Written." Four months later, "A Portrait of a Bum" appeared in the *Overland.* Three months after that came "The American Clowns of Criticism," followed by "Portrait of Another Bum." These early publications in the moribund *Overland* were not particularly remunerative, but they gave the author the encouragement to persist in his writing, and in 1934, he was propelled into the national spotlight when *Story* magazine printed "The Daring Young Man on the Flying Trapeze," a story told as the inner monologue of a young writer who is dying of starvation in San Francisco. Although it is a bleak and mournful subject, in Saroyan's hands the story takes on a light and optimistic tone, despite its irony. The editors of *Story* encouraged him to send more manuscripts, and he replied that he would send them a story a day for the next thirty days—and he did. His practice at that time was to sit down at his typewriter, conceive of a situation, type it out as it evolved in his mind, and then, without even rereading it, send it off. In less than a year, his first collection of stories, also titled *The Daring Young Man on the Flying Trapeze,* was published, establishing him as an author who could treat dark subjects such as the Depression and the spread of Fascism, yet still offer hope through a sense of humor and stoicism.

Saroyan's rise after his first recognition was as meteoric as Jack London's had been. Between 1934 and 1940, he published seven collections of short stories and two plays, *My Heart's in the Highlands* and *The Time of Your Life*, the latter taking place in a San Francisco waterfront bar (based on Izzy Gomez's saloon). Both plays were major hits, and *The Time of Your Life* was awarded the Pulitzer Prize. When Saroyan was notified of the award, he telegraphed the committee that he refused the prize, in a typical nonconformist stance, saying that "commerce had no business patronizing art." Of course, his refusal garnered more publicity than the prize itself could have done.

By this time, Saroyan had established himself as the American spokesman for the individual. While his contemporaries were writing in honor of the Common Man, he wrote of individual common men and their idiosyncrasies. His work was sentimental, whimsical, ironic yet warm, and it touched something in American readers that made them want more. They did not realize it yet, but what gave his works such intense appeal was that every one of them was, unfashionable as it might be at the time, an allegory.

In 1940 he published what is probably his best book: *My Name is Aram,* a collection of short stories, all with the same characters, that describe life in the Armenian community of Fresno. This book, along with many of his short stories about Armenian-Americans, established Saroyan as the first generally popular writer of an American ethnic minority. Aspiring young writers from all over the country began to write letters of admiration to him. Saroyan wrote encouraging responses to those who seemed serious and talented, in particular to a young playwright named Tom Williams, who would later adopt the pen name "Tennessee."

When the war broke out, Metro-Goldwyn-Mayer offered Saroyan sixty thousand dollars, a fortune at the time, to produce a "home-front morale-builder," and in less than sixty days he turned out *The Human Comedy*. He assumed that he would direct the film, and when he found out that the studio had no intention of leaving their property in the hands of an amateur, he offered MGM eighty thousand dollars to buy back the rights to his script. They refused his offer and went on to produce an Academy Award-winning film. Saroyan turned around and rewrote his script as a novel. It quickly became a Book-of-the-Month Club selection. In *The Human Comedy,* he did not glorify war, as most contemporary works did, but treated it rather as a tribulation that ordinary people are obliged to undergo from time to time, a tribulation that permits people to achieve heights of courage and forbearance. The warm, sentimental vision of family life he depicted was the sort he had never known as a young child, and that he would never be able to accomplish as an adult.

In 1927, while Saroyan was still struggling in the San Francisco Public Library, a young Kenneth Rexroth hitchhiked from Chicago to Seattle with his wife Andrée. When they were ready to return, they decided to do so by way of San Francisco. They loaded up their backpacks and descended the coast. They intended to stay only a few days, but when they were offered jobs (decorating furniture), they remained long enough to fall in love with the place. At twenty-two, Rexroth already had an impressive background. In school he had revealed an insatiable intellect and a revolutionary spirit. Like Saroyan, he spent more time in libraries than in classrooms because he could learn faster and wanted to pursue his own course at his own pace. He began translating French poetry at the age of fifteen and by the time he arrived in San Francisco he had become a bohemian extraordinaire, with experience as an actor, painter, poet, translator of Japanese and classical poetry, mountain man, cowpoke, speakeasy manager, con man, and monastic novice. He also dabbled in philosophy and revolution, vacillating between Communism, anarchy, and the International Workers of the World, but eventually grew dissatisfied with each of them. In his wanderings through

Kenneth Rexroth

the Southwest, he had fallen in briefly with the crowd that orbited around Mabel Dodge Luhan in Taos, New Mexico.

Mabel was the daughter of a wealthy New York family who dreamed of being a modern-day patron of the arts in Medici style. When her first husband was killed in a hunting accident, she moved to Italy with a second and turned her villa into a salon for wealthy people and artists. Weary of Europe, she moved to Greenwich Village and became a patroness of revolutionary causes, attracting Emma Goldman, Walter Lippman, Lincoln Steffens, Margaret Sanger, Alfred Stieglitz, Isadora Duncan, and John Reed to her circle. During World War I, she became bored with politics, moved to Taos, and determined that Fate had brought her there to rediscover the ancient wisdom of the Pueblo Indians which would revitalize decaying Western civilization. She married an Indian, by now her fifth husband, built a seventeen room estate with five guest cottages, and began to "collect" famous people again. Her prize catch was D. H. Lawrence, whom she hoped would become the spokesman for her project of revitalizing the Western world. When Lawrence failed to become a prophet and returned to England, Mabel turned her attention to Robinson Jeffers, but got no further with him than she had with Lawrence.

It was while Lawrence was still there that young Kenneth Rexroth came on the scene. He was not particularly impressed with the English novelist (although he was later to become the editor of Lawrence's works) nor with the hangers-on at Mabel's compound, but while staying there, he became a close friend of Mary Austin, who was living in Santa Fe at that time. He respected her genuine understanding of Indian languages and culture, and she guided his reading and research in these areas.

Rexroth and his wife had been active members of the bohemian literary-artistic world in Chicago and sought a similar group in
San Francisco. They found that the group was quite small. There
were artistic types who gathered in North Beach cafés and speakeasies, especially Izzy Gomez's saloon; but for the most part, San
Franciscans still thought of George Sterling as their great poet, an
idea that repulsed Rexroth. More sophisticated residents preferred Robinson Jeffers, but Rexroth could not abide Jeffers' work
either. The couple had rented a studio in the Montgomery Block
and begun to make friends when they met the sculptor Ralph
Stackpole, who "knew everybody in town from top to bottom and
took us everywhere." Curiously, one of the local writers who most
impressed Rexroth was the patrician Gertrude Atherton, who was
then in her seventies and living as a permanent guest in U.S.
Senator James Phelan's estate in Saratoga, Villa Montalvo.

The Rexroths were attracted to San Francisco by its free and
easy non-puritanical atmosphere and its active theater life—
American, French, Italian, and Chinese. What held them was the
easy access to open areas of natural beauty. The whole west coast
of San Francisco at the time was a stretch of open sand dunes,
except for the Cliff House area. They enjoyed riding horses there
and then began to explore the wilds of Marin and San Mateo
counties on foot and on horseback. They eventually discovered
the Sierras and began making annual pilgrimages to the mountains, which were deserted in those days except for Yosemite
National Park.

Since both Rexroth and Saroyan took advantage of the fact
that Izzy Gomez never charged the artists who dined in his place,
the two writers eventually met and became friends. Both were
still unknown to the public at the time, struggling to survive the
Depression, but when Saroyan published *The Daring Young Man
on the Flying Trapeze* in 1934, he leapt from obscurity to national
fame overnight. Rexroth recalled standing one day at Geary and
Stockton, staring in awe at a window in San Francisco's finest
department store, the City of Paris. In the window was a display
of mannequins swinging on trapezes, under which eight rows of
the book were on display. He was astonished when Saroyan came
up to him saying, "Oh, Ken, I'm so glad I ran into you. I've just

come from my bookie, and I got wiped out. Could you lend me two bits for carfare?"

XXXV

To Arms

Employment problems in the Bay Area were eased considerably when the newly-elected Roosevelt administration appropriated federal public works funds for two major construction projects, the Golden Gate Bridge between San Francisco and Marin County and the San Francisco-Oakland Bay Bridge. The two spans initiated the inevitable demise of the distinctive ferryboats which set out from the Ferry Building at the foot of Market Street to a dozen ferry landings across the Bay, the most extensive ferry system in the world. At the same time, the bridges ushered in an era in which automobiles and trucks would supplant not only ferryboats but railroads and streetcars as well. As the San Francisco-Oakland Bay Bridge neared completion in 1936, considerable interest was aroused in hosting another international exposition.

The parallels between the 1915 Panama-Pacific Exposition and the 1939-40 Golden Gate Exposition are remarkable: the former was conceived to celebrate the completion of the Panama Canal and to show the world that San Francisco had arisen from the ashes of the 1906 earthquake and fire; the latter celebrated the recently-completed bridges across the Bay and sought to show the world that San Francisco had not only survived the Depression but was well on its way to complete recovery. In both cases, after the planning of the exposition had begun, a world war broke out that would involve the United States shortly after the fair buildings had been torn down. Both fairs took place in a brief window between disasters.

The location of the second fair was not in San Francisco itself but literally in the middle of San Francisco Bay. The Bay Bridge, eight miles long, the world's longest steel bridge at the time, is anchored in the middle to Yerba Buena Island, where Joaquin

Miller had initiated Arbor Day in California with his tree-planting ceremony. Adjacent to Yerba Buena, a new island was created by dredging up fill from the bottom of the Bay to create a flat four-hundred-acre space connected to Yerba Buena by a causeway. And in honor of San Francisco's famous visitor, Robert Louis Stevenson, it was named "Treasure Island." This flat space in the Bay served not only as a fair site but also as a home base for Pan American's new China Clippers, four-engine seaplanes which had just begun trans-Pacific passenger service, the most elegant passenger service in the world: aboard the China Clipper, airline passengers were served their meals in a formal dining area with starched white tablecloths, fine china, and crystal glassware.

The theme of the Fair was "Pacific Unity," but by the time it opened in February, 1939, Japan had occupied much of the coast of China and was pushing relentlessly inland in search of a unity among Pacific nations in the form of a Japanese empire. In Europe, Hitler had already taken over Czechoslovakia and was only months away from invading Poland. But just as World War I had seemed remote to San Franciscans in 1915, the news of warfare in Europe and Asia did not much occupy the minds of visitors to Treasure Island admiring the four-hundred-foot Tower of the Sun, centerpiece of the exposition; the dozens of Art Deco buildings exhibiting the latest advances in science and technology; the Fine Arts building, where original works by Botticelli, Michelangelo, Titian, Tintorello, and Donatello were on loan from Italy; the Cavalcade of the Golden West, an outdoor show with a stage longer than a football field that held two hundred and fifty actors, two trains, and innumerable horses, and had a "curtain" of fountains that created a forty-foot wall of water; the Folies Bergère; Billy Rose's Aquacade; and the "Gayway," a collection of carnival rides and games. The Fair ran for two years, and on its last night, residents on both sides of the Bay watched as all the lights on Treasure Island were very slowly dimmed until only the Tower of the Sun remained illuminated throughout the night.

A year later, the United States was plunged headlong into World War II with the Japanese attack on Pearl Harbor. Suddenly Treasure Island was a Navy base, and the entire region became a hub of war effort, with military installations from one end of the Bay to the other and major shipyards in San Francisco, Oakland, Richmond, Vallejo, and Sausalito. Overnight, the Bay Area became the world's largest shipbuilding center, and the "Okies" and "Arkies" whose sufferings Steinbeck had portrayed in *The Grapes of Wrath* quickly found not only a welcome, but jobs at wages they could never have imagined. Southern blacks were recruited to work in the defense industries and poured into the area in search of good wages, often occupying the homes of recently "relocated" Japanese-Americans.

The five principal writers in Northern California at the time, unlike their predecessors, did not associate much with one another. Saroyan was friendly with Rexroth and had visited Jeffers at Tor House, but they belonged to no school or common movement. Most of the earlier male writers in the region had been members of the Bohemian Club, but Jeffers, Hammett, Steinbeck, Saroyan, and Rexroth were never invited to join and would have declined any such invitation had it been forthcoming—they were not joiners. However, in the fever of patriotism and national unity brought on after Pearl Harbor, each of them responded to the war effort in his own way. Robinson Jeffers had tried to enlist in the Army Air Corps during the First World War when he and Una were establishing themselves in Carmel. The Air Corps had turned him down so he settled for the Army Balloon Division, but the war ended before he could serve. World War I intensified his feeling that humanity was a "sick microbe" and a "botched experiment that has run wild and ought to be stopped." This gloomy outlook was not lightened when the war ended. He continued in his pessimism, and as early as 1933 began to predict another devastating world conflict. A few months before Pearl Harbor, his collection of poems *Be Angry at the Sun* came out, in which he decried the repetition of the madness of global war. This time, he saw his twin sons go off to the war that he had dreaded for a decade.

Dashiell Hammett responded to the call to duty. He had enlisted in 1917 to escape a dull job; this time he seemed to be trying to escape his own success as a detective story writer. He was forty-seven years old, alcoholic, and had received a medical discharge after World War I, but the Army accepted him. Since Hammett had been active in several Marxist and left-wing groups, J. Edgar Hoover had serious doubts about Hammett's loyalty to the American way of life. Consequently, the FBI made sure that Private Hammett stayed well away from any sensitive service. He was stationed in Alaska in the Aleutian Islands in a unit designed to warn of any Japanese activity in the area. Once again, the ex-Pinkerton man was out in the cold on stakeout.

John Steinbeck joined the war effort with his pen as a weapon. In 1942, he published *The Moon is Down,* a propagandistic novel about the Resistance movement in occupied Norway and followed that with *Bombs Away,* a nonfiction book of combat experiences in the Army Air Corps. During his service as a war correspondent in Europe for the New York *Herald-Tribune,* he gathered material for two postwar books, *Russian Journal* (with Robert Capa) and *Once There Was a War.* In 1944, Steinbeck returned to California to write the screenplay for Alfred Hitchcock's film *Lifeboat,* followed by a satirical story of the family of a Mexican-American boy who is awarded a posthumous Congressional Medal of Honor, *A Medal for Benny.*

Just before he was inducted into the Army in Sacramento in 1942, William Saroyan married Carol Marcus, a young debutante who had played a small part in Saroyan's production of his own play, *Jim Dandy.* The two could not have been more different. She was an innocent blonde, seventeen, who had grown up on Park Avenue. Saroyan was twice her age and still tied to the old-country values of the Armenian community. It was bound to be a stormy marriage, but while he was separated from her by Army service and their relationship was carried on by mail, they got along very well. His incapacity to accept any authority other than his own however, did not lead him to an illustrious military career. The highest rank he achieved was private first class, and he could not even hold on to that.

He was sent to London in the Signal Corps Film Division where he was the roommate of another Film Division enlisted man, the writer Irwin Shaw. The two of them managed to survive the London Blitz and were sent to Paris the day after it was liberated; they took up residence in the headquarters for war correspondents, the Hôtel Scribe. The "commander" of the literary Americans in Paris at the time was Ernest Hemingway who had ensconced himself in the Hôtel Ritz, accompanied by a group of resistance fighters of whom he had taken charge in Normandy. Hemingway had taken offense at what he considered to be snide references to him in *The Daring Young Man on the Flying Trapeze* and had denigrated Saroyan several times in print. When the two met, they were dining in the restaurant at the Hôtel George V, and when Hemingway, who had considerably overindulged in *apéritifs,* noticed Saroyan, he bawled out, "Well for God's sake, what's that lousy Armenian son-of-a-bitch doing here?" The verbal assault escalated, and Saroyan and his companions rose from their table. A brawl ensued which had to be quelled by the *gendarmes,* and both parties were ejected from the hotel. Thus ended Saroyan's wartime combat experience.

Kenneth Rexroth was a dedicated pacifist. When World War II broke out he obtained conscientious objector status and went to work as an orderly in the psychiatric ward of San Francisco County Hospital. He was not subject to the hysteria that was sweeping the West Coast after the bombing of Pearl Harbor. He knew many members of the Japanese community in San Francisco personally and understood that they posed no threat to national security. Furthermore, he was fully aware that the internment of Japanese-Americans in Relocation Centers was merely another chapter in the history of official bigotry and discrimination against Chinese, Japanese, and Filipinos that had taken place since the Gold Rush. He devoted the early years of the war to operating a kind of Underground Railroad for Japanese-Americans who would otherwise have been sent to Relocation Centers. He and his wife opened their house to Japanese who were not sick enough to be hospitalized but too ill to report to Santa Anita Racetrack, where all persons of Japanese ancestry were housed in horse stalls until the trains came to take them off to bleak camps in remote areas. Japanese-Americans who were attending college away from the West Coast could get an exemption from the camps, and Rexroth began enrolling young people in correspondence courses in art, photo retouching, dress design, and knitting. These courses were essentially scams that were advertised in pulp magazines, but they served to exempt his charges, whom he sent to Chicago to stay with his friends.

During the war, many conscientious objectors were sent to work camps, one of which was located at Waldport, Oregon, one of the rainiest spots in America. For some reason, the Selective Service sent all of the artistically inclined C.O.'s to this camp, unwittingly creating an art colony. When the young men were given furloughs from their camp, they would come to San Francisco and look up Kenneth Rexroth who was known to them by the two books of poetry he published at that time, *In What Hour?* and *The Phoenix and the Tortoise.* When the war ended, many of these young men settled in San Francisco. They were instrumental in founding little theater groups and a generally anarchist magazine called *Circle,* published from 1944 to 1948, which established connections with European avant-garde poets and painters, especially French surrealists. From *Circle's* contributors came the group that founded radio station KPFA/FM in Berkeley, the first alternative radio station in the area.

XXXVI

Back Home

When the war ended, San Francisco was no longer what it had been. A million servicemen and women had passed through on their way to the Pacific Theater, and those who survived passed through again on their way back. Many, having seen the city, remained there. The influx of thousands of defense workers had changed the city also. It was no longer a place where no self-respecting woman would think of being seen downtown without hat and gloves. But it was the place where the agency designed to bring about lasting world peace, the United Nations, was created, the delegates having met and signed the charter in the Opera House. The city was still vibrant and exciting, but different. Gertrude Atherton, now in her late eighties, came out of retirement to recall the old San Francisco in two nostalgic reminiscences, *Golden Gate Country* and *My San Francisco.*

In 1946, Robinson Jeffers reached the height of his renown with an adaptation of Euripides' *Medea.* He had seen the actress Judith Anderson, who was married to a University of California professor at the time, perform as Clytemnestra in a local production of his *Tower Beyond Tragedy* and was greatly impressed with her ability to bring his lines to life. The two became close friends, and Anderson convinced him to write the story of Medea, the sorceress who, when she learns that her husband Jason is planning to marry another woman, murders their two sons to punish him. Jeffers had never before produced any work by request, but this project, written specifically for Judith Anderson to perform, excited him and he completed the script in a few months. The play opened on Broadway in 1947 with John Gielgud playing Jason opposite Anderson's Medea. Despite its classic setting and the fact that it was in verse, Medea was a huge success. It ran for seven months on Broadway and then went on the road. Other companies were formed for productions in England, France, Germany, Denmark, and Italy. The name Robinson Jeffers became familiar to millions who had never heard of him before.

Dashiell Hammett did not enjoy such a postwar renewal. His health was poor when he was discharged from the Army and it was not helped at all by his heavy drinking. Although he was no longer able to produce anything himself, Hammett devoted himself to assisting the playwright Lillian Hellman, with whom he was living. Because he had supported left-wing causes all of his life, Hammett became a target of Joseph McCarthy's Senate Subcommittee on Un-American Activities. McCarthy arranged to have Hammett's books removed from all State Department supported libraries—Sam Spade and the Thin Man had evidently become subversive characters. Refusing to provide "evidence" to the Senate Investigating Committee about the activities of his friends during the twenties and thirties, Hammett took the Fifth Amendment. Despite his poor health, he was sentenced to six months in prison, after which he spent his remaining years in New York.

John Steinbeck returned from his war correspondent duties a disillusioned man. He was sick of the war and threw himself into a project of nostalgia. *Cannery Row* is the story of Doc, a reclusive marine biologist—unabashedly based on Steinbeck's friend Ed Ricketts—and a group of derelicts living in the abandoned cannery buildings along the Monterey wharves during the Depression. On a literal level, *Cannery Row* seems to be an attempt on the author's part to wash the war out of his mind with whimsical humor and a tolerant view of rascally characters who have no purpose in life but to survive and have nothing to do with the world of respectability, high ideals, or passionate causes. Steinbeck was conscious of Robert Louis Stevenson's prediction that the simple life that he found in Monterey in 1879 was too fragile to last and that "the poor, quaint, penniless gentlemen of Monterey must perish, like a lower race, before the millionaire vulgarians of the Big Bonanaza." Steinbeck was harking back to the final chapter of the "poor, quaint, penniless gentlemen of Monterey." But on another level, *Cannery Row* is a pastoral view of organic ecology, an attempt to reconcile the affairs of men with the inevitable processes of nature. Its theme is similar to those of Robinson Jeffers, but its style is vastly different. Throughout the novel and the misadventures of its characters, Steinbeck weaves images of an implacable nature, indifferent to human concerns:

> The tide goes out imperceptibly. The boulders show and seem to rise up, and the ocean recedes leaving little pools, leaving wet weed and moss and sponge, iridescence and brown and blue and china red. On the bottom lies the incredible refuse of the seashells broken and chipped and bits of skeleton, claws—the whole bottom a fantastic cemetery on which the living scamper and scramble.

Cannery Row was Steinbeck's last great work, although he wrote a number of books after it: *The Red Pony, The Wayward Bus, The Pearl, Burning Bright, East of Eden, The Short Reign of Pippin IV, The Winter of Our Discontent,* and *Travels With Charley.* None of these works, popular as they were, could measure up to the literary quality of *The Grapes of Wrath* or *Cannery Row.* Steinbeck left California for New York, where he spent the rest of his life, although most of his postwar books were set in California. In 1962, he was awarded the Nobel Prize for Literature based on the body of work that he had produced, the first native California writer to be so honored.

During his time in the Army, William Saroyan worked on a novel about a nonconformist not unlike himself, drafted into military service, who serves in the European campaign and is taken prisoner by the Germans. It was called *The Adventures of Wesley Jackson,* and it was a critical and financial failure. The light, effervescent style he had perfected had left him, and *Wesley Jackson* seemed like one long whining complaint, with the U.S. Army as villain while the German soldiers came across as really nice fellows. Like Hammett and Steinbeck, Saroyan moved to New York. He quarreled with his wife, who had borne him a son and a daughter, and divorced her. Two years later, learning that she was in love with another man, he convinced her to remarry him and return to California with him. The second attempt at marriage was no more successful than the first, and Saroyan ended up alone dividing his time between an apartment in Paris and two adjacent tract homes he had purchased in Fresno, one for himself and the other to store all of his artifacts which would one day become the property of the Saroyan Institute. Although he continued writing until his death in 1981, none of his later works ever equaled his early ones. For many critics, Saroyan was not really an American writer because he failed to observe the conventions of Western literature. But in his own way, he was as American as Mark Twain or Jack London; he represented the immigrant and the children of immigrants, and was thus a spokesman for this most American of experiences. In this manner he enlarged the definition of American literature.

XXXVII

The End Of The Past

The period after World War II in California resembled that which followed the Civil War: most of the major writers moved away, leaving a poet behind to carry the torch—Ina Coolbrith in the 1870s and Robinson Jeffers in the 1940s. All of them stayed away but one who returned rather grudgingly—Ambrose Bierce in the nineteenth century and William Saroyan in the twentieth. In each period, with the departure of the luminaries it seemed that a "golden age of California literature" had ended, but new authors came along and a rebirth began. Frank Norris, Jack London, Mary Austin, and Gertrude Atherton were the new blood of the post-Civil War period. Following World War II, it was Kenneth Rexroth, Henry Miller, Walter Van Tilburg Clark, Wallace Stegner, and Lawrence Ferlinghetti who were responsible for what has often been called the "San Francisco Renaissance." The G.I. Bill provided scholarships for all returning servicemen and women, causing a rapid growth of universities and colleges throughout the country. Notable among these was San Francisco State College, originally housed in a former elementary school building near the foot of Haight Street. Walter Van Tilburg Clark, author of the classic novel *The Ox-Bow Incident,* came to teach English and creative writing there after the war. While there he wrote his other best-known works, *The City of Trembling Leaves* and *The Track of the Cat.* Clark, an ardent admirer and friend of Robinson Jeffers, interpreted the poet's work and significance and helped considerably in the acceptance of Jeffers' poetry by the academic community. Wallace Stegner came to Stanford in 1945 to teach American literature and creative writing and produced a series of novels: *Big Rock Candy Mountain, A Shooting Star, Angle of Repose,* and *The Spectator Bird.* The work of these two men revealed, as never before, the West as a psychological—not just as a geographical and historical—phenomenon.

Henry Miller arrived in California at the end of the war and settled in the Big Sur country on the coast south of Monterey. Originally a New Yorker, he had spent most of his life in Europe and had gained a reputation for writing obscene books, all of which were banned in the United States until the 1960s. His semi-autobiographical narratives, though frank and explicit, were eventually accepted as

Henry Miller

something more than pornography. He was fifty-three by the time he became a Californian, and his major works, *Tropic of Cancer* and *Tropic of Capricorn*, were behind him; but he established himself as an idol to young revolutionaries with the publication of *The Air-Conditioned Nightmare* and *Remember to Remember,* in which he criticized American values with a vitriol that readers had not seen since the days of Ambrose Bierce. He then turned more philosophical in his autobiographical trilogy: *Sexus, Plexus,* and *Nexus.*

Miller chose the wild and sparsely populated Big Sur area because of its unspoiled natural beauty and because he could manage to live there with his wife and children despite having virtually no income. The Millers lived in a five-dollar a month shack at the edge of a cliff, and Henry would haul groceries—when a check from *Circle* or some other avant-garde magazine enabled him to afford them—a mile and a half uphill in a child's wagon. Deeply in debt but unwilling to leave the Eden he had discovered, Miller was astonished to receive a letter one day from the Obelisk Press in Paris announcing that they were holding forty thousand dollars in back royalties for him. He had published *Tropic of*

Cancer and *Tropic of Capricorn* with them just before Paris had fallen to the Germans, and had never heard from them again. He assumed that the German Occupation had destroyed the company and had no idea that his books were best-sellers in Paris to the thousands of American and British soldiers who visited the city. Two devaluations of the franc greatly reduced his windfall, but eventually he received enough money to buy a small house on a few acres in Big Sur. Eventually, royalties from his *Rosy Crucifixion* trilogy, and from *Big Sur and the Oranges of Hieronymous Bosch,* permitted him to live out the rest of his life in relative comfort.

Lawrence Ferlinghetti was born in Yonkers, New York in 1920, the son of an Italian immigrant who died shortly before his youngest son was born. Ferlinghetti's mother was too ill to care for her children, and the family was broken up. Ferlinghetti went to live with a great-aunt who, shortly thereafter, returned to her native Strasbourg in France. French became the boy's first language until he was six when he returned to New York with his aunt, who placed him in an orphanage while she looked for work. Eventually, she was hired as a governess to a wealthy Bronx family who accepted the boy as well, taking him in hand and sending him to a prep school. After graduation from the University of North Carolina as a journalism major, Ferlinghetti joined the Navy just before Pearl Harbor and by the time of the Normandy invasion, June 6, 1944, was in command of a submarine chaser that was a part of the Allied armada.

Three months after D-Day, Ferlinghetti was off the coast of Cherbourg when he received the news that Paris had been liberated and that he and his crew were granted forty-eight hours shore leave. He and his second in command managed to commandeer an unattached jeep and headed for Paris. In what seemed a catastrophe at the time, the jeep broke down and the two officers had to content themselves with spending their liberty in Brittany. In St.-Brieuc they went into a café for dinner. Ferlinghetti noticed that one of the paper tablecloths had a poem scribbled on it—a poem signed "Jacques Prévert." He took the tablecloth with him. In a sense, from that moment, his life began

Lawrence Ferlinghetti

to take a new direction. After the war, he took an M.A. in English at Columbia University, focusing on poetry. He decided to continue his studies in Paris. The G.I. Bill would pay for his tuition and books and give him sixty-five dollars a month to live on, and his head was filled with thoughts of expatriate writers sitting at sidewalk cafés writing and discussing literature: Hemingway, Fitzgerald, Joyce, and Pound. A further inducement to study abroad was the fact that French universities did not require attendance at many academic courses, but permitted doctoral candidates to concentrate on their theses. Immersing himself in contemporary symbolist and surrealist French poetry, he chose "The City as Symbol in Modern Poetry: In Search of a Metropolitan Tradition" as his thesis topic. In addition to his work at the Sorbonne, he studied painting at the Académie Julien, which Frank Norris had attended fifty years earlier. He received his doctorate in 1950 and then returned to the United States, where he settled in San Francisco.

It was *Circle* magazine that brought Rexroth, Miller, and Ferlinghetti together to form the nucleus of a movement that would burst upon the scene in the 1950s. The first issue featured Miller, and the second featured Anaïs Nin, who was living in San Francisco at the time. The magazine attracted an international set of artists: Darius Milhaud, who was teaching at Mills College in Oakland; Lawrence Durrell; William Carlos Williams; e. e. cummings; and the poet-in-residence at the University of California, Josephine Miles, the first woman to obtain tenure in the University's English Department. When *Circle* magazine folded, it was replaced as a center for aspiring poets and essayists of an anti-establishment bent by another magazine, this one called *Ark,* considerably more political and more radical than *Circle*. Many of those who had written for the first magazine continued to publish in the second, but a new and more permanent center for literary outsiders was created when Ferlinghetti opened City Lights Bookstore in North Beach, the first all-paperback bookstore in the United States. City Lights, which was an avant-garde publishing company as well as a bookstore, along with the bar across the alley from it, Vesuvio Café, became the locus of what in succeeding years would grow into a full-blown counterculture literary movement. One of City Lights' first publications was Ferlinghetti's translation of French poet Jacques Prévert's *Paroles*, including the poem Ferlinghetti had found on a paper tablecloth in St.-Brieuc.

For a while after World War II, it seemed to most people that California was ready to "settle down." The troops were home and peace was firmly established. Now there was economic opportunity for everyone. The G.I. Bill would stave off the unemployment that had followed World War I. Veterans could get a free college education and could buy a new, modern tract home on the outskirts of California cities for no money down. The Okies and Arkies were middle-class now, the farm labor done by *braceros* who returned contentedly to Mexico after each harvesting season, their pockets full. It was clear to optimists that California was in for a long period of peace, prosperity, and the cultivation of Protestant middle-class values.

But the tract homes for veterans provided a new Gold Rush. Developers discovered that there were fortunes to be made in buying up farmland and laying out rows of cookie-cutter houses with back yards and two-car garages; a vast suburbia grew up rapidly all around San Francisco Bay. Farmers and ranchers resisted the transformation of their land into "bedroom communities," but when their land was taxed on the basis of its potential value for housing, they could not hold out. Much of the world's richest soil was covered with houses, streets, and shopping malls, all connected with an ever-increasing sprawl of freeways. As industries moved out to the suburbs, San Francisco and other Bay Area cities began to disintegrate. Affluent citizens moved out while the cities developed ghettoes of poor and minority residents.

Moreover, the commercial leaders in the new high-rise buildings downtown were now faceless corporations that were involved in the city only as a place to house their headquarters. There was no longer the same spirit of business support for the cultural life of the city that there had been before the war, when most of the major businesses were family-owned and had grown up with the city: Levi Strauss; Zellerbach Corporation; Gump's; the City of Paris and the White House; the coffee roasters Folgers, Hills Brothers, and MJB; Anchor Steam Beer; Roos Brothers; I. Magnin and Joseph Magnin; Ghirardelli Chocolate; Golden Grain Macaroni; Fireman's Fund Insurance; and Books Inc., which could trace its lineage back to Anton Roman's Montgomery Street bookstore. San Francisco seemed a city surrounded by and under siege from the suburbs, and a growing polarization between those who lived in the crumbling city and those who came in only to work affected the literary crowd that was centered in North Beach. Eventually, this polarization led to an open revolt against the middle class in the 1950s and 60s, a revolution that began at City Lights Bookstore and then spread throughout the world.

The revolt was perhaps inevitable because San Francisco had not, like most American cities, been created by groups of settler families who developed a mature and stable society. Its history was rather one of displacement that began with the transformation of a native population by the invasion of the Spaniards who, with their missions and forts, converted the Indian population and imposed a new way of life on them. The Spaniards were replaced by Mexicans when the missions were secularized and huge land grants were made; the entire Bay Area belonged to a small number of families then, particularly Vallejo, Peralta, Estudillo, Castro, Martinez, Bernal, Noe, and Sanchez. After 1849, these huge landowners were rapidly replaced by the sharpest of the *gringos*, who poured in for the Gold Rush and immediately began squabbling among themselves over who was going to dominate. The railroad builders won out and were eventually replaced by bankers, stock brokers, and developers. And so the cycles continued: a new group arrived, took hold, and immediately resisted the admission of any group that threatened to replace it. Perhaps no one has expressed this phenomenon more personally than the singer, actress, playwright, and poet Maya Angelou in her autobiographical *I Know Why the Caged Bird Sings*. In it, she describes how the Fillmore district, which for years had been San Francisco's Japantown, changed rapidly as Japanese residents were sent off to relocation centers and replaced by Southern blacks, pouring in to work in defense plants: "The Japanese area became San Francisco's Harlem in a matter of months." Angelou was just thirteen when she arrived in San Francisco, which she found to be "a state of freedom."

While World War II and the sprawling suburbia that followed it brought convulsive changes to the San Francisco region, one vestige of the old days remained, a direct contact with the "Wild West." In the small cabins her father had built at the "Hights," Juanita Joaquina Miller kept his memory alive. She was seventy years old in 1950 and would live another twenty years. She had been there since 1911 when she came to care for her aging father. After his death she married twice, but each marriage ended shortly after it began. "If I was ever in love," she told a reporter, "it was with my own father." Her love for him was faithful to the end. She wrote an adoring biography, *My Father,* in 1941 and sold the "Hights" to the city of Oakland with the understanding that she could live there for the rest of her life and could erect a Sanctuary of Memory, a stone structure to hold her father's possessions. On her finger she wore a silver ring that contained her father's fingernail clippings. Next to her house, she had a small outdoor theater constructed where she could exercise her talents for singing, dancing, and acting by producing her father's plays or her own. In 1930 she even managed to convince members of Franklin D. Roosevelt's White House staff to have the Works Progress Administration build the 2,000-seat Woodminster Amphitheater with an elaborate waterfall fountain at the "Hights," by then known as Joaquin Miller Park. Each year, Juanita staged a pageant in honor of her father's birthday. The children of the area nicknamed her the "White Witch" because when they trespassed on her property, she would appear with a broom to chase them away, her face covered with shortening to preserve her complexion.

So, while a group of young poets, essayists, and jazz musicians laid the foundation for the next literary generation in the coffeehouses of North Beach, across the Bay in the hills of Oakland a rather silly but very devoted old woman kept alive the flame of her father's reputation that had been built on self-aggrandizement and outrageous publicity-seeking. Typically, Joaquin Miller had the foresight to create his own permanent monument with a resident curator who worshipped him. It was a good thing, for while the works of most of his fellow California writers are still read, his own are largely forgotten.

Juanita Miller is gone now, but Joaquin Miller Park remains in the Oakland hills, and the California Writers Club, continuing Miller's tradition, has planted a redwood tree there for each of the area's major writers, from Bret Harte to Dashiell Hammett. A few miles away, the seedy waterfront of Oakland where Jack London grew up is now the city's tourist center, Jack London Square; nearby is Bret Harte Boardwalk. In San Francisco, visitors can pay their respects at Ina Coolbrith Park and George Sterling Glade on Russian Hill, Robert Louis Stevenson's monument in Portsmouth Square, the plaque to Gertrude Atherton in Lafayette Park, or the one to Isadora Duncan on Taylor Street. To the north are the appropriately-named redwood forest of John Muir Woods in Marin County, the Robert Louis Stevenson Museum and State Park in St. Helena, and the Jack London State Park in Sonoma County. To the east is the Annual Jumping Frog Contest held in Angel's Camp, and to the south, Jeffers' Tor House in Carmel, the Steinbeck Museum in Salinas, and the Robert Louis Stevenson House in Monterey.

Longtemps, longtemps, longtemps après
Que les poètes ont disparus,
Leurs chansons courent encore dans les rues.

BIBLIOGRAPHY

HISTORICAL BACKGROUND

Angelou, Maya. *I Know Why the Caged Bird Sings.* New York: Random House, 1969.

Asbury, Herbert. *The Barbary Coast.* Garden City: Garden City Publishing Company, 1933.

Bacon, Daniel. *Walking San Francisco on the Barbary Coast Trail.* San Francisco: Quicksilver Press, 1997.

Benard de Russailh, Albert. *Last Adventure.* San Francisco: The Westgate Press, 1931.

Bronson, William. *The Earth Shook, the Sky Burned.* Garden City: Doubleday and Co., Inc., 1959.

Carpenter, Patricia F. and Paul Totah. *The San Francisco Fair, Treasure Island.* San Francisco: Scottwall Associates, 1989.

Caughey, John and Laree Caughey. *California Heritage.* Los Angeles: The Ward Ritchie Press, 1962.

Churchill, Charles B. "The Limits of Empathy—Richard Henry Dana in California," *The Californians,* Jan.-Feb., 1992: 45-49.

Dana, Richard Henry. *Two Years Before the Mast.* Boston: Houghton, Mifflin and Company, 1911

Ewald, Donna and Peter Clute. *San Francisco Invites the World: The Panama-Pacific International Exposition of 1915.* San Francisco: Chronicle Books, 1991.

Foley, Doris. *The Divine Eccentric: Lola Montez and the Newspapers.* New York: Ballantine Books, 1

Gentry, Curt. *The Madams of San Francisco.* Garden City: Doubleday & Company, 1964

Gordon, Mark. *Once Upon a City: A Wild Ride Through San Francisco's Past.* San Francisco: Don't Call It Frisco Press, 1988.

Gregory, James N. "Dust Bowl Legacies: The Okie Impact on California, 1939-1989," *California History*, Fall, 1989: 74-85.

Hart, James D. *A Companion to California.* Berkeley: The University of California Press, 198

——————. *The Popular Book: A History of America's Literary Taste.* New York: Oxford University Press, 1950.

Lewis, Oscar. *Here Lived the Californians.* New York: Rinehart & Company, 1957.

——————. *San Francisco: Mission to Metropolis.* San Diego: Howell-North Books, 1980.

——————. *Sea Routes to the Gold Fields.* New York: Alfred A. Knopf, 1949.

——————. *This Was San Francisco.* New York: David McKay Company, 1962.

Lockwood, Charles. *Suddenly San Francisco.* San Francisco: The San Francisco Examiner, 1978.

Martin, Cy. *Whiskey and Wild Women.* New York: Hart Publishing Company, 1974.

Michaels, Leonard, David Reid, and Raquel Scherr, eds. *West of the West: Imagining California.* San Francisco: North Point Press, 1989.

Miller, John, ed. *San Francisco Stories*. San Francisco: Chronicle Books, 1990.

Nasatir, A. P. "Alexander Dumas Fils and the Lottery of the Golden Ingots," *California Historical Society Quarterly*, June, 1954: 125-142.

O'Brien, Robert. *This Is San Francisco*. New York: McGraw-Hill Book Company, 1948.

Ogden, Annegret. "Why Napkins are Small in San Francisco: The Voice of World Traveler, Ida Pfeiffer," *The Californians*, March, Sept.-Oct, 1990: 14-15, 57

Presidial Weekly Clarion, April 27, 1906.

Scharlach, Bernice. *Big Alma: San Francisco's Alma Spreckels*. San Francisco: Scottwall, 1990.

Starr, Kevin. *Americans and the California Dream, 1850-1915*. New York: Oxford University Press, 1973.

—————. *Inventing the Dream: California Through the Progressive Era*. New York: Oxford University Press, 1

Wollenberg, Charles. *Golden Gate Metropolis*. Berkeley: University of California Institute of Governmental Services, 1985.

LITERARY HISTORY

Bennett, Robert A., ed. *The Bohemians: American Adventures from Bret Harte's Overland Monthly*. Walla Walla: Pioneer Press Books, 1987.

Duckett, Margaret. *Mark Twain and Bret Harte*. Norman: University of Oklahoma Press, 196

Ferlinghetti, Lawrence and Nancy J. Peters. *Literary San Francisco*. New York: City Lights Books and Harper & Publishers, 1980.

Golden Gate Trinity. *Oakland Tribune,* Sept. 25, 1966.

Haslam, Gerald W. "Literary California: The Ultimate Frontier of the Western World," *California History*, Winter, 1989-90: 188-195.

——————, ed. *Many Californias: Literature from the Golden West*. Reno: The University of Nevada Press, 19

——————. *The Other California*. Reno: The University of Nevada Press, 1994.

Herron, Don. *A Guidebook to the Literary World of San Francisco and its Environs*. San Francisco: City Lights Books, 1985.

Jackson, Joseph Henry, ed. *Continent's End: A Collection of California Writing*. New York: McGraw-Hill Book Compa Inc., 1944.

——————, ed. *The Western Gate: A San Francisco Reader*. New York: Farrar, Straus and Young, 1952

Jones, Idwal. *Ark of Empire*. New York: Doubleday, 1951.

Lee, W. Storrs. *California, A Literary Chronicle*. New York: Funk & Wagnalls, 1968.

Lewis, Oscar. *Bay Window Bohemia*. New York: Doubleday, 1956.

Noel, Joseph. *Footloose in Arcadia*. New York: Carrick and Evans, Inc., 1940.

Powell, Lawrence Clark. *California Classics*. Santa Barbara: Capra Press, 1982.

Rathmell, George. "The Overland Monthly: California's Literary Treasure," *The Californians*, March-April, 1991: 12-21.

Sawyer-Lauçanno, Christopher. *The Continual Pilgrimage*. New York: Grove Press, 1992.

Walker, Franklin. *San Francisco's Literary Frontier*. New York: Knopf, 1939.

——————. *The Seacoast of Bohemia*. Santa Barbara: Peregrine Smith, Inc., 1973

Western Literary Association. *A Literary History of the American West*. Fort Worth: Texas Christian University Press, 1987.

Xavier Martinez. *Oakland Tribune*, Oct. 30, 1966.

WORKS ON OR BY INDIVIDUAL AUTHORS

Ina Coolbrith

Coolbrith, Ina. *A Perfect Day*. San Francisco: John H. Carmany and Company, 1881.

——————. *Songs From the Golden Gate*. Boston: Houghton, Mifflin and Company, 1895.

——————. *Wings of Sunset*. Boston: Houghton, Mifflin and Company, 1929.

Rhodehamel, Josephine DeWitt and Raymund Francis Wood. *Ina Coolbrith: Librarian and Poet Laureate of California*. Provo: Brigham Young University Press, 1973.

Bret Harte

Harte, Bret. *East and West Poems*. Boston: James R. Osgood and Company, 1871.

—————. *The Outcasts of Poker Flat and Other Stories*. New York: Airmont Publishing Company, 1964.

Stewart, George R. *Bret Harte, Argonaut and Exile*. Boston: Houghton Mifflin, 1931.

Charles Warren Stoddard

Stoddard, Charles Warren. *Exits and Entrances*. Boston: Lathrop Publishing Company, 1903.

———————————. *For the Pleasure of His Company*. San Francisco: Gay Sunshine Press, 1987.

Mark Twain

Fanning, Philip Ashley. "One Story Mark Twain Wouldn't Tell," *The Californians*, Vol. 12, No. 1: 38-47.

Gillis, William R. *Memories of Mark Twain and Steve Gillis*. Sonora: The Banner, 1924.

Kierman, Kathy. *Mark Twain on Writing and Publishing*. New York: The Book of the Month Club, 1994

Lauber, John. *The Making of Mark Twain*. Boston: Houghton-Mifflin, 1985.

Lennon, Nigey. *Mark Twain in California*. San Francisco: Chronicle Books, 1982.

Moore, Jim. "Mark Twain and the Em Quads: A "Square" Deal, " *The Californians*, May-Aug., 1991: 48-54.

Neider, Charles. *Mark Twain at His Best*. Garden City: Doubleday and Company, Inc., 1986.

Smith, Harriet Elinor, Richard Bucci, and Lin Salamo. *Mark Twain's Letters*. Berkeley: The University of California Pre 1990.

Taper, Bernard. *Mark Twain's San Francisco*. New York: McGraw Hill, 1963.

Twain, Mark. *Roughing It*. New York: New American Library, 1962.

Joaquin Miller

Frost, O. W. *Joaquin Miller*. New Haven Conn.: College & University Press, 1967.

Guilford-Kardell, Margaret. "Calla Shasta—Joaquin Miller's First Daughter," *The Californians*, Jan.-Feb., 1992: 40-42.

—————— "Joaquin Miller: Fact and Fiction," *The Californians*, Nov.-Dec., 1991: 6-1

Johnson, Bènet. "Free Spirit? Juanita Joaquina Miller," *The Californians*, Jan.-Feb., 1992: 27-33.

Juanita's Loyalty to Joaquin. *Oakland Tribune*, Oct. 1, 1967.

Marberry, M. M. *Splendid Poseur: Joaquin Miller—American Poet*. New York: Thomas Y. Crowell Company, 1953

Stern, Madeleine B. *Purple Passage: The Life of Mrs. Frank Leslie*. Norman, OK: The University of Oklahoma Press, 1953.

Prentice Mulford

Mulford, Prentice. *Prentice Mulford's Story*. Oakland, CA: Biobooks, 1953.

——————————. *The Swamp Angel*. Boston: F. J. Needham, 1888.

Ambrose Bierce

Grenander, M. E. "Ambrose Bierce and Charles Warren Stoddard: Some Unpublished Correspondence," *Huntington Library Quarterly*, May, 1960.

Saunders, Richard. *Ambrose Bierce: The Making of a Misanthrope*. San Francisco: Chronicle Books, 1984.

Robert Louis Stevenson

Bell, Ian. *Dreams of Exile. Robert Louis Stevenson: A Biography*. New York: Henry Holt and Company, 1992.

Bevin, Bryan. *Robert Louis Stevenson: Poet and Teller of Tales*. New York: St. Martin's Press, 1993.

Field, Isobel. *This Life I've Loved*. New York: Longmans, Green and Co., 1937.

Issler, Anne Roller. *Happier for his Presence, San Francisco and Robert Louis Stevenson*. Stanford: Stanford University Press, 1949.

Lapierre, Alexandra. *Fanny Stevenson: A Romance of Destiny*. Translated by Carol Cosman. New York: Carroll & Graf Publishers, 1995.

Makay, Margaret. *The Violent Friend, the Story of Mrs. RLS*. Garden City, NY: Doubleday & Co., 196

Osbourne, Lloyd. *An Intimate Portrait of RLS*. New York: Scribner's, 1924.

Sanchez, Nellie. *The Life of Mrs. Robert Louis Stevenson*. New York: Charles Scribner's Sons, 1920.

Stevenson, Robert Louis. *From Scotland to Silverado* (edited by James D. Hart). Cambridge: Harvard University Press, 1966.

Wood, James Playsted. *The Lantern Bearer: A Life of Robert Louis Stevenson*. New York: Pantheon Books, 1965.

John Muir

Muir, John. *The Mountains of California*. New York: Doubleday Anchor Books, 1961.

Helen Hunt Jackson

Jackson, Helen Hunt. *Ramona*. New York: New American Library, 1988.

Frank Norris

Norris, Charles. *Frank Norris of "The Wave," Stories and Sketches*. San Francisco: The Westgate Press, 1931.

Norris, Frank. *The Octopus*. New York: Airmont Publishing Company, 1969.

——————. *McTeague, A Story of San Francisco*. New York: Doubleday, 1899.

Rathmell, George. "Frank Norris, Apprentice Novelist," *The Californians*, Vol. 11, No. 5: 40-45

Isadora Duncan

Duncan, Isadora. *My Life*. New York: Boni & Liveright, 1927.

Jack London

Gillespie, Elgy. Jack London's Broken-Hearted Daughter. *San Francisco Chronicle*, June 10, 1990.

London, Jack. *The Call of the Wild and Other Stories*. New York: New American Library, 1960.

——————. *The People of the Abyss*. Westport, CN: Lawrence Hill, 1977.

——————. *The Valley of the Moon*. New York: Macmillan, 1913.

London, Joan. *Jack London and His Times*. Seattle: The University of Washington Press, 1968.

van Dillan, Lailee. "Becky London: The Quiet Survivor Talks About Her Father," *The Californians*, Jan.-Feb., 1992: 34-39.

Gertrude Atherton

Atherton, Gertrude. *Adventures of a Novelist*. New York: Liveright, 1932.

——————————. *My San Francisco, A Wayward Biography*. Indianapolis: Bobbs Merrill, 1946.

——————————. *The Splendid Idle Forties*. New York: Macmillan, 1902.

Shumate, Albert. *A San Francisco Scandal: The California of George Gordon*. Spokane, Washington: The Arthur H. Clar Co., 1994.

Mary Austin

Austin, Mary. *The Land of Little Rain*. Boston: Houghton Mifflin, 1903.

Langlois, Karen S. "A Fresh Voice from the West: Mary Austin, California, and American Literary Magazines, 1892-1910," *California History*, Spring, 1990: 22-35.

Yone Noguchi

Atsumi, Ikuko, ed. *Yone Noguchi, Collected English Letters*. Tokyo: The Yone Noguchi Society, 1975.

Noguchi, Yone. *The Story of Yone Noguchi*. London: Chatto & Windus, 1914.

Gelett Burgess

Burgess, Gelett. *The Heart Line*. Indianapolis: The Bobbs Merrill Co., 1907.

Robinson Jeffers

Jeffers, Robinson. *The Collected Poems of Robinson Jeffers*, Volumes 1-3. Stanford, Stanford University Press, 1991.

Karman, James. *Robinson Jeffers: Poet of California*. San Francisco: Chronicle Books, 1987.

Dashiell Hammett

Hammett, Dashiell. *The Maltese Falcon*. New York: Vintage Books, 1930.

Johnson, Diane. *Dashiell Hammett. A Life*. New York: Random House, 1983.

John Steinbeck

Champney, Freeman. "John Steinbeck, Californian." *The Antioch Review*, Sept., 1947: 345-362.

Covici, Pascal, ed. *The Portable Steinbeck*. New York: Viking Press, 1946.

Henderson, George. "Steinbeck's Spatial Imagination in The Grapes of Wrath," *California History*, Winter, 1989-90: 211-223.

Hunter, J. Paul. "Steinbeck's Wine of Affirmation in The Grapes of Wrath." In *Essays in Modern Literature*, edited by DeLand. Florida: Stetson University Press, 1963: 76-89.

Lisca, Peter. *Nature and Myth*. New York: Thomas Y. Crowell, Publishers, 1978.

St. Pierre, Brian. *John Steinbeck, The California Years*. San Francisco: Chronicle Books, 1983.

Steinbeck, John. *Cannery Row*. New York: The Viking Press, Inc., 1945.

—————. *The Grapes of Wrath*. New York: The Viking Press, Inc., 1939.

—————. *Tortilla Flat*. New York: Covici, Freide, 1935.

Kenneth Rexroth

Hamalian, Linda, ed. *Kenneth Rexroth, An Autobiographical Novel*. New York: New Directions, 1991.

Morrow, Bradford, ed. *World Outside My Window: The Selected Essays of Kenneth Rexroth*. New York: New Directions, 1987

William Saroyan

Bedrosian, Margaret. "Saroyan in California," *California History*, Winter, 1989-90: 202-209.

Darwent, Brian, ed. *Saroyan: The New Saroyan Reader*. Berkeley: Creative Arts Book Company, 1984.

Floan, Howard R. *William Saroyan*. Boston: Twayne Publishers, 1966.

Foster, Edward H. *William Saroyan*. Boise: Boise State University, 1984.

Saroyan, Aram. *William Saroyan*. New York: Harcourt, Brace, Jovanovich, 1983.

Henry Miller

Miller, Henry. *Big Sur and the Oranges of Hieronymous Bosch*. New York: New Direction, 1957.

Lawrence Ferlinghetti

Silesky, Barry. *Ferlinghetti, The Artist in His Time*. New York: Warner, 1990.

INDEX

George Rathmell received his BA from UC Berkeley in 1956 and his MA from San Francisco State University in 1970. His specialty is California history and literature, and his articles and short stories have appeared in *The Californians, Soundings,* and *Coast* magazines. He is the author of BENCH MARKS IN READING and THE TENDER AND FAITHFUL HEART.